"I WAS SOLD IN CHINA"

GEMMA DUNN

提防

I have tried to recreate events, locales and conversations from my memories of them. In order to maintain their anonymity in some instances I have changed the names of individuals and places, I may have changed some identifying characteristics and details such as physical properties, occupations and places of residence.

ISBN: 9781072787211
ISBN 13

DEDICATION

For my incredible parents Lesley and Stewart, who I am proud to also call my best friends. Without your unwavering love, support and encouragement, my life would not be half the adventure it has been. Thanks will never be enough. I love you with all my heart.

I write this also in memory of my big sister Niki. I wish you could have been here to see my dream happen. Mums, Pops, Phill, Andrew and I, love and miss you everyday.

CONTENTS

I was stagnating at home in England. Waiting for 'something' to happen but not doing anything to tempt it. So that's where I hit upon the idea of somehow working my way around the world, that didn't involve living off the pittance of picking fruit or working in a seedy bar. I'd travelled to 20+ countries from Europe, to Africa, to Asia and no longer wanted the transient traveller experience – I wanted to really understand what it was like to truly live another culture.

One late summer, I realised I had to make efforts to make it happen for myself and I signed up to an online TEFL (Teaching English as a Foreign Language) course with the aim to get qualified and travel my way around different countries. I mean really living in them, not just touring through, which I didn't believe gave you a true picture of the country you were wandering through. Plus, having already turned 30, I was over the post school/university gap year mentality of boozing my way through countries and wanted to learn something about other existences that were different from my own.

As it happened, my younger brother and his girlfriend had also hit upon the same idea and for my birthday in September, signed me up and paid for, an equivalent course with another company. Luckily, I managed to get my money back from the one I had recently bought and went for their choice as a refund was impossible for them.

I was fully aware that simply sitting on a website for a certain number of hours didn't qualify anyone as a teacher, but it would give me the basics of what I needed to be a foreign language teacher and where university obtained teaching certificates were not so necessary. Of course, the earning capabilities would be less, but I felt time was of the essence and didn't want to delay by formally re-qualifying just for the purposes of earning an extra few pennies abroad. After all, it wasn't the money I was going for, it was the experience.

In my limited free evenings from my more-than-full-time job I sat and plugged away at the online TEFL course. It consisted of reading materials and short multiple-choice exams after each learning section, requiring a minimum pass rate in order to move onto the next section and ultimately achieve your basic teaching certificate. This was also the minimum requirement of jobs I had browsed on-line, from Europe to Asia, so I was confident that this was the first step in my adventure to somewhere else.

Being a pedant for grammar and spelling the course drove me to distraction. It was full of spelling and grammatical errors and I found it ironic that it was testing ME for my English abilities. I also found it to be so ambiguous I wanted to shake the person who had created it and ask them how they expected people to pass. As it happened, you could pass without doing very much at all. The web pages didn't quite work as was obviously intended and you could flick to the answers before you completed the exams. It didn't block you from moving on to the next page before you had ticked your boxes. It was farcical really. But hey, it didn't cost me anything. It was simple, and if something this basic was a pre-requisite to teach then I figured I would be fine in the real world. I was relatively literate, had a neutral English accent and was not nervous to stand up in front of strangers and convey knowledge.

The course took me less than half the number of hours I needed and once completed, I set my sights on finding a job.

Although I, very arrogantly, had assumed I would be fine out in 'the real world', I was a little apprehensive to sign up to a year's contract in a country I didn't even know. I was also anxious about doing something I didn't genuinely know if I was any good at, or could do it some justice.

So, when I found, with the same company I did my online course with, a six-month placement as a trainee teacher, I thought I had struck gold. The timings were also perfect in that they were doing a mid-term intake in February, whereas all other schools had recruited by September. I was concerned that if I had to wait until next September, almost a year away, I would have settled too much into my life at home and probably would be reluctant to make the break. As of right now I had no commitments to relationships, I had the desire to get out there, so it was "now or never" in my eyes.

Before I applied for the internship, I heavily researched both the job and the English company whose sister school I would be placed in abroad. The company itself had glowing references on various forums. Being the nerdy accountant I was, I even checked its company records online to see if the income it generated represented an established and apparently successful school – which it did seem to appear. So far, so good.

The job itself also seemed ideal. The choices for the mid-year intake were Thailand or China. Having spent two months traveling around Thailand, China seemed to be the obvious choice for a new adventure. The details of the package as an intern teacher were also reassuringly good and had a supportive in-country team which was essential to me, being a lone travelling female. The sister school was also in Beijing, so no back water local yokel town, but a previous Olympic city for which I had high hopes that it was relatively visitor friendly.

There were numerous additional reassuring perks to this placement, too. For a trainee salary large enough to survive on, the school would provide me with accommodation, sharing with a fellow teacher (instant friends) with Wi-Fi and all necessary mod-cons and no more than a 20-minute walk from the school. A 2-week induction to the city and the schools, lesson shadowing, lesson planning tutorials, a teaching competency certificate at the end and a portfolio of work for later applications. All for the cost of admin and visa applications, which, although costly, could be earned back soon enough. It sounded ideal and less of a daunting commitment than signing up to a year somewhere I perhaps didn't enjoy and having no teaching support. This was the one.

With the Beijing internship in mind, I tweaked my CV to bring to the forefront my training, coaching and teaching experiences from my jobs and my hobbies and presented a CV that was convincing enough to show I had potential and submitted it to the TEFL company. The next step would be a telephone interview, followed up by a face to face interview in London and then an offer if I was deemed suitable.

A few days later I received a phone call from the recruiter, Nic Bacon. A well-spoken, sure-fire ex public schoolboy. He was very warm and friendly and chatted me through the details of the opportunity. I asked as many questions as I could and he responded in a manner that I liked. Thorough, helpful and enthusiastic. The school in Beijing was actually the Asia headquarters and was the only branch that actually had two TEFL company representatives in country, based in the school. I took this to be a good sign too.

An hour later and after a very pleasant conversation, I enquired when it would be possible to come to London and formally interview, if of course he thought that was appropriate. He told me that would not be necessary, that I was clearly suitable, he trusted in my motives to go and not drop out of a contract mid-term and announced that should I be interested, one of the two jobs available was mine.

I was ecstatic, if not surprised, and accepted a day later after going through the finer details and discussing the practicalities of upping and leaving my life and my home in England. My parents and family were very supportive, used to my itchy feet and all were of the opinion 'why not' when I was still young (ish), had no ties and the opportunity was there.

With six weeks left to go until Christmas and only ten weeks until I left for Beijing, I started to put the wheels in motion to rent out my house, resign from my job, pack up my home and leave everything behind. During this time, I paid over my visa fees and waited for my visa paperwork to come through, which I would then have to take to the Chinese embassy in London to get the formal visa stamped into my passport. It's notoriously difficult to get a visa for China so I was nervous about that process and the time constraints during Christmas to ensure I could fly mid-February. Add to the fact I had to renew my passport before I did this, as it only had a year left before expiry – and if I planned to travel further or stay where I was, a passport renewal in a foreign country was not an ideal situation.

The visa paperwork was very slow to come through and took a lot of back and forth emails with the TEFL Company to get everything I needed together. My new passport was a piece of cake thankfully and it was back in my hands two weeks after application. It was now early January and my leave date was looming. As soon as I had it in my hand, I jumped on a train to London and headed for the embassy, along with half of the country apparently. I was unable to get an appointment that day and had to return home empty handed. Before I left I had begged for a specific appointment time in the next few days so that I would not have another wasted trip. I also investigated the express visa service which meant that by hanging around for a few hours, I could apply and receive my visa and passport back on the same day. It wasn't cheap and I was slightly annoyed that I would have to incur this cost because the TEFL Company had been so slow in getting their own act together. But hey ho…if I wanted to go, this was the process I had to go through. Besides, I'd already committed a lot personally to this, I'd resigned from my job, my house was half packed up, I'd found tenants to rent it to almost immediately and balls were rolling

Four days later I was back on a train to the embassy in London to hopefully get my visa sorted once and for all. I got there in good time and miraculously my appointment was spot on at the scheduled time. It seemed to be going well; I could be home earlier than I had planned. In fact, I was home even earlier than that…my appointment lasted all of three minutes when an eagle eyed official spotted that a page of my visa documents did not have a rubber stamp on it from the institution applying for it. Computer said 'no'. I was stunned, and livid. The documents were all in Chinese characters so I could not have spotted it was a requirement myself, but instead I had put my faith in the 'experts' supplying it. After all the hassle, my second costly trip to London, I still hadn't got my visa. I was leaving in three weeks... everything else had been planned – this was going to foil everything!

The second I left the embassy building, once again empty handed, I put in a call to Nic Bacon and let rip. I told him this whole process was turning into a joke; was this even a real opportunity or were they taking me for a ride? For a so-called professional outfit, it was not operating so. He was mortified and incredibly apologetic. His explanation was that it was a new visa process they were following and they had got it wrong. He assured me he would get it sorted ASAP and get me the documents back.

Six days before my flight was due to leave to visit a country I had no legal access to, my documentation finally came back, fully rubber stamped and signed. The earliest appointment I could get at the embassy was two days before I left. I had no choice but to take it and cross everything that it would get processed and returned the very same day.

Less than 48 hours before my scheduled flight time I was strolling out of the embassy with my visa firmly planted in my new passport. Talk about cutting it fine.

In my relief, I failed to read the signs in my gut that something just didn't feel right... I just believed that I'd had all my challenges up front and that the rest would go swimmingly... I couldn't be any unluckier, surely?

Sadly, I could not have been more wrong.

For that reason, I feel compelled to candidly share with you my tale. I need the world to know what I went through so I can protect others, who might naively do what I did, despite the planning, the research and the consideration I put in to my trip.

No-one is infallible. The truth was, I was conned, vulnerable, scared, became isolated in a foreign country, disgusted, assaulted, hunted by police and immigration… but I made it out the other side. Others might not be so lucky. If I save one person from experiencing what I did, then my work here is done.

Travelling, absorbing yourself in new cultures, and living existences alien to your upbringing - is hard. Whilst my story is my own personal experience and the opinions I give are my own perceptions of situations…they are no less valid. Please do not ignore my warnings.

The Con

I HAVEN'T FOUND SWEET – BUT I'VE DEFINITELY FOUND SOUR

The Con

My feeling of unease came before the plane even landed. My eager stare out of the plane window as we circled above the former Peking, provided me no insight to the city I would be living in and teaching English in. We touched down in the midst of a midday cloud with haze so thick that the terminal building loomed like an eerie imposing shadow in the distance, devoid of features or detail or an horizon beyond it.

I remember having the fleeting thought that there might have been an apocalypse mid-flight and we were the only survivors.

My first post-flight gulp of fresh air indicated that this was in fact not a cloud after all - but a mass of suspended particles that actually had a taste, a sulphurous smell that I could physically feel entering my mouth, my nose and my eyes. I unconvincingly told myself that it must be airport pollution.

Little did I know. The clouds of pollution in Beijing are not discerning in their locale, nor the result of aeroplane emissions alone, and that this oppressive blanket would follow me for the entire duration of my stay in what was to become apparent, an equally oppressive country.

Exiting customs, I eagerly sought the Western face of the school coordinator who had arranged to meet me. Although I had just disembarked a plane from London, I could no longer see any other Western faces. The faces I could see, from my vantage point several inches above the crowd, were either donned with surgical masks or busy spitting phlegm from the deepest parts of their lungs on to the terminal floor, wiping excess saliva onto the nearest surfaces. The unrelenting cacophony of mucus removal from every direction was as retch inducing as the stench of the air inside the building - stale sweat and urine from the open squat holes in the bathrooms.

The quicker I could escape its confines the better.

I had expected to be met by the Australian TEFL representative but instead left the airport in the company of a very Chinese looking lady called Louise. Allegedly, she works for The China Agency, the Chinese partner TEFL 'X' work with (news to me – which will slowly become my favourite phrase over the course of the next few hours and days), and who is responsible for settling us foreigners into our jobs and housing around the city.

She was very typically Chinese and smaller than my hand luggage which posed a problem when she offered to carry my bags for me (I gave her my travel neck cushion and I'm pretty sure she struggled with that). As my host for the next couple of days, I'm pretty glad I didn't finish her off with any of my overweight bags at our first meeting. I was clearly going to need her help over the coming weeks. But boy did I underestimate just what that meant.

On stepping out of the airport (and away from the first sightings of surgically-masked people), I was met with glorious sunshine in zero degree temperature and some welcome, if not slightly distinctive in smell, fresh air. It was so eerily hazy though that as we drove away from the airport in the taxi, all I could see behind me was the outline of the airport, like it was the only building in the vicinity and floating on a cloud. It's a nice-looking place, obviously upgraded for the Olympics and giving visitors hope of a reasonable level of civilisation once they reached Beijing.

I grabbed on to that hope like all the others before me. I was on a big life-changing adventure...and it had better be good.The drive was relatively short, an hour or so, and took us deeper into the haze. There was no way of seeing civilisation, the surrounding areas or even where we were headed it was so thick. I knew the sun was shining but I didn't know where in the sky it was and it felt like it could be any time of day. Had I not been wearing a watch, I would not have known that it was barely after midday. I know my wish for it to be night time was a fruitless one though – I was exhausted after my sleepless flight.

Louise took me back to her own apartment on the outskirts of the city, pretty much one of the last subway stops from the centre of Beijing, just to give you an idea. The streets by this point I could now see, were buzzing, dusty, overcrowded, full of crazy and dangerous traffic - and unnervingly loud. Her apartment was in a block a hundred metres or so off the main road which was like an oasis of calm in the madness.

On first glance her apartment seemed what I had assumed to be authentically Chinese and very cute. It was in a 5-storey building and was a 2-bedroom apartment with character, low furniture, with classically Chinese features, a kitchen for shorter people and cutesy red wall hangings.

I briefly met her husband Wilson (Chinese) who took the job of bringing in my bags, and was then showed to my room. It was small, with questionable sheet cleanliness (fag burns galore in the layered and stained concoction of bedding), and packed with their unused furniture. It was as equally cold inside as it was outside. But hey, it was a bed, it was in an apartment of a person who I would be needing - and regardless, I had no choice. I was in another country, being taken in by a foreigner – who was I to judge their hosting standards? Louise pointed to the bedroom and strongly suggested (commanded) I get some sleep, and that she was going out for lunch with her husband, and that she would see me later. And they went. Just like that.

I realised I had no keys to get out so I figured my only option was to actually sleep – and by the way I felt, that wouldn't be a bad option (if of course I hadn't been cringing inside at the state of the bed). And so, I slept. Trapped alone in this strange place, whose address I didn't know, which I couldn't leave, no phone signal, with nothing to eat or drink and wearing as many clothes as I could unpack to keep out the frostbite of an unheated building. Needless to say, I was not feeling too sure about this whole scenario…

Next thing I knew I'm waking up a couple of hours later to the sound of Louise and her husband having returned, and as their tiny home is also "The China Agency" office(!), they were both busy conducting interviews in their living room with a string of foreign male visitors, in order to place them to teach in far flung parts of China.

Tiled floors and booming male voices are not a good mix for the sleep deprived. When I popped my head out of my room, Louise thrust a spare set of her apartment keys in my hand, told me abruptly that the next time I would be needed was tomorrow afternoon, to sleep as much as I could now, and suggested I go out and get myself some food when I was ready, before turning her back on me to answer the intercom for her next interviews.

I retreated to my room confused, clearly in the way, and somehow amidst the noise fell asleep again, only to wake up to an empty and pitch-black apartment due to my stomach aching for food and my throat as dry as Gandhi's flip flop. So much for asking my host for tips on where to eat and food shop in the area. I guess I was going to have to brave it alone without any sense of orientation, map and full of apprehension.

Before I went out, I thought I'd take a shower and hoped that maybe she would be back when I was done, but the shower in the apartment looked terrifying - more than a little dirty (along with everything else in there) and strangely unused. No soap, no shampoo bottles - no evidence of regular washing. I was relieved to see two toothbrushes in the filthy sink however, so gained back a little hope of personal hygiene. Taking a shower at this point was a little too daunting for me at my stage of belly aching hunger and pending frostbite so I decided to brave the streets instead.

My dark walk through the maze of apartment blocks into the buzzing streets had me feeling like an alien. Everything was in Chinese, although why I'm surprised by this, I'm not sure. This is not the cosmopolitan Olympic city of Beijing I imagined, although I believed I might be on the outskirts of the city so I guess it being so 'local' made sense. My walk showed me that I was definitely the only Western person in the area, but contrary to stories from friends who had been here; my clearly Western appearance was barely acknowledged by the hordes of people streaming past me.

The dogs of course smelled something up I'm sure of it (perhaps due to my lack of washing), and I became to those who saw me, an apparent one-woman dog walking service. If only I knew whom to charge for it, I would have become instantly rich.

I later learned that Westerners are renowned for smelling of dairy. Our milky tea and cheese obsession perhaps? Either way, I wonder if my fresh-from-England scent was what attracted the hounds. My fluffy friends could neither confirm nor deny this so I can only assume this was the reason why.

In my determination to get food, I followed in reverse, with my trusty pack of hounds in tow, the people with supermarket carrier bags. It was easy to find but I was disappointed on arrival. It was on the first storey of a seemingly abandoned building with, on closer inspection, people walking out with bags and trolleys full of hardware items.

First task failed! As I turned my back, I saw a KFC and despite my hunger, was determined to keep searching for something a little more authentic than processed 'chicken'. Armed with good intentions I circled back in the vague direction of my temporary home through a market buzzing with people, the smell of food and steam and smoke disappearing above the throngs of very short, dark haired people.

I'd already decided that I would stick to rice or noodles for my dinner just to err on the safe side of 'being authentic' whilst not giving my stomach a rude awakening to China through the gift of unidentified meat that I had been warned about. This apparently was too much to hope for. I was ignored, glared at if I paused at a food stall and anyway, I had no idea what to ask for.

Suffice to say, I'm ashamed, but I totally (and literally) chickened out. I swerved the trailers and stands of admittedly very pleasant-smelling unidentified meat and found myself back at the doors of KFC where I struggled through pointing to a menu and nodding to get my order placed. My stomach would be sure to tell me in the next few hours whether or not I chose right to eat at KFC... the 'chicken' wasn't a colour or taste I expected. I just hoped the fries wouldn't let my body down too.

When I found my way back to the apartment around 8pm, it's apparent Louise had returned – although just about to leave again. She announced she would popping out for a short while and that if the door buzzer rang around 10pm, I was to let a man in and get him to leave 2000 Yuan on the table, which I was to count before he left. I was more than a little concerned. In a flash she was gone again and I was left wondering what on earth this whole scenario was all about - collecting money off men in the middle of the night, surely not?

Next thing I know, an older man lets himself into the apartment with a yappy dog and as I stick my head out of my room, it starts to make a bee-line for my ankles. Dogs seem to suddenly love me. The unannounced guest was armed with large bags of food which he deposited in the kitchen, he prattled at me in Chinese and let his dog attack me, looked me up and down, then disappeared as quickly as he had come. It was almost surreal. But he hadn't left any money?

With me thinking this was the man I was to let in, I began to panic that there was no money and maybe would I be accused of stealing it? I wasn't sure. My mind was in overdrive. I was therefore both shocked (and relieved?) when the buzzer later sounded. I answered the intercom and find myself speaking to an American man who was the money depositor.

Despite him being a particularly odd American (from NY – just for info – not as an explanation as to his oddity), I was grateful to finally speak to someone who could talk my language, who could tell me where exactly I was, and question until I ran out of breath all of the things I needed to know.

We swapped email addresses and he has offered to help where he can. He's been here three years and he hesitantly informed me that the money was for the rent of his apartment which Louise leases to him – just in case you were wondering. Not sure how convinced I was, he certainly looked awkward about it, but I was just glad this strange guy didn't make things difficult. I was glad when he had left and hoped he would be the last of the late-night male visitors.

When Louise finally reappeared, around 10pm she immediately sat me down and told me to rewrite my CV Chinese style 'to make me more attractive for my interviews'. I was confused...had I not already got a job? Was I not training and working at London Linked School, Beijing branch, that I had paid TEFL 'X' for? Been told the age of my kids? Been sent a link for the school I was working at?

Turns out not – and she knew nothing about that. Stupid me. Why when everything else leading up my arrival here had gone wrong, did I suddenly think that anything else I'd been told was true? What the hell was going on here and who the hell is this woman whose home I am in?

Louise informed me that I would have an interview with a school tomorrow and that I must prepare a demo class for them as they were over the age of 16, 'normal practice' for this age group apparently. Stunned again. Not only was it now 11pm at night, I now had homework to do, an interview to prepare for, I had no idea of the level of English knowledge this school/class had in order to pitch it right, I had no idea how to teach older kids and did not wish to – and I hadn't been given my two weeks of

Chinese orientation and training with which to do this beforehand. Oh, did I mention the orientation they promised me?

The two weeks' worth of induction, sightseeing and integration I thought I was having with other teachers like myself? Oh, well that's not happening either. I start teaching on Wednesday…and today is Sunday. Time to learn to fake an entire career in two days flat.I could feel the tears of fear and confusion bubbling.

Already seriously disturbed by my experience so far, I explained to Louise the completely different information I had been given before I arrived and she responded by mentioning that it might be possible to interview for primary children tomorrow afternoon instead (Monday).

I was relieved at this, but that didn't ease the fact I would be thrown in blind and this was not what I had paid for. Oh, and my teaching hours for either school I chose would be Wed-Fri 2-8pm and Sat and Sun 9-6pm with Monday and Tuesday off. The week off I had been told I would get in May was actually only possibly three days and those three days I had to make up beforehand, and the paid holiday days I was told I would have – they would be unpaid.

On a more positive note, she said I would be moving out on Tuesday into my own apartment. No more solitary confinement for me: clean sheets and the luxury of having food and drink was a fine thought. But would that be with the colleague that I was promised? I no longer had a clue.

From this point onwards, I didn't question anything further – my energy was completely sapped and my heart had sunk to unchartered depths. And she still hadn't offered me a drink.Once I had decided I couldn't face hearing any more after this, I retreated to my horrible bed. Fully clothed. In tears. Lonely. Regretting this whole mad decision to leave everything I loved behind me for six long months of goodness knows what. Let's hope tomorrow is brighter, maybe I'm just tired and confused and the language barrier is muddying the waters somewhat...because it certainly couldn't get any darker...could it?

AN INTERVIEWEE AND A WITNESS TO
A BEATING

The Con

So today is a new day and it's one day closer to the end of my trip – so I'm happier for that fact alone. Even having slept on it, it really feels like I've made a huge mistake. I'm hoping my spirits lift once I have seen the school, seen my own apartment, met other Westerners like myself and generally settled into a routine.

Although I was no longer confident of what form that would take. The dream of a safe escape to China to be trained as a teacher with a renowned UK company who would offer me some semblance of security was fast diminishing. Every Google search I had ever done on them had been glowing…no one warned me about this…

I later learned, and was to meet, the person responsible for the glowing reports, the happy fake blogs; the person responsible for policing the internet, and removing the honest reports which would have made me steer clear of this company. He was an employee of the London Linked School/ TEFL 'X' if you hadn't guessed it already. His name is William – look out for his multiple appearances later in my tale of doom. Coincidentally, he was also the guy who I had been expecting to meet me from the airport the day I arrived.

I wake up early as per their office hours when there are Chinese voices and phones ringing non-stop from about 7.30am. As my head is about a metre from the activity, more sleep is impossible. I still don't feel ready to show my face and so hide until I hear people leave.

Plus, it's so cold outside of my bed and the bundle of clothes I'd been sleeping under, that I have to work myself up to leaving it anyway - despite its stench and resident bugs, and even though I'm wearing a serious amount of clothes (which I mostly wore on the plane here but I am still the cleanest things in this hellhole). When I do leave the confines of my room to ask if I can use the shower, I'm told I will leave for my interview at 2pm. Yes, I can have a shower but immediately after that I must go and buy a mobile phone.

Wow…I'm to get a mobile method of communication, this is good news, despite having no idea who I would call - but comforted by the fact that I might get a glimpse of how to escape this apartment and its vicinity.

Getting clean again went ok, but getting dry was a little more difficult. Not only was it too cold to drop my towel to get dressed, I managed to blow one of my travel plugs with my travel hairdryer when I tried to use it to warm myself and the room that I was in. Thankfully I didn't blow the whole apartment's electrics but I couldn't risk trying again on my 2nd and last travel plug. Too much of my link to civilisation relied on power from it so I tied up my wet hair and vowed to buy a hairdryer on my next outing, which was to come in a short while.

Louise and I left the apartment at midday to go phone shopping, which was back in the area I had walked my stray band of dogs around last night. I purchased a cheap phone under her direction (local calls only) and was informed that it was her way to keep tabs on me and I must always answer if she calls me. Louise pointed me in the direction of a department store with heavy duty sleeping bags hanging from the doors to keep the cold out, and she once again instructed me to get food.

The basement of the well disguised department store was apparently a supermarket. If only I'd known this little gem when I needed food and drink last night. But on the plus side, I found a hairdryer. No more wet hair in this bitter cold country, and a much needed heat source. It felt like Christmas. Albeit a seriously miserable one.

I returned to the apartment long before my 2pm leave time to go for my interview. By 3.30pm my escort had arrived. Looks like timeliness is not too important here. Unless of course you're late for your lessons and you are then fined – according to The China Agency contract clauses. Which is the only clause I thought was fair enough. But rules for one don't suit another though it seems.

Some further examples of the clauses were:

If you don't give 24 hours notification of illness from work then you will both be unpaid, but also fined a tenth of your salary. God forbid the Chinese quease kicks in on the morning of lessons or if you have an inconvenient unscheduled illness.

Should any classroom apparatus, such as chairs, desks or other equipment be damaged under my watch, I am liable to pay for the replacement.

If you request more than three days leave, then your pay will be delayed by the number of days you requested. I'm unsure of this logic.

If you ask for more than five days leave in the first six months, you will be fined an entire month of pay.

Cancelling the working contract within six months will incur a month's worth of pay.

Pay day will be on the 20th day of the month following the month the pay covers. So, almost three weeks after fulfilling the work required.

So basically…the cheapest way I can escape is to walk out on the 20th day of a month and forfeit 20 days salary. Assuming I could even trust the agency to pay me at all.

You can see why even going for an interview to get a job that would trap me into this debacle was not an exciting adventure.

My escort was called Charles. Another classic Chinese name. His English is pidgin but from what I can gather he will be introducing me to the subway and taking me to my interview. The subway was a breeze on the journey there, but despite my new friend Charles being a Beijing-er, we got hopelessly lost in the business district of the city where I was to have my interview.

I later learned an interesting cultural point here that contributed to our disorientation. Even though Charles was asking for directions and people were giving them to him, we were sent off in completely the wrong direction on many occasions – despite people seemingly being confident of knowing where our destination was. It turns out that rather than say: "I'm sorry I don't know where 'x' is" they will blatantly lie to your face so as to save face. There is no admission of incapability or lack of knowledge – just a dishonest response that wastes your time. How jolly handy.

On finally, somehow, reaching our destination, it was then that I learned my interview was not actually at the school itself, but in an office block, so I'm still none the wiser as to where I'm going to end up.

The interview was a joke. After turning up embarrassingly late, then not being able to fill in a Chinese form, ten minutes of explaining my teaching experience of wild African children apparently qualified me for teaching in my new school of 3-14 year-olds. I had the job. Albeit one I was totally unsuited for.

We 'celebrated' with me buying Charles a Starbucks. It had been a while since I'd had a nice warm drink (or anything other than smelly tap water drunk out of my hand) so I was desperate for it and happy to pay for his too. Charles requested a 'coffee with alcohol' from the counter. I was surprised this was possible but we were in Beijing after all, maybe coffee was different here. But no, there is no alcohol coffee to be had. When Charles looked confused at the cardboard sleeve, he was offered to go around his cup to protect his hand from the heat, I realised I had got myself a coffee house novice. The straw he plunged in the top of his scalding coffee was the next subtle clue.

I hadn't yet learned, due to my limited exposure to Beijing so far, that a common and much more affordable way to get coffee in this country was in a plastic bag - with a straw in it. In retrospect my reaction at the time, although not expressed, was judgemental and naïve.

The trip home from the unprofessional and farce of an interview on the subway was horrendous. Bang in the middle of rush hour, the Beijing subway is a violent place – and not through vagrants camping out in the tunnels as you might imagine drunk or begging for money, but from smartly dressed businessmen and women. Getting on the trains is a surge, a push and shove and an aggressive squeeze into place, with no notice taken of people trying to get off first, it's survival of the fittest down there. If you think the London Tube is busy at rush hour, then this is 100 times worse. Luckily there is only a small gap to mind or I'm pretty sure there would regularly be bodies on the track.

The most disturbing experience I had that will stick in my mind forever, was from a tiny teenage girl who did her brave push for entry onto the train past a large businessman (large for a Chinese male but still a good foot or two shorter than me – boy do I feel like a giant here at 5'7" tall). As she did so, she clipped his bag with her own – as is inevitable in surging crowds such as these.

What I didn't expect was the way he turned and instinctively responded by smacking her in the head with his briefcase, not once, but four times. After the first time I thought he would realise he had hit a young girl, maybe apologise, maybe look a little ashamed, as he well should, but no, he went in for more, foaming at the mouth as he did it. He only stopped his attack when the alarm sounded for the doors to close and in a final act of anger; he kicked her hard in the legs from the place on the platform that he had disembarked to.

I felt sick. And no-one helped her. No-one even batted an eyelid. A weak squeal escaped my lips but Charles gave me a look to say 'Shut up!' so I quickly dampened it. I was in shock. Why did people stand by and let this happen?! Why did he think that was okay and more interestingly, why did she not react…? Seriously, where the hell am I? Such disgusting behaviour I hope I never see again.

Alas, little did I know then that this was tame and I would encounter much, much worse, and that China held even darker brutality and risk that I would come to experience during the rest of my stay.

On finally returning to my (hopefully) temporary home, Louise congratulated me on my new job and confirmed I would start on Wednesday and that she would show me around my potential new apartment tomorrow afternoon.

This, by the way, was an hour's commute and then a further 45-minute walk from the school. Once again, what happened to the 'no more than 20 minutes' promise? I was furious. I calmly told her of the hundredth promise that had not been kept and made it clear this was unacceptable. She then suggested that the alternative was that I stayed with her for another month and commuted from her place (same distance as the apartment she had found me) and see how I coped with the commute.

I told her I wanted my own place as soon as possible so I could settle and that as kind as her offer was, it was not an acceptable option. I didn't mention the filth, frostbite or malnutrition I was bound to start suffering if I stayed. She has no idea how to host.

She said I could go to my room whilst she gave it some thought. Thanks. As if I hadn't already had enough of enforced solitary confinement... and to think I hadn't even broken the law to deserve this treatment. And if I wasn't crazy yet I sure would be if my life carried on this way. I wondered if amongst the junk in the room there would be some wall padding from previous occupants who had been in my situation.

About 8pm she appeared at my door with the most bizarre and ridiculous contract I had ever seen, written up for a year. Worse than the sample one I had already been shown and now this one was for a whole year rather than six months. I'm totally at my wits end by this point – and I think she is with me, too. Her usual 'clients', whatever she recruits them for, are obviously more of a pushover than I am. However, she adjusted the contract to add a six month break clause to it, just below the list of fines I could expect to receive if I so much as sneeze in the wrong direction. I'm not sure whether or not to be grateful or just get on the next plane home.

Faced with an outrageous contract and the events of the last few days... I finally began to feel scared. It began to dawn on me that I had effectively been people trafficked, hadn't I?

At this point I truly believe she was sick of me and wanted to solve me as a problem, and showed me an apartment she had found online which was a five-minute walk from my new school, a five-minute walk from the horrific subway, but in the very centre of Beijing. It looked simple, it had a single bed in a tiny room with no curtains and I was to be sharing the apartment with an unknown Chinese woman – not a 'colleague' as advertised when I took and paid for this placement. But you should all be learning by now that anything you thought you knew about what I was doing is rubbish.

Apparently, no-one shares with colleagues, they all share with professional Chinese people and that is their preferred option? News to me. But what can I do? I want to go home but have no idea how to go about this... if I stay, I either take this apartment, or stay here for another month, or commute for two hours a day and risk bodily harm every time - and I'm tired of fighting everything I come up against. I get to see it tomorrow afternoon (after a visit to the school I had to beg for, so I am prepared for where I need to turn up to) and if it's remotely acceptable then I'm just going to take it and try to start my life in Beijing.

It's cost me a lot to get here, I feel I have no choice but to see this through. I have no home to go back to, no job, and I'm scared that if I do go home, I will be too nervous to leave the UK again – and travelling was my passion. But ultimately, my pride is completely destroyed and I'm too ashamed to admit I have failed and been conned.

There is no-one I know of that I can get any more help from out here, and despite my troubles so far, I need to give this a good try. If all else fails, I need to get some independence from my current predicament, then I will be free to flee if I want to.

So that's my next plan.

3

NO HOME AND NO CHOW MEIN
EITHER

The Con

Surprise, surprise, the following day didn't bring much of anything to be positive about.

I got myself up and ready to leave the apartment at 12 noon as instructed last night, for both my visit to the school and my apartment viewing. I am still apparently the only person to have used the shower and Louise is still wearing the same red jumper and baggy tights she was wearing since she picked me up days ago. That should confirm to you the conditions I currently reside in.

At 12 noon Louise informed me that I would now be leaving at 3.30pm and was told 'go to your room' until 'it's time'. So that's another good few hours spent in the confines of my dingy room, and a lost opportunity to find civilisation and sightsee just to get myself out of here.

Instead I'm writing these pages so that in the event of my demise there is evidence of how it happened. It is also the only thing I can do right now to keep my sanity and occupy my time. On my stroll to the subway at the allotted time, I realise it has now been over 24 hours since I last ate. I had a packet of crisps from the supermarket for lunch yesterday…a nutritious diet I know, but there is little other option unless I risk a KFC again. This combined with the tap water is not making me feel well at all. The silver lining of this cloud is that my trousers already feel a little looser.

Halfway through my trip I was to meet my alcoholic coffee buddy Charles at a midpoint station so he could escort me to my new school. After yesterday's saga of getting lost in Beijing I didn't see how this was a wise choice of company but again, I had little choice and was beginning to get used to the fact that I had no control over my existence here at this stage. If I played this game right, I'd be able to escape at the next given unwatched opportunity – when I had moved out of the apartment on the promise of faking being a legitimate teacher for The China Agency.

When I met Charles, he proudly informed me he had already completed one mission today – showing another new teacher an apartment, but which a few moments later, the guy later called to turn down. This didn't fill me with too much hope about my own pending viewing, but today I was trying to remain positive. Mind over matter, right? I had a goal now. Play the game, win freedom.

We eventually made it to the school after Charles asked for directions from almost every person he met on the street. He is definitely a simple soul and it also turns out he needs glasses but refuses to wear them – which is why he gets hopelessly lost all of the time. He can't even read the road names and maps are a blur. Its feels great to know I have a network of incompetents supporting me. When we find the school for 5pm, it turns out to be the sixth and top floor of a shopping mall. It looks fun and friendly and I am greeted by a teacher called Justin (Chinese), who was genuinely lovely.

He talked me briefly through an example of the syllabus for a few of the age groups for ten minutes and then informed me if I return in an hour, I can observe a lesson. This seemed like a good idea, although frustrating to have to kill time again - but if I could track down Charles who was loitering nearby, I would make him get us some food.He passed that test with flying colours with some super Chinese food for both of us, for less than a fiver.

I doubt I will be able to eat it again mind you as the menu was all Chinese symbols and I didn't recognise what it was called. When I tried to request chow mein, the Staff looked at me strangely. Lee's Garden Chinese Takeaway back home has caused me embarrassment. My menu based Chinese language learning has not proved useful and who knew that numbers for menu items were not a universal language?

When I returned at 6pm to the school, I was invited to watch a kindergarten lesson of very lively four-year-olds. The three teachers in the room were all suitably animated for their audience, but there was no teaching, all they did was play games on the white boards with the kids for the hour.

I figured I could handle that if I knew how to use an interactive whiteboard and all the magical games it could offer. I'm not sure if I'm just supposed to somehow know all this stuff, but I envisage a lot of practice on my part outside of lesson times. I also reckoned that would be the easiest class to teach and still desperately needed to see other age groups in session.

After the lesson, the three teachers who had conducted the lesson approached me eagerly for feedback on their own performance, you know, because I was a qualified and experienced teacher from

England and my opinion was clearly important to them. In my realisation that I was absolutely not the person I had been sold to them as, and the nervous state that had put me in, I almost laughed in their faces. I also noticed I was the only Westerner in the building, so this would be a solo flying-by-the-seat-of-my-pants scenario with very little moral support from someone else who could understand my situation, my language or advise on cultural challenges.

Suffice to say, I'm feeling utterly terrified at the prospect of teaching now, even if I only have to fake it for a short while whilst I plan my escape. But, alas, no time to dwell on it for too long, I have an apartment viewing at 7pm so I had to make a swift exit.

In Charles' downtime whilst I was at the school, he claimed to have found the apartment block my viewing was in, but as per Charles' awesome directional skills, the five-minute walk, now in the dark, proved too much for him and we ended up strolling the dark and seedy streets of a residential area in north west Beijing for nearly an hour. This unscheduled tour made me wary of the area straight away so I think I had already decided there was no way I would feel safe living there, despite its proximity to the school.The apartment entrance was down a dark alleyway in an unlit area. It was on the 6th and top floor of a shady looking building and the hike to the apartment itself was not good.

Dusty dark stairwells, littered with broken bikes and dead pot plants revealed a less than impressive apartment. Filthy was not the word (the place I am in now is positively spotless in comparison). It was hard to tell the original colour of the toilet bowl, the kitchen walls were crawling with bugs and I'm sure the units only hung to the walls with grime, the one sofa it had was broken and stained - not even a student would have accepted to live here. Bearing in mind my university house back in the UK had been condemned by the environmental health, I feel I can judge.

Not only was it in dire shape, smelly and frankly crying out for condemnation by environmental health to put it out of its misery at least a decade ago, it turned out that I would not only be sharing with a Chinese woman (who spoke no English) but also a third person, a Chinese man too. Three people in an apartment no bigger than a postage stamp with whom I could not communicate and was pretty sure hadn't washed for quite some time.

Lack of cleanliness seems to be an enduring feature in my tale but having also lived in tents in Africa for weeks at a time; I can honestly say that my standards in foreign countries can be pretty low. But this was taking the biscuit.

I felt utterly destroyed. I had been determined that I would be positive about my new place (about something, anyway), but this was too much. There was no way in the world I would be taking this. Which meant I was stuck longer with Louise and her husband in solitary confinement. Is there no end to the misery? My China dream (more importantly my escape dream) was crashing around me and I hadn't even been in the country five minutes. Plus, I still hadn't spoken to my parents who I desperately needed right now.

On my journey back to Louise's I decided that I would have to try to get in direct contact with William, the TEFL 'X' contact here in Beijing. Bizarrely, when my phone had finally detected a signal, I had received a text message from him whilst I was in lessons saying he was 'so pleased to hear I have settled in so well'. Seriously?!!! I'm ready to get on the next plane out of here. What's taken him so long to contact me? He knows I don't have a number for him… he will also know I've been frantically trying to contact him after his no-show at the airport. And now what on earth has he been told? I've pretty much cried every time I have spoken to Louise, I have questioned everything she has put to me and made it damn clear that nothing that was happening was part of the teacher training contract I had signed (and paid for – more fool me).

I called him when my subway ordeal was over and I was on my walk back to the apartment. I let rip, in an ashamedly hysterical manner and told him that if he didn't help me immediately, I was flying home and raising merry hell when I got back about the con, that was the London Linked School, I was apparently wrapped up in.

I told him my tales and he sounded genuinely shocked. Either he is a super liar or he was honestly surprised to hear of my plight. He was a little confused that if I wasn't happy, I was feeling isolated and was nervous of teaching without an introduction, why on earth wasn't I attending the five days training that starts tomorrow?

Louise told me it wasn't happening and didn't exist and that I had to start teaching tomorrow…I'm livid. She had clearly lied to me to get me on her payroll quicker. And in addition, yes, according to Will, I should be sharing with TEFL 'X' colleagues, or alternatively living on my own near to the school. Not with strangers in some backwater dive. Was he thinking on his feet, or was this true?

As a result of my near on hysteria, William is meeting me tomorrow at the subway at 9.30am to escort me to the training college where I will meet other interns, after we have had a coffee together and got to the bottom of the lies and shock that are overwhelming me. I guess I wait and see tomorrow if he can be trusted, if this will speed up my escape from this apartment and ease my fears at even being here in this mess as well as get me on track with the internship as I had understood it. Time will tell. But I reckon tonight I will sleep easier, knowing there is help coming in the morning.

Fingers crossed it will actually be help and not another smokescreen in my Beijing horror story.

4

A RESCUE FOR BREAKFAST, EARS FOR LUNCH, WESTERNERS FOR DINNER

The Con

I woke up two hours before I needed thanks to a toddler tantrum directly above my head. I stupidly missed an opportunity to Skype home before everyone back in the UK went to bed since I have now managed to get hold of the Wi-Fi password, which I'm disappointed about. I'm just not thinking straight at the moment, plus, I'm avoiding having to act happy when I'm scared and exhausted and frankly embarrassed at my situation. The story so far has just grown too big to cover in one conversation.

I got back to my hovel too late last night to pick up food or drink from the supermarket so I had a growling stomach and only a bottle of flat coke to quench my thirst so that was another level of misery I didn't want to share.

I snuck out of my room as soon as the child woke me, to switch on the Wi-Fi, the best part of my day because I'm guaranteed word from home, even if not able to see anyone's faces.

Just as I snuck into the living area to turn on the Wi-Fi, I noticed a pile of bedding on the sofa. I had noticed it last night but thought nothing of it. Louise was under it (Wilson must have stayed away) because it turns out she had another waif and stray staying in her and her husband's room... an American girl! My first non-Chinese female sighting since I arrived here. I felt ecstatic. We barely had a chance to speak more than a greeting (we were not given a chance to be alone together or foster a conversation) and a 'see you later' but I hope to see her later this evening after my day trip to TEFL 'X'. I just hope she doesn't feel the shock I did... I wouldn't wish this on anyone.

Anyway, I'm showered, have dry hair and I'm wrapped up warm - it's lightly snowing today so it will probably be a cold one. I head to the KFC outside the subway which is my designated meeting point. William isn't here, but he is at a KFC at a subway station - just not mine. Mine is called Shuang Xiao, he was at Shuang Jing. Easy mistake to make I guess but they are 30 minutes apart so I'm in for a wait. I think he's probably just as nervous to meet me as I am him. It won't be a happy conversation but all I can hope is that it changes things.

I wait outside in the cold for about 20 minutes, grateful to breathe some fresh(ish) air after my stuffy confines. I just missed the morning shift at KFC so I'm having more coke, and it's only 10am. My dentist will love me when I get home. Almost as much as the employees love me in this KFC. I think I've been in twice a day since I got here, whether it's just for a drink, some 'chicken' or just a quick loo stop – of which there have been many urgent requirements.

Despite KFC being of Western origin, the toilets are distinctly disgusting - but needs must at times and they have forced me to perfect the squat technique. Every time I come here the cashiers shuffle round to avoid serving me. It's embarrassing. But I'm pretty good at pointing and paying, all accompanied with an apologetic smile from me and a stony stare from them.

The next little while is a whirl in my head. William arrived at KFC and instead of coffee, after having read the choice diary excerpts I had sent him the night before, whisked me straight off to TEFL 'X' headquarters, based in the London Linked School I was originally supposed to be teaching at. There I met with him and his colleague Jon, a Canadian, who listened to my tale of woe and jumped into action, arranging for the immediate collection of luggage and my passport from the hands of Louise.

They escorted me back to her apartment with the embassy number, the local police number and the number for their lawyers all prepared in case there was trouble – mainly because she had my passport. She had requested this on my arrival 'for visa purposes' – I hadn't wanted to give it to her but being vulnerable and at her mercy I felt I had no choice.

Several attempts by me to get it back had failed – I couldn't have even left the country had I wanted to, but had been assured it would be back in my hands if I took her job and accommodation. I began to be very nervous at the way they reacted. Like they were on a mission to save my life from the Chinese underworld. Returning to the apartment with men in tow made Louise visibly nervous and she tried to separate me from them so she could speak with me. The boys were having none of it (I later learned this wasn't to protect me – but themselves from the truths I might learn – read on) but remained calm and polite until I, and my belongings, were safely out and before I knew it, we were back at HQ.

There was a lot of nervous chatter about "what could have happened if" but I know the boys were just relieved all went okay on the rescue mission. I questioned them about how much they knew about Louise and they said that they had met her and she seemed lovely and they had no reason to suspect her of wrong doings. They avoided my questions about what she had to do with this whole internship thing I had signed up to with them…if I smelt a rat before, I was now smelling a whole pack of them. I got a distinct nagging impression that she was 'new' to them and in the back of my mind my suspicion was rising further as to what I had got mixed up in.

It turns out Mitchell, the other intern who arrived the same day as me, was also staying in accommodation Louise had arranged so they were curious to speak to him about his experiences. I thought this was strange because when I asked Louise for Mitchell's details so I could contact him, simply for moral support from another new person in this strange country, she had claimed she knew nothing about him. When I told William this, he looked perplexed. He had gone with Louise to the airport to collect both of us, but because we were flying into different terminals, Louise insisted he left her to be on time to meet Mitchell even though he was arriving a whole hour after me and that she would wait for me herself.

Putting together the pieces of information that I knew so far, a girl had previously stayed in Louise's dungeon and left the day before I arrived, and another girl had arrived the day I left…but it was only a string of men who visited her apartment for 'interviews' and she had sent them on their way as soon as she could. Was this woman collecting vulnerable foreign girls...? I shudder at the thought.

By now it was about 11.30am and Mitchell who was also due at the school was assumed lost, also un-contactable and now an hour and a half late for our meeting. Yet another concern for the already tired TEFL 'X' team. Mitchell eventually arrived and the mystery was solved. He had already run out of credit on his Chinese phone (which means you are not only unable to make calls, but are unable to receive calls or text messages either) because he had spent too long on the phone to his girlfriend in Hong Kong for moral support – for he too had been having an ordeal all of his own.

Once Mitchell and I had calmed ourselves from the morning's activities, Jon and William took us for lunch at their favourite Chinese restaurant, about 20 mins walk from the school.

I ate like a King and a Queen and all their footmen combined. It was the best meal yet (admittedly my first proper one in several days so it was bound to rate pretty high). I even had my first sip of Chinese beer. Apparently not China's finest ale, but it tasted like a little piece of heaven in a glass. I was seconds away from making a faux pas of drinking straight from the bottle when it was served to the table – thinking it was all mine, but here they serve it up in a very small, teacup sized glass. Nonetheless, it was better than the Coke I had been living off – although still a threat to my teeth.

The feast was huge: kung pao chicken, black pepper beef, dumplings, spicy lentils, spinach and hazelnuts, mustard wooden ear fungus, (and yes it tastes as bad as it sounds) finished off with a spot of jasmine tea, which tasted like potpourri, served in another teacup. Splendid. My first proper meal in what felt like months.

Conversation was just as good as the food. Jon from Vermont grew up on a mountain with no TV. He studied Chinese history at school and decided he wanted civilisation (!) so moved to Beijing and took up a job with TEFL 'X' at the London Linked School. I did question that logic but he has been here five years with his English girlfriend and has no plans to go home, so it obviously makes perfect sense to him and I warmed to him immediately.

William is Australian, and lived for a few years in Wales. Became fascinated by Chinese history and won a scholarship to study Mandarin at Beijing University, five and half years ago. He has no plans to leave either and is with his Chinese wife over here. I cannot warm to him though. There is something shifty and disingenuous about him.

Mitchell is 32 and has spent years living in various places around the world. He met his girlfriend when he was working in a backpacker lodge selling tours in Australia. She is from Hong Kong and he is from Kent, England. The purpose for him being here is that he gets a professional teaching certificate doing this internship and if he does a total of a year here in Beijing, his chances of getting a Hong Kong visa are greater. Only then can he apply for a teaching/working visa to join his girlfriend in Hong Kong. Otherwise he would have to marry her to live there. Although he is not averse to this idea, he doesn't want it to force the issue.

Mitchell is hilarious, I adored him straight away. Despite the fact he has this annoying habit of saying "true" in response to everything people say. (This is a 'true' fact).

This background information is pretty dull but will be relevant later in my tale…

Lunch and informalities out of the way, we all trudge back to the London Linked School to discuss where we are all at, and begin our one-week (which we thought was two weeks) training sessions. But not before Mitchell has let off some steam about… guess what…his experience with Louise.

On arrival in Beijing, he was whisked off to a studio apartment of his own by William, which was owned by Louise. He had the same problem of disgusting sheets and questionable cleanliness of the squat-like apartment. He too was sleeping in all his clothes, it was freezing, there was no hot water and he had to make an early purchase of a bottle of bleach to sanitise the place. It also turns out that the apartment is obviously up for rent and out of the blue he would find himself face to face with people letting themselves in to his apartment for viewings, several times a day, whether he was there or not.

One time he stepped out of the shower in his pants, only to face three Chinese people having a viewing. Another time he comes home from a jaunt to find his balcony door swinging open and urine splashed all over the toilet, and another time to an unflushed poo. He has taken to carrying round with him in his backpack all of his valuable belongings and hiding his other belongings when he goes out, just in case. He is pretty furious too.

In addition, Louise had arranged a job interview for him at a Korean school, the same day I interviewed for mine. His interview was tougher and he got thrown into a situation where he had to, without warning, draw up two lesson plans and to conduct two x 45 minute lessons. He said he winged it but was too embarrassed to tell us what he had done for it and swore never to be put in that situation again. More fury. He'd done a simple (and very poorly written) online TEFL course too which introduces you to the basics of the English language but in no way prepares you to stand in front of a class and teach. He had signed up for the same program I had which promised us an ease into teaching, not being thrown in the deep end and obviously sold to us as a job of a professional and experienced teacher to have half our salary stolen from us and live in a flea pit.

He's also not happy with his working hours. He had received his teaching timetable and he is expected to teach, unsupported, seven hours straight with no breaks Monday to Friday. This well exceeds the expected teaching hours we had been told we were having as trainees and doesn't even allow for lesson planning time. Bad, huh?

Mind you, my hours and expectations are even worse in comparison.

Just to focus on my teaching hours for a second, because over time I have got more and more cross about them. They have totally knocked the wind out of my sails. At least Mitchell is working just Monday to Friday and can see his girlfriend at weekends. My hours, from Wednesday through to Sunday, exceed even his designated hours and in addition ruin my weekend trip plans, and make things a little tough for when I have visitors – because they don't match their working weeks and time off, even though I was informed otherwise.

The problem is that I think at this point in time when things are pretty low, everyone I care about is magnified in importance to me (they were very important before, now they're critical to me). This lack of availability is making me feel like I've got a really tough deal and I might as well have stayed in England and slogged my guts out there instead. I had very little time then either but I had a nice home and good money and the people I care about close by, and standard working-week schedules that afforded me time to spend with them.

Despite this, I'm also beating myself up about the fact that I've lost sight of my reason for being here in the first place: to experience the world, to teach children and further my change of career and that maybe I just need to toughen up a bit. But everything is questionable in my mind right now. This whole thing has mentally been a lot of hard work and most importantly, a complete farce.

In isolation, the little detail of my working hours would be disappointing enough, but not a deal-breaker, but the cumulative effect of potentially living in squalor and everything else that's going wrong/not making sense, makes me feel totally lost. And I can't tell you how sick I feel at the prospect of being plunged into a classroom environment, apparently unsupported, that I haven't been properly prepared for. I know the same is expected of Mitchell and he is feeling just as uneasy so I don't feel like I'm being unreasonable. We signed up for something completely different.

This whole thing is nothing like I thought it would be. I'm even starting to question my understanding of everything I was sold on. Had I just got this all wrong and romanticised the whole thing in my head due to my eagerness to see the world and teach? I didn't know anymore. But the more I hear that Mitchell is in the same boat and equally confused and angry, the more I am reassured that it's not just my imagination and that something really underhand has happened to us.

In the meantime, Mitchell also told us of an apartment viewing Charles had taken him on the day before. He was shown into an apartment an hour and half outside the city, in the vague direction of the Korean school he had been interviewed for. It turned out to be a two-bed apartment, one room was occupied and in the living room there was a shower curtain cordoning off another bed and a baby's cot.

Not only that, but he described it as being like a concrete cubicle – with no plaster on the walls or tiles on the floor. He would however have his own room. Naturally even this did not placate him and he was furious that this would even be considered as appropriate for him. Especially as, again, we were promised something different. "An apartment shared with colleagues" doesn't really match here either, does it?

I couldn't wait to get Mitchell on his own to speak with him further – and totally candidly - about what on earth was going on here.

Mitchell and I had been due to be at the London Linked School for a whole day of training on various bits and bobs, but due to our late start there was not much time for us to really do anything. Plus, William and Jon were particularly laid back and slow at directing us to do anything. William did manage to fit in ten minutes of discussing how to do lesson plans, which basically could be summarised as: don't worry about them, just Google what you need.

I've decided he's an outright idiot – he's one of those kids at school who tries to be cool but can't actually pull it off because he's beyond socially awkward. That's not particularly useful for completely novice teachers and I can't help feeling that there was no substance or truth behind this supposed training week either. Were they just thinking on their feet in the face of an awkward situation? You have to wonder and probably conclude 'yes' just like I did.

The day was also cut short by Chinese Louise having promised Mitchell's evening to the Korean school he was to be teaching at and because of the distance he would have to travel to it, he had to leave at 3.30pm. He ran off sweating about how he would recognise Chinese symbols he had to look for to catch the right bus, the number of stops he had to endure, and if all else failed, the pronunciation of exactly where he needed to be for a taxi driver to take him, if indeed they stopped for this white man (which I would learn is frustratingly rare).

We were so deep in Chinese territory, with no maps, no tips or advice, I was impressed by his courage to go out into the even deeper darker suburbs, but more confused as to why he was still under the impression that this was expected of him – and Will and Jon did not correct him. Had he not learned from today that what Louise was putting him through, was not what either of us had paid to come here for?

When Mitchell had gone, I had to hang around and wait for someone to sort out some sort of accommodation for me that night which took another couple of painful hours. It also meant I got to meet the Director of Studies for The London Linked School called Jim, who was instantly pretty pervy and made me feel more than a little uncomfortable with such inappropriate stories and comments that he would have been sued on the spot in the English workplace. I think his opening sentence to me was "Are you on your period? Because if you are you know you shouldn't eat ice cream". No word of a lie. Apparently, a Chinese belief that I should take note of. This didn't bode well for the people who were now 'saving' me if he was one of their seniors.

Due to me viewing an apartment on Friday (having previously been arranged by Louise or TEFL 'X' - who knew?), the thought was that I could go to a hotel for the next few nights and assuming I liked the apartment I saw, I was to move into that on Saturday, so three nights in a hotel wasn't really a big deal – and frankly there were no other options for me. What I didn't realise was that only the first two nights were to be paid for and I would end up being stuck there much longer at my own expense.

William found and booked a hotel for me called the 7 Days Inn, a 15-minute walk from The London Linked School. Yes, it was close, and it was safe and presumably clean, but I couldn't face lugging my entire luggage there, so I took a moment to repack an overnight bag so at least I could manage for the next day and not have to carry unneeded items along the roads, and leave the rest in the school. Just as well because 15 minutes turned into a half an hour walk and on reaching the hotel, they took one look at me and announced they didn't accept foreigners. Apparently, a legacy from the Olympics a few years ago, but again, I was soon to learn that foreigners were not welcome in most places in Beijing by any stretch of the imagination.

So, on we go with another trek of the streets, past live chicken in a coup ready to be slaughtered at the adjoining restaurant, an astounding amount of sex shops, just to find somewhere that would take this lost and forlorn white girl. Weirdly, we found another 7 Days Inn another half hour walk away that would accept me and I finally got to settle into my new home. It was clean (ish), had fresh un-slept-in bedding, a real towel (as opposed to my travel towels) and a power shower.

Unfortunately, I was too depressed and exhausted to feel excited. The drama of the morning and the last few days, plus a wasted day with TEFL 'X' and the confusion of my situation was too much and I was so disheartened I shut my door and cried. Again. One day it will come as a surprise that I didn't have a day in which I didn't cry. I'm looking forward to that.

Moments later I get a skype call from my clearly very stressed, upset and worried parents. They had received my diaries for the first few days and were naturally very concerned. I naively had thought that if I gave an honest warts-and-all view of my trip so far it would make interesting reading because it would then have been swiftly followed up by a happy clappy diary entry of how everything had settled and was awesome.

Unfortunately, I had wrongly assumed that it would all turn good soon and hadn't anticipated a prolonged misery. Instead I had so far succeeded in leaving people I care about in a state of worry and concern and with no real solutions to my dire dilemma thousands of miles away. By the time we had all finished crying on Skype, I had about 15 minutes to decide whether or not I wanted to join a night out with the other Western teachers from the school. I had met a teacher called Samuel earlier that day at the school who had very kindly invited me to eat and drink with the rest of the teachers from the London Linked School at a nearby restaurant. At the time of his offer I had been very keen to do so, but right at this point in time, I just wanted to hide my head from the world.

After taking the deserved chastising from my parents, it took a superhuman effort and a fit of anger and defiance that China would not bring me down, that I decided to drag myself back out of the hotel to the scary streets to make the pre-arranged meeting time back at the school for when Samuel finished his teaching at about 8pm to join other people like myself for a good feed. As much as I wanted to, I simply couldn't bear passing up the opportunity to meet real-life Westerners and talking uninhibitedly about my ordeal so far. Plus, I needed to get this whole saga off my chest and to not feel so alone.

I was late to the rendezvous due to taxi drivers ignoring me on the side of the road, but Samuel was dutifully waiting for me to appear when I finally made it. I was so grateful to see him. Within two minutes flat he had bought me a bottle of local ale for the walk (as a cheer up drink) and we had begun our walk in the biting cold to meet the others in a nearby local restaurant.

As soon as I met him, I knew I had made the right decision to go out for the evening due to his warmth and friendliness, and when we arrived at a fellow teacher's apartment and I was met by six other Western smiling faces I felt my spirits lift. There really were other people like me out here, and just seeing them gave me hope of regaining a little of my sanity.

I briefly filled them in on my introduction to China, to which they unconvincingly behaved like it shocked them, passed me a mug of wine, and promised me a good evening. And it was. It was at their favourite local Chinese Barbeque 'restaurant', back in the direction of my hotel, where the food was piled high and drinks other than flat warm coke were flowing. There were six girls and two guys in the end, and we giggled and gossiped like we were old friends. The relief at this small mercy was overwhelming and reminded me of what I loved about travelling. You can immerse yourself all you like in the culture, but there's nothing quite like 'meeting your own' in countries alien to your own for a reassuring metaphorical hug.

Due to being so sleep deprived, I reluctantly left them pretty early to carry on their drinking until the early hours and made my way back to my hotel, feeling much better within myself. They had all plugged their phone numbers into my phone in case I needed them and promised to adopt me as one of them. One of the girls, an Australian girl called Amity who has been here for two and half years, walked me right back to the door of the hotel. She was so nice and I was really grateful to her for taking the walk through the dark streets just to see me home safe. I questioned her safety of making it back to the bar in the dark on her own and so late at night, but she said in the whole time she has been here she has never felt physically unsafe and violent crime is virtually unheard of. I did message the guys soon after she had left to make sure she was back safely, and sure enough she was.

I hoped against hope that this evening wasn't a one off and that these great people will become a part of my new life in Beijing, if of course I am to stay out here at all. Who knows what will happen right now? I'm now quite a long time into this whole ordeal and still nothing is clear.

As I tucked myself up in bed a couple of things really struck me about the people I had just met. Although they feigned shock at my start in Beijing, they didn't ask too many questions and didn't really comment too much on it. If I had met someone who had experienced being seemingly sold in China, having their passport taken from them and who had been collecting money off men in the middle of the night - I'm damn sure I would have grilled them. But these guys...either they already knew the details, or China had stopped surprising them with its drama. They also just rolled their eyes when I told them how I had been treated by the school since. The school is definitely not held in a good light either, from what I can gather. Although no-one really gave anything concrete away.

What I had learned from that night was that one of the girls, Aoife with the strongest Irish accent I have ever heard, was protesting the fact over dinner that her six-month teaching contract had just been renewed, and even though she had negotiated keeping her room in the schools apartment as part of the deal, the second she actually signed her new contract she had been kicked out with only a couple of days' notice. She had made immediate plans to sleep on Amity's sofa, starting tomorrow, on the other side of the city, in an apartment shared with Samuel and another teacher called Lana. But getting apartments in Beijing was so tough she had no idea what she was going to do now. She was not a happy bunny.

Aoife had actually successfully completed the program which I had arrived to do. I wondered if it was her fault, in that because she renewed her contract at the last minute, that perhaps that's why my job vacancy didn't come up and I got passed on to Louise instead? I wonder who else did that to cause the same trouble for Mitch. Certainly no-one knew who this Louise person was.

Amity herself was also clearly pretty mad at a situation the school had put her in. She refused to share the details with me so that I could make my own informed decisions which I respect her for, but I'm not getting a good feeling about the school at all. Still, good to know that I am right to be on my guard. I have no idea what is unnecessary paranoia anymore. One of the other girls Holly, who was more than a little drunk, kept asking and asking whether I had met Jim yet. She demanded to know if he had been inappropriate to me yet as apparently, it's a rite of passage. She didn't ask it in an amused manner – she asked in a disgusted 'I hate that man' tone. I really want to know more about that. I held off on relating my 'have you got your period' experience.

But regardless of their collective whines, as a group they were strong, supportive and protective of each other – that was so clear. I desperately hoped I could just slide on in to this safety net if I ended up staying. I needed people experienced in the ways of this weird world I had stepped into, and frankly, I did genuinely really like them all.

Another thing that really hit home tonight was that we were all equals. All but one of the people I met tonight were teachers and had met through the same school. It didn't seem to matter who any of us had been before we landed in China – it was irrelevant. It didn't matter if you had had a good career, a nice car, a home – or any of the things we tend to measure people by at home. You start from zero and it's your personality and attitude that counts now. Having travelled before, this was something I used to love. The ability to start again, the fresh start, to be who you really were now and not what history dictated for you. But in this situation, it stung a little bit. I think that deep down I needed to not be that gullible de-frauded girl who left England on a whim to bum around the world as an unqualified 'teacher'.

My self-esteem had taken a battering in the last few weeks; I had no power or real control over the outcome of my situation. I was embarrassed – and I needed my history and my past to be my crutch right now, to prop me up. Except no one here cared. Everyone had their own reasons for travelling – bad break ups, career drifters, grief, or simply a passion to get paid to travel. The reasons become irrelevant in a ropey smoky restaurant in darkest Beijing.

The only non-teacher in the group was a guy called Rob. Originally from London, he had been in Beijing for six months on a quest to learn Mandarin. He had been an expat Project Manager in Singapore previously, and intended to stay in Asia, where his employment opportunities were very lucrative. He had decided to take a sabbatical from work and gain a skill that would further his career. More often than not, his employees were Chinese and he thought by learning the Mandarin language he could progress his career better.

He was currently attending college every day whilst applying for his next expat role. He had managed to meet the rest of the group by coincidence when strolling past the very restaurant we met at tonight where everyone else was eating, and sticking out like a sore thumb with his white skin in a very local non-tourist area, he had been heckled and dragged in to the fold. I immediately liked him. He had eyes that shone and when he spoke to you and it felt like you were the only person in the room. We hit it off immediately. Both being serious career professionals taking a sabbatical in the crazy world of China we had something in common. I felt an immediate bond.

I felt like I was going to be safe so long as I was part of this group.

A stark realisation

Today is the day Mitchell and I have to venture to the other school in the very centre of Beijing for a morning of training before heading back east to HQ for the remainder. It's a day of Chinese language lessons, Chinese culture lessons and lesson observations. Apparently.

I leave to head to the school for 10am as instructed and crossed paths with Will and Jon on their way in to the hotel to pay for another night for me. That was a surprise as they made it clear they would be unlikely to be able to claim it back but didn't explain why, but I was thankful regardless. The reason for this was to become clear, shortly.

I somehow manage to find my way to the subway to begin my journey and meet up with Irish Aoife who I had met the previous night at dinner with the others. It was her soon-to-be-old apartment that Samuel had taken me to. I remember thinking how lovely it was and more like what I had been promised – which made me feel like I could quite rightly be stronger in my quest for an apartment for myself if that was the precedent.

Aoife was really nice – and was a shining example of how the internship program had worked previously. When she first came out here, she was employed by the London Linked School as per the internship agreement I had signed up to, and she too had purchased: had a two week training program, was placed in accommodation with colleagues from the school, had an immediate social network, had a teaching support network – and had so much fun she decided to take the offer of a full time teaching post with London Linked School and stay for another six months. I must admit I felt a little jealous. Why wasn't my experience working out like that? What had gone so wrong/differently for Mitch and me?

I later learned she had had a far from perfect experience, but my new friends chose to protect me from this whilst I was in my own turmoil. Her story will become clear too as this tale unfolds.

We get off the subway a stop early from the school so that Aoife can stroll me through the central streets of Beijing. And there I am greeted with the Beijing I expected. It's the 'China' I had hoped for, buzzing in an industrial but organised manner. There are lanterns and pretty lights hanging from the trees, the streets are wide and modern-ish, the traffic is chaotic and loud but far more organised than the suburbs I've seen – and I liked it instantly. It was only a 10-minute walk and only gave me a brief glimpse, but I felt relieved to see that it was just as I had hoped. It's like I needed to see it just to have a reason to want to see this whole experience through.

The school we were headed to was called The City School and is the second of the two partner schools of London Linked School out here, but based more centrally. It is on part of the 7th floor of an office high-rise building which is another strange place to find a school, but it seemed really bright and friendly and had a brimful of smiley teachers and kids. I liked that too. The majority of teachers flit between both schools so I saw some familiar faces from my visit to London Linked South East School yesterday. If only I had been placed at these schools as I was promised and my first exposure to teaching here had been this.

As per usual, Mitchell strolled in late to the City School. Fuming some more. His observations at the Korean school and subsequent viewing of an apartment last night and troublesome journey home to the far-flung outskirts of Beijing where he was staying, had got him home at gone 1am in the morning. He was then subject to early morning calls from Louise, pressurising him to sign contracts for accommodation and to attend the Korean school again this evening. He was understandably exhausted, angry and confused and spent a good hour on the phone to William/Louise et al trying to get some understanding of the situation and relieve some of the pressure he was feeling. He got nowhere and finally attended our Chinese language lesson in a less than impressed mood, but realising more than ever that these lessons would be essential to basic survival out here in a country where barely anyone, despite Olympic training, could communicate with us and it was a bridge that we ourselves would have to gap.

The lesson was taken by one of the administrative staff at the school (who had heard our plight from the other Western teachers and offered her own time to us). Her name was Susan (obviously not her Chinese name) and although not a teacher, definitely had great skills. She was a really sweet girl, I warmed to her straight away and I instantly felt I had found another friend here, and introduced us to the pronunciations of letters in the pinyin system of Chinese language.

This is where the symbols have been, only in recent years, translated into the alphabet as we Westerners know it. You will see this in many places in central Beijing, again, as a legacy of the Olympics. I have no idea how people navigated the city otherwise. Unless you had an English-speaking guide, you would have been unlikely to find it a very easy experience. Even now, it is only the market stall holders in the centre (catering for the tourists), or the very young population who speak any sort of English at all. I guess it would have been much like the experience I was having so far in the suburbs. It's almost like being deaf and dumb I imagine – hearing is useless and speaking is pointless. It's all facial expressions and hand gestures which often don't work well.

Our lesson took us through the pinyin pronunciation and the various tones that we should use depending on the type of asterisk above the letters. It's pretty hard to master and often times when we were asked to repeat the sounds, we ended up singing the response as it was the only way we could naturally find the dips and rises in the words. This was coupled with head bobbing and tracing the sound through the air with our fingers. We must have looked and sounded pretty stupid but it was still interesting for us.

We also learned that the number four is unlucky in Chinese culture because if pronounced wrongly, it sounds like the word death. The Chinese are so superstitious about this that in traditional buildings you will not find a 4th floor (and sometimes not even a 14th floor) and phone numbers that include the number four are not wanted. (Mine has a few in it – I'm hoping that's not an omen, but it certainly explains why it was cheap to get – Louise and the phone seller must have been laughing at me). We also learned that to have the lucky number eight (obviously I have none) in your phone number means you would have to pay a higher amount for your phone.

I love these little facts about a culture and wonder what obscurities we have in our own culture that people from elsewhere might find strange. This is exactly what I came here to learn – the nuances of other cultures. How quickly I had naively forgotten that there would also be negative ones that I was yet to learn. Those about being a white woman in Asia, that tourist spots and treatment therein was not as one would expect, that the government and regimes had created situations that survival would become such a daily battle for me.

It was a short but sweet lesson – and the most useful thing we have learnt so far – and before we knew it, we had to leave the City School to get back to the South East School on the outskirts of town. But not before we had ourselves a cheeky McDonalds on the way. I wouldn't dream of eating such quantities of fast food if I were at home, but needs must when hunger strikes and you're not sure where you can find your next meal. Plus, Mitchell was in no mood to experiment in the Chinese outlets. He was still fuming.

We ordered our meals and Mitchell bought an extra hamburger for his pocket to eat later as there are no food shops within a 10-mile radius open by the time he makes it home each night. Goodness knows how that's going to taste later, but again, if needs must.

In Chinese McDonalds, you get served orange squash with your meal too, which was actually a refreshing break, if not a surprise, so we both stocked up on that. It beat flat Coke in my eyes. Plus my teeth were hurting from the sweeteners I'd been consuming by the gallon recently.

It wasn't until we sat down to eat that we both spewed out our anger and confusion and frustrations of the past couple of weeks. This was really the first time we had spent any real private time together and it was like we were having a therapy session.

It's now abundantly clear to both of us that we have been led a merry dance – there is no internship program running this semester and both TEFL 'X' and London Linked School have tried to pull the wool over our eyes to this fact. They have kept us at arm's length intending us to have committed to contracts from Chinese Louise at The China Agency at a very low salary to us and a big commission to them, in the hopes that if/when we notice it will be too late for us to do anything about it.

This explains why William regularly avoided, sidestepped or

passed on our concerns with our experiences. He was buying time until it was too late for us.

Clearly this infuriated us, but where we hadn't had time to really talk to each other, or rationalise our joint situations, between just the two of us; it wasn't dwelled upon too much up to this point. Our realisation of some even more serious issues was yet to come, but for now, we were furious enough to start really standing up for ourselves. Especially now as we had both met Aoife who shared her experiences of exactly what we should have been experiencing – and trust me, these experiences couldn't have been more different if we'd been buried in a hole in the Gobi Desert.

We decided that our only hope of salvation was to head back to the South East School and TEFL 'X' offices to discuss this in depth until a resolution was found that suited us. We knew as soon as we arrived that they were nervous – I genuinely believe they knew we weren't far off discovering the whole truth and by the looks on their faces they realised now was the time. We sat with useless William and stated our understanding and demanded that something be done immediately to rectify the situation and that we were not willing to continue this façade until they gave us what we paid for.

William looked terrified and I was later to learn from my new English teacher buddies that the owner of the school had threatened his job if he didn't find a way of sorting this all out. 'This' being the stink that Mitchell and I were on the verge of creating both in China and in London. He told us that he would get onto it straight away with London, as soon as they came online for their working day and let us know definitively tomorrow what the plan was and how they would address our issues with the internship we had purchased. We told him he had better have an answer for us by then and he assured us he would let us know a time to come by the school tomorrow to discuss the resolution.

There was very little more we could do about it today, so we trekked off back to my hotel so that Mitchell could use the internet in my room. He hadn't had contact with the outside world for days and was desperate to speak to home and message his girlfriend.

In MSN conversations with his girlfriend when he could get Wi-Fi, she reiterated the point about Communist China bullying the weak – which was exactly what we vulnerable new foreigners were to them, and something we had been experiencing since our arrival from Chinese Louise. And the pathetic people who were William and London Linked School were relieved to let this happen to us as it removed a problem for them. Namely, Mitchell and I, who had paid for Visas and services for a job we didn't actually have. Oh, and it earned them a shed load of cash through selling us too. The full story is still yet to unfold so bear with me.

The only light I felt in my soul the entire day came from Mitchell, who amuses me greatly. Or maybe it's just the dire circumstances we are in that makes him funny, who knows, but I'm grateful for him being in this with me.

We talked about his previous work experiences and what brought him to TEFL 'X' in the first place. He explained that he used to work in a giant fridge at 0 degrees in an authoritarian environment with a six foot square bulldog-type sweaty boss who apparently always had his hairy butt crack on show. Mitch was exceptionally eloquent in explaining why he though China might be a better option for him.

The only job he ever enjoyed was one in the photo department at a large regional newspaper. He used to spend his days photoshopping pictures for print in the paper and made it his mission to turn one 'minger' a day into a hottie, whilst photo-shopping eyeballs into bushes, adult toys onto mantel pieces, six fingers on to people he hated and so on.

It was this job and the boredom beyond photoshop amusement that led him to TEFL 'X'.

To do these qualifications and join TEFL programs you must have a degree. He didn't have one and TEFL 'X' were the only organisation that accepted his photo-shopped certificates of his fake qualifications, and so here he is - in China in a right old mess with me.

He also admitted he was severely dyslexic and that in order to get a professional qualification he had to go for Teaching English as a Foreign Language. This would allow him to enter Hong Kong but he would have to stick to teaching smaller kids as he reckoned they would probably be the only ones to have a level of English lower than his. He says he can manage four letter words but beyond that he's lost. God help his future pupils.

Meanwhile he is still tapping away at MSN with his girlfriend – before sniffing his armpits and complaining that he smells. He's already broken wind more times than my stomach has growled with hunger (which is a lot) so I could have told him that myself, without having to get up close and personal with his armpit.

It turns out he hasn't washed well since he's been here. First up, he hasn't brought a towel with him and is running out of socks to dry himself with. Secondly, he claims he can't wash properly because his toilet is blocked and his horrible bathroom is too small. I wasn't clear of the relationship between the two issues until he explained that the first day he arrived (with gastroenteritis, no less) he managed to block the toilet up using his notebook as toilet paper – as there was none in his apartment.

In China you don't throw anything in the toilets, so you can imagine how several A4 sheets of standard paper affected the flush. The explanation continued that because the bathroom was so small (he could reach all four walls of the bathroom by standing in the centre with him arms outstretched and turning in a circle – and he's about a foot shorter than me so you can imagine how tiny it is) so when he had a shower, the water jumped straight into the full toilet and splashed back out again, thus covering himself and his toothbrush with blocked toilet water. I get now why his hygiene is lacking... I stopped him when he explained what he had to do when his notebook ran out.

But anyway, I digress, the problem in hand of the TEFL 'X' teaching and housing problem, was up in the air and we had to wait until the following day to discover our fate. William had texted us both to tell us to come in at 4pm to talk about it. I replied to him and asked why so late - as by that time I would have had to have paid for another night in the hotel and plus that's an awful long time to stew on what was going to happen to us. William replied to say that the news would be favourable if we didn't mind waiting that long and he had checked some things with his bosses in the UK.

Mitch's only response to this was that he had broken a rib in a moped accident in Thailand and fallen down a toilet in Japan and all had turned out fine in the end (questionable) and that he trusted this would too.

Sounded hopeful. But it's lucky I already knew not to hold my breath on anything here.

5

NO LIGHT YET

The Con

Another wasted day, quelle surprise. Mitch appeared at my hotel about 1.30pm to use the internet. He had no idea how long it would take him to make the journey from his apartment, so had set off early and arrived an hour earlier than I expected him. I had to make him wait outside my room until I was dressed from the shower before I could let him in. The hotel had a weird glass bathroom so not only could you see directly into the bathroom from wherever you stood in the room, you could also hold a conversation with someone in the bed whilst you were sat on the loo. So, with nowhere for me to hide my modesty, he was definitely not coming in until I was decent.

Because he was using the electrical sockets in the bedroom for the computer, I had to dry my hair in the bathroom which is something I hate to do. Something about water and electricity mixing? I told Mitchell that I was drying my hair and that if anything happens, does he know what to do. He told me calmly not to panic and that he knew how to call for an ambulance in Japanese. Pretty far to go to get treatment but apparently, it's my best option.

We left my hotel about three-ish to begin the walk to the school via a supermarket, as I hadn't eaten since our lunchtime McDonald's trip the day before. En route, around 3.30pm, we received word from William that our meeting had been delayed until 5pm. This annoyed us as it was getting later and later in the day, and also meant we could have actually done something with our day instead of hanging around my ashtray of a hotel. We killed time drinking; yes you guessed it, coke in the local KFC, until our time was up. The food chain clearly hadn't linked the poop squat training to me and was still letting me in.

Arriving at the school we were ushered into Pervy Jim's office by meek William and asked to summarise our requests. Had we not made them clear yesterday? We were coming for a 'favourable solution' not to start this whole process again! William's excuse was that the contact in London we had been dealing with, Nic Bacon (stupid name – should have known not to trust him – I had several dealings with him before I left England and even they weren't wholly positive) had been off yesterday and William had only just got hold of him.

All he had to say was that he had discussed with us exactly what we were experiencing now when we had originally invested in the internship program. I felt the anger rise. Mitchell and I both had emails and conversations to the contrary – selling us a completely different experience - so were furious that once again there had been a fob off, or more lies – but either way we realised we were no further forward.

Pervy Jim also tried to lie to us in his hideous whiny voice that of course we were on the internship program and that the schools we were being sent to were affiliated with the London Linked School (he allegedly had paperwork agreements to prove it although conveniently could not produce them when we demanded to see them right then) and that yes we would be supported and that there was in fact a two week training program he had arranged – so what was the problem? For a start the 'program' he waved at us was the teaching rota – nothing to do with us, and bearing in mind he didn't even know what my proposed school was called, there was no way we believed the schools were 'affiliated'.

Lies and more lies. We both pressed our points that the schools we were going to had given us seriously long hours to work (that exceeded our intern agreement and for an intern pay – we didn't realise at that point that the remaining half of our pay would go to Louise) and expected us to be fully experienced, and that we were based nowhere near the support network promised and that living with completely unchecked Chinese strangers was not in our internship program details.

We went around and around in circles when Mitchell, clearly exasperated, annoyingly stated that he might view his suggested accommodation again over the weekend and seriously consider starting at the Korean school just to get some sort of stability. I was in despair…this knocked me back and put me in an awkward situation of being the only troublemaker. It also, in effect, meant he had accepted the change to the terms of the internship and would make my battle harder - if I had any energy left at all to pursue it. I understood that his personal need to make this situation work for him was different from my own – he had his girlfriend and relationship to think about – but I didn't have anything of the sort to fall upon. But by him ducking out, I was totally alone.

It was on that low note that William informed me that Chinese Louise had found an apartment for me to view that evening and William would accompany me. I reluctantly agreed to view it, just for the sake of doing my bit to try and cooperate, knowing that I was now literally on my own fighting this battle. I also hoped it would be an utter dive so that William could see for himself just exactly what we were having to put up with and being forced to accept.

So off we went that evening to the far north west of Beijing to see a potential contender for my new home. It was a good hour and half from the London Linked School we were at and was during a very awkward and busy commuting time of day. William made idle small talk the entire time and I took no interest at all. He was clearly uncomfortable. I asked a few indirect questions trying to glean more information from him about the cover up with the company that was going on and he confessed that this was the first occasion that they had needed to use Chinese Louise and her China Agency recruitment company – and he'd had no idea there would be so many problems. He looked broken but I didn't care. He had been one of the causes of my own seriously dire situation so I felt not an ounce of sympathy towards his own employment situation.

The apartment, which was described as being 'much more appropriate' by Chinese Louise, after reaching the subway where my school was based directly outside, was a further 20-minute taxi ride away. Much further than again we had been promised. On arrival we walked into a gated community of 20 storey high tower blocks. The apartment was on the 13th floor, which was unlucky, in many ways. We were greeted at the apartment by the agent, who opened the front door to a waft of damp and decay so strong that if there had been anything in my stomach it would have made a visit back the way it came.

The bathroom was dimly lit due to broken light bulbs, had no ventilation and was crawling in green mould and damp stains, so big they stretched taller than my 5'7" in height. My 'room' backed straight on to this and although a good size looked like a squat with a blanket roughly draped across the window and filthy, unpainted and mouldy walls. There were four closed doors off the grim and dark corridor which housed an unused fridge and a filthy microwave discarded on top of dumped broken furniture. Behind one door was a kitchen which had been locked as it was never used as such and instead was a storage room. The other three doors apparently led to three double rooms in which one or two Chinese may live, with their pets. Need I explain more why I didn't want to live there?

I told William to get me out of there – after he had the audacity to ask me, in front of the agent, if I would like to take it. I asked him straight out if he would live there himself. He ummed and aahed and said if the price was right, he would make do if he lived on his own. When I asked if he would let his wife live there alone, he looked suitably embarrassed. When on earth would this dishonesty and cover up end? I despise this guy.

He ever so courteously paid for me to get a taxi all the way back to my hotel where I sat in more numb silence. It took me through the heart of Beijing, I'm sure just to tease me, as it looked wonderful at night. After getting hopelessly lost I finally recognised a supermarket that I knew wasn't too far to walk to my hotel and got the driver to throw me out there. Fortunately, I managed to run in and grab some drink and some snacks to take back to my hotel with me and on my way home called Mitchell to tell him of my latest experience.

It was then that he told me that he had given his own situation some further thought and he was definitely going to take the Korean job and the apartment just so this was all over with and he could get on with his life and begin his quest to make it to Hong Kong. He was tired of fighting and needed the experience too much to risk losing the opportunity and the 'great job' he thinks it could be. He also negotiated himself a pay rise with the agent so he was semi-placated. So, it looked like I really was on my own from now on.

Immediately after I got off the phone to him, Chinese Louise called me and told me that I was too hard to find apartments for so she would give me a housing allowance to find one myself and it was basically over to me, the non-Mandarin speaking Westerner from whom she was stealing more than 50% of my wages. I was going to be poor, helpless and homeless in big Beijing.

My troubles never seem to improve, they just seemed to change shape on a day by day basis. I'm so unbelievably tired.

6

PLEASE LET THAT LIGHT NOT BE A TRAIN

The Con

Another fitful night of sleep saw me waking up much later than I had hoped. Today was a trip to the school to beg the Director of Studies, Pervy Jim, to help me out personally. After speaking to Mitchell last night, I realised I have to fight this one on my own and so that is what I am going to do until I have some sort of resolution to this situation that is satisfactory to me. And the sooner I do that, the sooner I might actually relax a little, have a day off from the constant emotional hassle - and do some sightseeing.

I've been here so long already and I've seen practically nothing of this city. It's the least I want to do before I run and I'll be damned if this whole drama is for nothing.

I arrived at the school around 11am and Jim was available to chat. He sat me down and heard my plight: That if I couldn't live with another Westerner in suitable accommodation, then I wished to live on my own, in close proximity to the other Western teachers (which was also in the vicinity of the two main schools) so I would have a support network, both socially and for my teaching.

I also requested my school be changed to one closer to this location, seeing as I could not be placed in a tutored school as promised, or otherwise my daily commute would be three hours a day and I was not prepared to do that and again, it was not what I had been promised, nor what I had paid for. I reiterated and reiterated until I was almost in tears that I already felt abandoned in this strange city and after my terrible experience I wanted some sort of resolution and stability ASAP or I was going to have to report this whole fiasco when I got back home, if only to protect others from my own naivety.

He asked what Mitchell thought and I told him I needed to be considered as an individual from now on. That Mitchell had his girlfriend from Hong Kong visiting most weekends and that he was not as needy as I was of a social support network, especially as a single white female out here who didn't yet know the language. Which was true. Mitch had called me and told me he was just going to take his shared accommodation, take the job at the school and launch himself into it as he did not believe he would get a resolution anyway. This helped me in one way – one person to fix is easier than two but made me feel really lonely in another sense.

Jim was a little pathetic in skirting around the subject, not looking me in the eye, talking in his gratingly whiney voice and gave me no straight answers to my questions. I had heard he was a slippery fish, so I played the game too, knowing that if he was pressed and pressed, he would cave in because he was a weak and pathetic individual. (My new friends words, not mine). So, I listened intently and straight faced when he told me his lame, sickeningly inappropriate and irrelevant stories and miraculously somehow managed to turn every anecdote he told me into another reason as to why I needed help or to be closer to other people so I could one day happily tell the same stories he did.

Despite the fact I shouldn't have to be playing this game in the first place. Plus, I made it subtly clear legally they had all made a dog's dinner of Mitchell's and my situation and I wasn't going to be budged until I got what I had paid for. Or, silenced, if this all went wrong. Other disturbing things I had learned about Jim made me question his ability to get a job anywhere else, or at least in more scrupulous organisations than this (you can draw your own conclusions as to why), so I hoped that he would feel a personal inclination to do something to fix this mess because it saved his bacon too.

While we were discussing at length my location in the city and my distance from the security of other London Linked School teachers, he took the gut churning opportunity to spread a map across my legs, touch my knees more than an accidental number of times and practically sniff my neck (so close I could smell his breath) whilst he introduced me, via the map, to the 'cool' night time hangouts in Beijing.

I'd definitely got his number by this stage and realised he was not going to be able to help me with everything I needed, nor did I want anything more to do with him than necessary. Whilst keeping a safe physical distance from him without making it obvious, I decided to bring back his focus to my immediate living arrangements and not let him wander off on tangents that didn't immediately interest me or help me. Or, give him an excuse to touch me anymore.

It took time, and many awkward silences I forced him to fill, but he finally mentioned that perhaps the solution to my living arrangements was to live with the old intern Aoife who had just been evicted from her own accommodation (by him it later turns out – for no good reason other than the fact he is unhinged, but had since decided that he could house six school admin staff there for his easy access – think what you will) and was in desperate need of a place too.

What he didn't let on was that Aoife had already mentioned this to him yesterday as a solution to her own problem – the one they had caused by screwing her over by evicting her from a home they had told her she could have for the next six months. I think it took a while for him to bring it up because he was reluctant to bother helping her, but now there were two problems he could solve in one.

He called Aoife immediately and explained the possible solution. As she was in the middle of packing her life up in her old apartment, she asked if he could bring me to her apartment for 2pm to talk it through. Although sharing with her was ideal for me, she was based a long way from me school wise (she was City based which was centrally placed, I was potentially on the western outskirts) and she had been experiencing living in the thick of the social life, so I got a little concerned that even though I would have someone to live with, it would probably be me who had to compromise on location (if my school didn't get changed).

It would still be one hell of a commute for one of us every day. I tried to keep an open mind though and see what 2pm brought me. The apartment was only a 10-minute walk, no subway, from the South East School so that was one journey I didn't fear making. It was also a little step forward in my dilemma.

I decided to kill a bit of time before my walk to meet Aoife by popping out from the school to find food (yes, food, KFC admittedly but sustenance nonetheless) which unfortunately was interrupted by an appearance by Pervy Jim where he joined me at my table and regaled me with disgusting stories containing too much sordid detail about his relationship with his hot Japanese 'wife'.

She is apparently not really his wife but someone he met at a fetish party in Beijing - and who the other teachers rumour to be a pair of swingers. The interruption to my relief time was not pleasant and I suspected was rather less of a coincidental encounter and more of a contrived effort to stir me up a little bit more, and made me feel even more disconcerted that a man who is as questionable as him works with children.

I felt this way now, but was still to really see and hear the hideous details of his actual behaviour at the school with the children and the female staff. My gut was more powerful than I had realised and it had nothing to do with the volume of KFC's I had been consuming recently.

A few minutes before 2pm Jim and I left the school to walk over to Aoife's apartment. It was a little awkward arriving and being put in front of her not knowing how she really felt about the prospect of living with me now it was actually a possibility. But as soon as Jim left, the conversation relaxed and we found a solution that suited us both.

Because I had a greater amount of salary to play with (thanks to Chinese Louise now relinquishing my - still pitifully small - housing allowance to me) and Aoife was now a formal teacher, we had more money to play with in terms of getting respectable accommodation. She was happy to move away from her current area because the solution we found was actually a more straight-forward commute for her to the City School and if there were two of us joining a social event with the others, we would always be catching taxis together and we estimated the cost would only be a pound each per night (Beijing is so cheap!).

With regards to subways, my school (if I had to accept the job) was literally across the road from a subway station and the area we were looking to live was bang in the middle of both our schools – maybe three or four tube stops each. I was amazed she didn't mind moving away and seemed quite keen to have a Western roomie – she had Chinese girls for the last seven months and there had been a distinct culture clash.

This would however mean I would potentially be staying at the school I had been given. Like Aoife said, even in her internship she was thrown in at the deep-end, it was nothing resembling the internship she had paid for and she had been terrified too – and she survived. She said she was supported by the other Westerners and that she would do the same for me. In light of the fact I have very little choice, I felt relieved that my major concern of somewhere to live and settle down in could be solved within the next few days.

I still had no idea why I was pursuing the idea of this 'internship' debacle in China anyway and hadn't just gone home. That I was displaying the actions of a desperate, prideful idiot was all I could put my finger on.

Once we had settled on a location, Aoife immediately enlisted the help of the Chinese girls on the admin staff at the London Linked School who would find us an apartment to our specification – two double rooms, clean, kitchen, washing machine and Wi-Fi – in one of two subway locations. Both of which Aoife really likes and both within easy reach of our schools.

The only downside was that we would have to find three months' rent up front and a deposit (which are easy to get back if you have Chinese allies requesting it, impossible if you are a Westerner), which is a lot of cash to be passing over in one go and not something I had been prepared for, or aware of, before I came to Beijing (surprise surprise). But apparently this is normal – and this is why Chinese Louise was giving me such slums to view – because they were cheaper (by more than half the value of my housing allowance) and it was therefore less of an outlay for her and she would get it back from our salaries within three months or so anyway.

The remaining three months surplus was cash in her pocket, or if we continued for a year, that was nine months of more than half our salaries going to her for nothing. But regardless of that detail which I try not to think about, you can move into apartments almost immediately out here - the quicker the better in fact, so I didn't have to personally shell out for nights in the 7 Days Inn for much longer. Which I was now having to pay for myself, because, in their opinion, I had turned down alternative accommodation (veritable squats they would't keep their dogs in) therefore I had created my own problem.

During our discussions, Aoife made me cups of tea (oh how I've missed them) and boiled me up some dumplings that tasted just like beef ravioli. She also marked my map with all the areas I would definitely want to go to when I finally had time to be a tourist: the silk markets (cheap shopping), a massive lake with bars and restaurants which would be beautiful in the summer months (which are only weeks away now), must-see tourist attractions, The Village (an ex-pat community), and the locations of where the other teachers lived. She also showed me how close we were to an Ikea where we could buy our very own bedding and other essentials from. For the first time in a long time, I started to relax and dare to be a little excited about my next few months.

Whilst I was there, I also logged on to Facebook via her VPN, which hides your IP address and allows you to view sites that are banned by the Chinese government – Facebook, Twitter, YouTube etc. – any site that allows freedom of speech, basically. When I checked my emails, Facebook had emailed me to confirm that I had in fact logged in from a location in Los Angeles…weird. That must be where we are hidden. This was something I was going to have to get used to doing. It seems anything controversial written about China is tracked – I needed one just for my diaries at the rate I was going. I didn't want to risk my safety again, anymore than I had been already on a daily basis.

At about five-ish, I left Aoife to continue her packing and headed back to my hotel for rest and writing. Not before she gave me a spontaneous hug. Another thing I have missed so much! Not quite the hugs I missed from the people back home but amazing nonetheless. I think tonight I shall finally sleep well – with a belly fully of tea and nice food. And looking forward to an early morning skype date with one of my favourite people back home and perhaps maybe a spot of sightseeing? Or was I getting ahead of myself? Fingers crossed, today really did bring me nearer to the end of one of my crises.

The
Dawning

7

THE LIGHT WAS A TRAIN

The
Dawning

I woke early for eagerly awaited Skype dates with home and they didn't disappoint. After my horrid week, to see familiar faces I hadn't seen since I arrived here was a welcome sight. After so much drama it felt like I had been in Beijing for months rather than weeks and it made me feel sad. If I stayed here for the full six months goodness knows how I will feel when I actually get to see them, and my other favourite people, in person. Although I do have hopes of a visit from some of my closest people to share this place with me. Despite it being a cruel wish to them.

The weird thing was that even though I had been excited to Skype, I didn't look or feel my best – and I don't just mean I didn't have any make up on and I had a bed head. It took me a few minutes to get the courage to actually dial and face them. I felt like I looked drained, I felt like I would have nothing to talk about other than that which had consumed ME for the past little while – and I didn't want to disappoint them with a shadow of my former self and totally disregard their own life.

Sounds dramatic, but it's all too true. Tales of woe are fine when you can pick them up and put them down when you feel like experiencing them through words alone. But to actually arrange a time when you know they will have to be spoken out loud is harder when they involve people you love - and they become all-consuming and all you can talk about.

It's this inbuilt need to share a problem to halve a problem, which is a fallacy. On the few occasions I have managed to Skype my parents I've felt the same. Even though they are used to every one of their kids pouring out dramas to them at some point during a week, to be so far away and be like this feels like I'm torturing them and myself. I know too well that the poor recipient of my calls will know me well enough to see right through my faked positivity and I will send them off feeling deflated and helpless, which is a horrible thing to do to someone.

It's funny how in business I am the Queen of poker faces, but when it becomes personal, the story gets etched in my face for the world to see. This is something I definitely need to work on for the sake of others. My experience here is not only hurting me, but others too - and that is my fault. The guilt I feel is enormous. But what they don't realise is that the fear for myself and my mind is even bigger…but it's something I daren't admit to them.

Having gone to bed feeling a lot less anxious, I think my recent pattern of sleep has really affected my ability to get a good night in. Waking up this morning was hard, but inspired due to my contact from home. But immediately after I had finished the call, feeling a little blue and missing home, I climbed back into bed for an hour or so.

The next thing I know, Mitchell was calling me. He had already texted me at 8.30am, whilst I was on Skype, asking me if he could come around and use my internet again and chat. I had ignored him because I just wanted to do everything in my own time today and maybe do a little sightseeing to my own agenda. I eventually relented though as I know what it's like to be without contact to the outside world, especially when you need moral support. Despite him apparently leaving me in the lurch.

I waited for him to arrive, looking forward to sharing my news that I too had decided to make the best of my current situation (I couldn't afford otherwise because of both my purse and my pride) and was just going to get involved with China as it had been presented to me. I naively hoped that today would be the first of our positive conversations, and also the time that he would visit me, not smelly, or farting on my chair.

On all of the above counts I was wrong, although it wasn't my chair, or hotel room he festered in after all.

He called again and had me meet him at London Linked School down the road. This was annoying as I had hoped to hop on a train and see the mysterious and beautiful Beijing I had glimpsed and heard so much about. But alas, this was not to be.

Mystified at the urgency and concern in his voice when I finally did answer his call, I headed straight there to find Mitchell surrounded by his luggage, preparing his overnight bag to check in to the same hotel I was in.

And finally, our whole Chinese mystery was to unravel…

Mitchell had his girlfriend from Hong Kong over to stay for the weekend just passed. She learned three languages at school to a higher standard than our poor attempt in England to learn French or Spanish. They were Cantonese, English and Mandarin. The latter being pretty useful to us right now. He had collected her from the airport and taken her back to his squalid apartment (he has no class) and first thing Saturday morning they had made several important trips.

The first trip was to a hotel to book in for Saturday night, understandably, as she had refused to spend another night in a hovel. The second trip had been to the apartment he had been given the keys to, and was expected to sign contracts for, near the Korean school, arranged by Louise. With his girlfriend in tow it had been established that his apartment, as with one of my dodgy apartments, had the same set up. Up to two people per room, plus their handbag sized dogs. So, he would be living in an unfinished three-bedroom apartment with four others and two yappy dogs.

As an aside, there is a law here in Beijing, due to its overpopulation, that if you must have a dog, it must be a tiny one – no big ones. If you break this law your dog will be removed, stolen off the streets if necessary. You are also only allowed one of them. Again, if you flout this law one of your dogs at random will apparently be plucked from you. Harsh, but the apartment blocks are overcrowded with people anyway and pets just makes them worse. It seems everyone in Beijing has an accessory pooch, dressed in Armani (Armanl, Amarni, Almani depending on the fake market you go to) for you to fall over in the street or at least walk their own un-poop-scooped muck around.

Anyway – back to the story. After learning the set up in real terms from his girlfriend he was pretty cross. Add to that the constant harassing calls from Chinese Louise to sign the contract on the apartment, the contract on the Korean school and get out of his studio apartment, he was feeling pretty pressured into an uncomfortable situation.

As a result, meeting up with Chinese Louise becomes their 3rd trip of the day. Again, with his girlfriend's excellent command of Mandarin, he established a few very interesting details:

Chinese Louise had no idea what we had paid for regarding an internship with TEFL 'X'. She had simply been approached mid-January to supply accommodation and jobs for two teachers arriving from England in February and for which TEFL 'X' would be awarded, by Louise, on successful placement in schools by her, 2000 Yuan each, the equivalent of £200 for myself and £200 for Mitchell.

This is a significant amount of money in China where total daily living costs are no more than £5, if that. Therefore, in effect, TEFL 'X' would have received a finder's fee for trafficking two foreigners straight into her hands and who she was set to cream off our salaries a considerable amount herself over the duration of our contracts. Mitch's girlfriend had also understood that TEFL 'X' and London Linked School had no job openings to fulfill the internships we had paid for (and they had known this long before Mitch and I were interviewed and sold our placements). It wasn't particularly news to us, but to hear it formally was quite something.

She confirmed we had been sold as fully fledged, experienced teachers to the schools we had interviewed at. (Having a TEFL certificate is apparently the only pre-requisite, although even this could be faked – as Louise never actually asked to see either of ours). The fact that we expected to have 'reputable' training throughout the six months was news to her and not something she would want the schools seeing happen as she would 'lose face' as to the quality of her people (she still sold people who were totally inexperienced and unqualified anyway but that's her issue).

She confirmed that after our arrival when I myself posed a tricky customer, William had admitted to her that 'they think they are on the old internship program, but don't worry, we will calm them down and tell them this is part of it' via email. Which I now have in my email inbox, courtesy of Mitchell, via Louise. It's in black and white the con London Linked School and TEFL 'X' tried to pull on us. I hate them. I hope they rue the day they did this…

She informed Mitchell that she had been approached by TEFL 'X' last Friday evening by both useless William and Pervy Jim to fake documentation that claimed the schools we had been placed in were formally affiliated to TEFL 'X' and the London Linked School, so they could continue their ruse that the internship involved affiliated schools and that they were protected somehow if we ever tried to kick up a stink back home in England. Chinese Louise had refused to do this for them. Maybe she wasn't totally lacking integrity of all kinds.

In her naïve view that by helping Mitchell, she could guarantee having us both start at our schools as per her 'contracts' and save her face, she forwarded on ALL the incriminating mails to his account.

Boom. Highly regarded TEFL 'X' and internationally highly regarded London Linked School (albeit via fake reports and blogs) reputations were at our finger tips to destroy.

But now we had to figure out exactly how to use this information, when the best time to strike would be, and who we could hit the hardest with it to get what we want out of this sorry mess.

Embarrassingly, we had been conned. By a UK company.

I had mentally prepared myself to live with Aoife and throw myself into my job, and so had Mitchell up to this point. Learning all this new stuff we now felt China had completely soured for us and that we were both so exhausted with it that we just wanted our money back and to go home. But when we really considered pushing for that option, we both felt we would be cheating ourselves. We had geared ourselves up to gain value and future experience and to go home now would mean we would have to wait months to try again when the new terms across the world restarted.

We both needed these six months under our belts, and it had cost us a lot to even get here in the first place - leaving the UK had not been easy for either of us to do and we could not be sure our previous employers would take us back seeing as we were definite flight risks. Despite the fact we could potentially get our money back and more in the UK after this con-job fiasco, this in itself would take time and money that neither of us had, or could afford to spend in an uncertain state of limbo.

We started to consider our alternative options:

The London Linked School is the only school in Beijing to run the CELTA exams – the Cambridge University affiliated English Language Teaching exams. The one-month intensive course fee was the same as the fee for our six months training, that we had already paid. Had we asked for that we would have a worldwide recognised certificate and go home in a few weeks and teach back in the UK, or anywhere else in the world, still having experienced China (albeit not very positively), but not really having lost anything financially.

This option was unlikely but the highest we could aim for whilst here and the only thing that seemed a step forward in earning back our money if our legal plight back home failed. And anyway, legal matters would have to be taken up in the UK, not in crazy China where forcing someone to lose face is a no-no. And, who knows how the Chinese legal system works, but we certainly doubted its integrity – especially in support of foreigners.

Our alternative was to push for an internship that didn't exist but that we had paid for. The chances of that were obviously zero.

So, we concluded that we would argue for CELTA and be grateful for an official internship at the very least as we were now here and couldn't really afford to do much else. Unfortunately, they had us trapped. We would still of course try to seek compensation for these days of torment and our personal costs but we knew nothing could be guaranteed. These companies could clearly not be trusted to do the decent thing.

The internship was still, maybe crazily, our favoured option – as why else would we have signed up for it in the first place? True, we didn't trust the quality anymore, but from a general social and teaching experience perspective, it still seemed we could make something of it as others had before us. We were forcing ourselves to be positive, I know, but we were feeling hopeless and needed something to grab on to.

And also, if we stuck with it, our warts and all experiences that we would both share on completion would be much more rounded and a more indicative story of the chaos that is China and the unscrupulous people who run the schools and TEFL companies back in England. And you can be sure that we would tell that story to anyone who would listen…no way did either of us want anyone else going through what we had to go through.

The TEFL 'X' and London Linked School reputations could wait to be 'handled' until we had what we wanted and were home safe and sound. Our safety being uppermost in our minds. Dreams of an expose in newspapers of the dangers of TEFL abroad for Mummy and Daddy's little baby dance in our minds a lot. We feel the need to protect others from this nightmare. How realistic this is or whether this happens or not is a whole other thing. But it's whatever keeps us going now that matters.

Once we had considered what we wanted to fight for, we discussed our approach to fighting for it over a dirty great, greasy, gorgeous pizza. I was trying to think in my own mind how I would handle approaching this situation. On one hand I had weak people who would lie and skirt around issues for as long as they could, and we needed action ASAP. On the other hand, I had Mitchell whose loose lips could potentially sink our rickety junk ship. I figured the best way of handling this would be for us to read, from a well-structured and comprehensive document we had prepared in advance of our confrontation meeting, (which we had planned for 9am the next morning) that would remove the risk of being spoken over or detracted from.

And so, we set to work. We penned it first over dinner with the intention of me going back to the hotel and typing it up until it was presentable. This was a task I dare not leave to Mitchell with his vocabulary only stretching to four letter words and his tendency to talk his way into trouble rather than out of it. A trick he had never learned the way I had through my jobs, was the power of silence. Letting other people feel awkward enough with silences you posed was a sure-fire way to get what you wanted as they always felt the need to fill them and give you ground. And we needed every inch of dusty Chinese ground we could get.

Just as we returned to the hotel and after Mitchell had checked his emails for the umpteenth time, we then received the biggest shock since we had arrived here. An email from Chinese Louise, whose phone calls Mitchell had been ignoring all day in a bid to avoid having to sign ridiculous contracts. It turns out, due to being unable to contact either of us for some time now and finding her studio accommodation abandoned by Mitchell, she had quite rightly assumed we had no intention of honouring what she had arranged for us. Her email was addressed to wet William and copied both myself and Mitchell. It was a threatening email to the extent that if we did not start work this week and sign her contracts, that TEFL 'X' had to pay her a sum of money for her 'services' since we arrived and due to her loss of reputation and loss of face in front of her client, she would use her contacts to revoke our visas.

Ouch.

But mostly: Oh shit.

8

SHOW TIME

The
Dawning

D-day has arrived.

When my alarm goes off, I can barely open my eyes. It feels like someone has removed my eyeballs in my sleep, rolled them in a dusty Chinese gutter and very kindly popped them back in for me. They hurt badly.

Four hours of restless sleep after contemplating my future is not enough to go into battle with and still look like a convincing opponent. I needed to up my game.

Mitchell arrived at my door early, not buzzing with excitement as I had expected him to be, but looking already defeated. I think the prospect of being an illegal alien in China was a little too much for him. My little sidekick ball of energy was failing me as much as I was failing myself.

Time to go through our notes on our walk to the school and pump ourselves up a little, I reckon. We only had to find energy for an hour or so this morning - surely we could do that?

We had decided we were meeting with the head honcho of the

London Linked School and would not take no for an answer. We had already figured out who this guy was. He was called Alfie (bearing no resemblance to the EastEnders barman and his synonymous witty quips) whose wife runs the highly regarded international London Linked School back in the UK.

They are co-owners and run multiple large schools across the world. Regardless of how their bizarre marriage actually works, to damage one London Linked School back in our home country would severely damage their reputation across the world – especially seeing as English teachers are generally native English speakers and their market back home was where we could do the most damage. Our aim was to indirectly make them realise that we could be their Achilles' heel and use that to get what we were owed in return. Grand plans, huh?

We walked into the school and headed straight to find Alfie, passing a secret and nameless supporter on the way. Throughout this saga 'nameless' has been a whispering supporter for us. Not allowed to talk to us directly, this person always finds a way to whisper us support, tell us who we should be speaking to and feed back to us what the other staff are thinking or doing after each meeting we have had so far. 'Nameless' had already warned us they are scared of us, they know we should be getting what we came here for, and gave us the details of this Alfie guy to speak to. 'Nameless' whispers his support for our confrontation as we walk by.

Alfie greets us nervously with a smile, clearly hoping that we haven't come for him. But we have. And we make it clear we need to speak to him that very minute and it may take some time. I have my business face on. The personal one is taking a nap, probably, but I'm glad it's not around for this. It would only let me down.

He takes us to an office and we sit. Before he can continue his nervous pleasantries we not-so-subtly let him know that we will not be partaking in extensive 'isn't the weather nice today' small talk and that we have direct and urgent business to discuss. In the meantime, word of our arrival has sparked some interest in the school (they have been watching this unfold for many days and are all rooting for us) and we see a few familiar faces making awkward attempts to watch and listen to the pending performance.

Not-so-strangely, wet William is not around this morning. He's either gone to fabricate other false information online or more likely to go and kowtow to Chinese Louise – and with any luck she's stamping on his head whilst he does it. Either that or he has been sacked, as per the rumours of his impending doom we've been hearing for days, caused by his treatment of us since we arrived, and the embarrassment he has caused the school.

My conscience feels nothing at this. We are now far too many long days down the line in a hell that he could have avoided had he only been honest and not the spineless creature he is. I worry about whom else this has happened to that didn't fight so hard. Who knows? Maybe we can fight for them too and the poor souls that will undoubtedly follow – unless we get the message out there that these companies simply cannot be trusted.

Once Mitchell and I are seated, Alfie calls in another Director of Studies called Noel – clearly wishing to even out the opposing sides. But even so, numbers do not matter to us now and as I'm well aware of these classic tactics, they do not bother me.

I announce that Mitchell and I would like to read a statement, in its entirety to them, that it is a comprehensive document (its soooo long – too long probably but there's a lot to cover and my mind wasn't exactly in prime condition when I wrote it), and that we will take comments and questions at the end.

The looks on their faces say they are not prepared for this soft looking blonde to command anything of them.

And so, I begin.

"Mitchell and I have spent the past days doing research, seeking formal advice and evaluating our position here in China with TEFL 'X' and The London Linked School.

As you well know we purchased the following China 2012 internship:

SHOW DOC – cue Mitchell.

We both had phone interviews to discuss the above program where all the items were re-confirmed to us. We then accepted and paid for our places, with a considerable sum of money, to cover visas and legal documentation.

Following this, we both received multiple communications from both China and the UK, right up until our departure, specifically from Nic Bacon, regarding the details of the internship we had purchased and our pending employment at the London Linked School.

At no point were we informed that the internship program had been cancelled some months ago. We only pieced this information together weeks into our trip after a web of ongoing lies and misleading information - and once we had already experienced serious emotional and physical hardships.

We came to China in good faith that the internship would be honoured and were given no reason to believe otherwise.

Both TEFL 'X' and the London Linked School had every

opportunity to inform us that the internship did not exist, long before we paid our fee, paid for our visas and turned our lives in the UK upside down - at considerable sacrifice and expense to ourselves. We genuinely believed we were doing it to further our teaching careers with a reputable company and school.

Since our arrival in Beijing, Mitchell and I have been kept at arm's length from each other, TEFL 'X' and the London Linked School, whereby we were both placed in the hands of a 4th party: The China Agency, of which TEFL 'X' and the London Linked School, by their own admission, had no previous dealings with, or knowledge of, before they were engaged for the purposes of Mitchell's and my arrival.

This has led to extremely disturbing experiences for us both where we were both placed in far from satisfactory accommodation with questionable safety for ourselves and our belongings.

To give a brief example from each of us:

Mitchell was taken to a studio apartment by William, belonging to Louise of The China Agency. It was not equipped with necessary basics, it was of unsatisfactory cleanliness, and he experienced, on numerous occasions whether he was present or not, strangers letting themselves in to his apartment for viewings, with no prior warning or consent – or with any regard for his privacy, personal safety and security of his personal belongings.

I was taken to Louise's own apartment and quite literally confined to a filthy room for the duration of my stay. On one occasion when I was left alone in the apartment late at night, I was instructed to answer the door to an unknown male who would visit to deposit money on her table. In addition, she took my passport from me.

It was clear from these first few days, and the absence of contact from TEFL 'X' or London Linked School that we were now in the hands of an unknown 'partner'. Unable to communicate with anyone.

Since we arrived in the country, we have also been victims of undue pressure, harassment, misinformation and extreme emotional and physical stress. To the extent to which the person who we relied on for accommodation and contact with the outside world, pressured us to sign contracts, interview for jobs that we were not experienced enough to take, (and that we thought we already had), and pressuring us to view and accept permanent accommodation of a highly unacceptable standard.

We were both extremely vulnerable and confused. This was not what we had expected as it was not what was offered on the internship program we had signed up for. This should NEVER have happened.

It was several days until either of us even met with TEFL 'X' – our supposed caretakers in this country, who to their credit, did extract me from my accommodation and place me in a hotel immediately – but one that I am now having to personally pay for. As now is Mitchell, if only to safeguard ourselves and our belongings.

We all know there is no Internship program for us, and we have been continuously lied to throughout our stay in Beijing.

Louise was unaware there was a training program for us – or of the details of our internship package – and for this we have evidence. We were both expected to start full time teaching last week in schools who believe us to be fully experienced teachers…causing us further emotional stress and confusion.

We have evidence to suggest that The China Agency has only

recently been contracted to work with TEFL 'X' to 'fix' the situation you have got yourselves into and have dragged Mitchell and me unwittingly through the mess with you.

A one-week training program does not constitute an internship of ongoing support that should last six months. Neither does being placed as unsupported 'experienced' teachers in random schools across Beijing. We also have evidence to suggest that they are not actually affiliated schools that we have been placed in, and activity is being done by TEFL 'X' and London Linked School to retrospectively forge a relationship to satisfy our questioning.

I could read you more details of our tale but I think by now you have a keen idea that many reputations are at stake here. Rest assured Mitchell and I have both kept extensively detailed diaries of our experiences here on a day by day basis and now have a wealth of 3rd party documentation to support our findings.

We now do not trust that TEFL 'X' or London Linked School are able to deliver the quality internship we arrived in Beijing for, and paid for. Therefore, please take this as notice that we will not be accepting or undertaking any contracts for teaching or accommodation that we have been pressurised into undertaking via The China Agency.

We suggest that you consider, as part compensation for the physical and emotional stress and the personal expense we have both suffered as a result of your combined actions, placing both Mitchell and myself on an intensive CELTA training program, with accommodation for the duration of a standard that is acceptable to both of us with regards to cleanliness, location, and is suitably equipped for our stay. We also require reimbursement of our personal costs of accommodation in the hotel we are now both in and reassurance that as per Louise's threats via email last night, our visas are not harmed in any way. (Who, as per TEFL

'X', should not have had anything to do with them in the first place.)

I am sure you can appreciate that this decision needs to be expedited and we require a decision by midday today. With no delays, fob offs, or lies as per our previous experiences.

If we do not reach a satisfactory conclusion, we will be taking this further."

And breathe. I've paused, I've emphasised, I've made 'don't mess with me' eye contact (or so I think) and God only knows what a bitch I can look like when I do that. I did everything I've been taught over the years, but nothing taught me how to deal with these nerves. Or is it hunger? I'm not sure. Even so, the audience is silent and edgy and I think I may have got away with it all. Mitchell has his nervous excitement back – so I guess he's happy with the performance of our very last minute and late-night homework assignment.

I remain in silence and so does Mitchell as per my strict instructions. That works too and suddenly, as we sit in silence, the options and resolutions and references to preserving reputations pour out of a clearly panicked Alfie's mouth. Noel has a poker face. He's good. I'm impressed. But I already know what side he is on and it's not this man's. He's another one with his own agenda – it doesn't necessarily match ours, but it's not totally contradictory either.

Profuse apologies follow from Alfie, a promise to honour the internship is given, a promise to move us into accommodation tonight is promised too, together, promise of employment at London Linked School is given, and reimbursement of all personal expenses is promised. Everything we have expected since our arrival and subsequently fought for is being offered to us. Mitchell and I re-confirm the details out loud for a second confirmation. We tell him we appreciate his time and will be at the school tomorrow with our response, ready to move into accommodation the moment we arrive, if we have, during our consultation with each other, decided that it is a satisfactory resolution for us both after our ordeal.

We get up to leave. Alfie stands to shake our hands, apologises again – and we are gone. Escaping unnoticed to the confines of TEFL 'X''s office so we can finally let our shoulders sag and take a few deep breaths.

Jon is there. He asks no questions other than how he can help us when we leave the office for the day.

He took our phones and voice recorded us some useful Mandarin phrases to help us get by. Once Mitchell had unpacked himself another day's clothes, we finally left the school. After I've stolen a loo roll, though. They don't give you enough here in hotels and I have no idea how to ask for more. I'm so bad I know. But really? It's the least they owe me - and I can't tell you how good I felt ramming it into my handbag.

The rest of the day is drama free. A coffee with Mitch to go over our meeting and discussion on whether to take the offer of the internship (we will have to take it, we have no choice and we did pay for it after all), a supermarket trip to buy fruit (my first healthy food in a long while) and back to the hotel for a nap, a read of my book, and some diary writing.

A thankfully uneventful day from here on in one hopes – although Mitchell and I are braving the outside world in a few minutes for a spot of dinner - and time with him is never quite 'uneventful'. I wonder what inspirational stories he can tell me tonight. He's already informed me that he had to go to the supermarket to buy pants just now, thanks to us not having had access to a washing machine for quite some time (I've been washing my clothes in the shower in case you're wondering).

The sizes were L, XL or XXL. He plumped for large which turned out to be the same size as a ten-year-old. His voice may be a little high this evening… brilliant. Like he's not mildly irritating enough already.

9

TOO TIRED TOURISTS

The Dawning

Today is the day we should be getting confirmation of our new accommodation and should be our final day of being subjected to this dank hotel (and all of the prostitutes business cards being shoved under our doors on an hourly basis) – and dreams of having access to a washing machine and being a step closer to making ourselves our very own cup of tea being realised.

When we hear no definitive word from the school by midday, we alas, have to book ourselves in for another night. We have heard that we can visit the school to get our expenses reimbursed though, so I guess that's some form of progress. I've spent over £150 on this cheap ass hotel so far, and seeing as that could feed a person for three months out here, it's quite a lot of money I'm looking forward to getting it back. IF I get it back, I should say.

So, once again, Mitchell and I took our daily walk to school. The place where we don't go to teach as we expected we might, but instead only visit to partake in more battles to get what we came here for.

We are 15 minutes down the road and Mitchell realises he has left the key for his luggage back at the hotel. He has been living out of an overnight bag since he moved into the hotel and collects fresh clothes each day. I can't face walking back with him so I let him run back alone. Turns out he has to pull all manner of kung fu moves to get his ten-year-old-sized pants on each morning, and wants to grab his dirty ones to hand-wash for the sake of having children in the future. I have no idea how he managed to 'run' back at all.

When I get to the school without Mitchell, I kill some time with Pete, another teacher who I had briefly met at the BBQ restaurant all those days ago. He asks for an update on our current situation and looks appropriately disappointed for me when he hears it is not yet over. He also fills me in on what he sees and hears of the saga from his side. He informs me that Chinese Louise visited the school yesterday afternoon after Mitch and I had left and caused a huge scene.

She arrived out of the blue and demanded to see William and Jim. Once locked inside the TEFL 'X' office she went totally crazy – shouting and screaming about how TEFL 'X' and the London Linked School had caused her to lose face, reputation and income - and not repaid her any of her expenses nor the cash she paid to 'buy' us in the first place. She demanded 20,000 RMB (which equates to £2,000) as compensation. Reportedly William was near to tears by the time she had delivered a threatening ultimatum for them and left.

I can't say I'm too disappointed to hear this. I'm glad there was a public demonstration that showed what sort of woman she was and also how badly William and Jim had played this whole thing. I'm also not surprised she was angry – through pimping out Mitch and me as fake teachers she stood to take home over half our salary each month, barely leaving us with enough to survive on. She had lost a lot of potential money. I'd be mad too.

Just as Mitchell is arriving at the school and heading straight for his luggage, Noel appears and asks to speak with me in private for a moment. He sits me down in an empty classroom and begins to discuss accommodation. It turns out they have found a place for Mitchell, in the school's accommodation, in the heart of Beijing, and very near the partner school we will both be teaching at. It is with an older man who is a CELTA trainer at the school and who can have him move in ASAP as the room is empty.

But as for me, Noel asks if I would like to either move into the other staff accommodation (the apartment near the London Linked School that Aoife has just been evicted from) and live with a few Chinese girls (all housed in one room together), but that my room won't be ready for a few more days, or would I like to begin apartment hunting with Aoife and move in somewhere else with her.

Despite the full circle I have come in over the past few days and with Aoife of course being my favoured option, I find myself hesitating and weighing up the options in relation to which one is going to mean I have a home faster. I'm that desperate for stability. Realistically though there is very little difference in time scales here as if you view an apartment in Beijing, you literally move in within the next couple of days, if not immediately. So, I choose to go with the Aoife plan. I wanted to live with Westerners as I wasn't too heart warmed about the alternative due to more horror stories I had heard from others.

Noel and I discuss areas we can view and what my next moves should be. Aoife is working today and tomorrow but is apparently happy for me to view potential apartments and trusts my decision if I see one that suits and have to put an instant deposit down. Which is nice of her – but puts all the responsibility on my head regarding organising viewings, picking one in a reasonable condition, having the best location etc. Am I really the best qualified of the two of us to do this? Undoubtedly not. But again, I come back to the time issue and if that's what it takes, that's what I'll do.

The next step of the plan is that Noel will email to Aoife and me some links to apartments he has seen online and the flat-hunt can begin in earnest tomorrow – everything is always infuriatingly 'tomorrow' 'tomorrow' 'tomorrow'.

In the meantime, a very relieved Mitchell is informed of his apartment being available for him and ready to be moved into ASAP. Because we have already paid for another night in the hotel, Mitchell decides that his daily visit to the school tomorrow will see him collecting the rest of his luggage and taking it to his new place instead of right that minute. I was secretly glad he chose to do this because it meant I had company for one more night at least, and that we could finally get some sightseeing done today.

Alfie showed his face to us as well today. Couldn't be friendlier. But then so was Chinese Louise and look where that got us. I will reserve further judgment for now. Plus, rumour has it that Alfie is terrified of his Chinese business being damaged. Remember my comments about his wife running the London Linked School and living over there whilst he lives over here?

Well it turns out our old buddy Alfie (according to my sources) is allegedly wanted for fraud in many countries, and is a wanted man by some very dark people in Russia where another school is.

So, despite being a multimillionaire through the Language ventures, China is his only safe country at the moment... Interesting, huh? No idea how much of it is true but I shall certainly be looking into those little nuggets.

Which actually I have already done, being the accounting nerd I am. I researched Alfie and his wife and his known associates extensively since this all began and he and his shady cohorts have a less than honest sounding past. Between them, they appear to open companies, operate, then administrate/liquidate them, leaving a trail of well up to 20 companies in tatters (I stopped counting after a while) and presumably countless creditors unpaid. As limited companies, they personally do not suffer and technically can start new companies the same day and continue like nothing happened, basically having got services acquired through their 'failed' companies for free and cut-price assets to boot.

It's morally reprehensible but a very lucrative operation that takes advantage of loopholes in company law. They disgust me. I wonder how many people they have screwed over in the past and how many people lost a lot of money to these immoral masterminds. So, the allegations of reprehensible behaviour abroad in less regulated countries comes as little surprise to me. It makes me sick that they can all continue to make bundles of cash in this manner and potentially destroy others along the way. And nobody is stopping them.

With the daily school visit done and our pockets replenished with some of the cash we were owed (but no spare loo roll this time, unfortunately) Mitchell and I, after far too many days spent dodging the Chinese underworld, finally arm ourselves with our cameras and head out to the tourist sites of Beijing.

Within an hour and half, we are emerging from the subway at Tiananmen Square with plans to whiz round the Forbidden City which is at the head of the square and if there is enough time, even do the famous silk markets on the way home.

Sadly, these were too high hopes for two mentally exhausted people. We stood gormlessly looking in the direction of Tiananmen Square in the distance after exiting the subway, in silence, before turning to look at each other and in unison announcing 'I can't do this today'. Our experience in China this far had taken its toll, had definitely been tough and we could barely face walking anywhere. We wondered if we had some food inside of us, we may feel different though, so headed to the famous Walking Street in the very centre of the city. There are food and market stalls galore, hidden behind the buzzing businesses of the main and modern looking commercial road.

Such a naïve decision. Walking Street smells great and the markets are really bright and inviting – but don't let that fool you into eating the terrifying food there. The first stall we were called over to had buckets on top of the counters which I thought were just decoration. On closer inspection I can see that each skewer standing in this bucket has a string of three or four scorpions poked on it. Worse – if you tap the top of the kebab stick, those scorpions that haven't died through their being impaled, start wiggling their legs and stinging tails. It sent shivers down my spine and flipped my stomach – and not in a good way.

The stall-holder, then, seeing my reaction, suggested I may prefer the kebabs under the counter instead. That would be snake kebabs, then. And that would be a 'no' from me. I gave a polite weary shake of my head in response to the offer of cockroaches, crickets, bats, worms and beetles and other unrecognisable grubs too.

No amount of hunger, ever, would make me knowingly swallow any of the above 'delicacies'.

It's not long after our swift run through the market that I notice Mitchell has turned pale and the little sparkle of his that has kept me going since I met him, has gone. He has a headache (but then he hasn't changed his pants yet so I'm not really surprised) and I can see he just wants to go home.

He looks terrible and instead of heading on to the Silk Market I decide I will escort him all the way home. Plus, I do actually need to go to the toilet and I have no idea where the safest ones are around here. Public loos are horrifically disgusting here – although they are here in abundance they comprise of a dark un-aired room with no cubicles, paper or wash basins, and half a dozen squat holes in the ground next to each other. Although a very social toileting experience, the stench of stale urine and faeces everywhere is beyond acceptable for a civilised Westerner. And so I plump for going back to the hotel too. This is probably a good idea for me also because when I come to move into my own 'home' I struggle enough with my luggage as it is, let alone with market bought goodies in there as well. The markets will have to wait for now.

After returning to the hotel for an hour's nap, Mitchell is feeling well enough, although not restored to perfect working order, to join me in heading out to the BBQ restaurant with the other teachers, where I went last week. It's my future roomie's birthday so I definitely wanted to go and celebrate with her.

It was once again a very fun evening indeed. So much fun in fact that somehow Aoife persuaded me to promise to try our first scorpions together before our six months here were up. And somehow, I agreed. Overtiredness is all I can blame.

That's what the last few weeks have led me to – very stupid promises. So, before I made any more that I would regret, and lost any more of my lungs to the super smoky barbeque restaurant air, I went home.

Early, as usual. With Mitchell in tow, as usual. I think I'm really going to miss my little shadow.

SICK IN - AND SICK OF - BEIJING

The
Dawning

W hat. A. Day.

I don't even know where to begin – and if you think the pattern of luck is changing – you would be sorely mistaken.

Mitchell knocked on my door as he checked out of the hotel for his final time. He was heading to the school for 11am where he would be escorted in a taxi to his new abode. I was supposed to be going with him to check on my own status, but I was too depressed at his abandoning me in my nicotine stained hotel room that I hadn't even bothered getting showered and dressed. I was just going to phone in instead and await instruction.

He looked better today and had a spring in his step, not just attributed to better fitting pants. It was no wonder really. His life in Beijing (and the dream of his future in Hong Kong) was about to start properly as of today. Mine was still stuck in limbo for the foreseeable.

Once he left, I crawled back into my bed. So many nights of not being able to sleep properly, walking for miles and feeling despair and shame every minute of each day made me not want to face the day at all.

I did however find it in myself to call Noel and find out what I needed to do. The answer was to make my way to the City School to meet with Aoife and go over accommodation details whilst she was between classes. I knew she had a full teaching schedule so I didn't hurry, and only reached the subway stop for the school by 1pm.

This is when the first part of my worst day yet happened. On my very first solo trip through the city of Beijing.

In China, the second you step off the plane, you will notice spit all over the pavements, both indoors and outdoors, in restaurants and on the streets. This comes as no surprise if you're not deaf and can hear every second person hacking up their lungs and projecting their salivary, phlegmy load onto the ground below them.

When you first start hearing and experiencing the phlegm balls flying around you, and once your stomach has leveled out its disgust, you instinctively check your feet for a hit, but after a while, although you cringe inside every time you hear it – you stop the checking and carry on your business.

So that's what I did today on exiting the subway station for my ten-minute walk up to the school. Ignored it. Felt disgusted by it as usual, but tried to block it out.

Next thing I know, as I'm turning towards the main street from a feeder road from the subway, I feel a tap on my arm. I turn to find a Chinese guy pointing nervously to my legs. And yes, you guessed it. I had been the victim of a direct hit from a booger bouncing China man. And I'm not talking just a little bit of transparent saliva. I'm talking enough greeny phlegm to drown a small child in. On my leg. And it's staying put. Like a massive, thick, glob of glue and it's so bright green and striped with brown; it could have come straight out of the lungs of someone dying of a terminal lung infection.

The world stopped. I felt that telltale constriction of my stomach, the gag, the instant prick of tears in my eyes and yup, I was sick. Sick BAD. I vomited so hard into the gutter of this roadway, with all these people milling past me and watching that my neatly pinned bun on my head fell out, my handbag swung off my shoulder precariously close to last night's dinner and my knees almost gave way.

I stand there doubled over, vomiting, sobbing and coughing, my nose running like a turned-on tap and beg myself not to have to kneel down because if I do, this disgusting mess on my calf will get attached to my upper thigh and the vileness will be doubled – and the sickness is guaranteed to double also.

I somehow manage to stagger my way to lean on the side of a dusty shop where I try to compose myself. Still gagging, still crying, but feeling confident that there is no actual vomit going to happen again for the moment.

That's when, in my wisdom and dire straits, I rummage for my phone and take a photograph. Yes, you understood right. A photograph! Why, in the mess that I was in, did I think taking a photograph of my leg was a priority?! It's hardly like it was top of my list of things to do right then and that I would look on it fondly in weeks/months to come…I mean seriously?! What the hell was wrong with me? Fury made me simply want to document the horror – no-one would believe me otherwise.

Once that utterly ridiculous moment of madness had passed, still queasing, I decide to start on the more pressing priority of cleaning this scum off my leg to get it out of my sight and halt its slow soak onto my skin through my leggings. My handbag thankfully houses metres of emergency loo roll so after wrapping it around my hand many, many times, I didn't wipe, but actually plucked this lump of grotty phlegm off my leg. Unfortunately, that meant getting a pretty good close up view of it and then when I could feel it sliming around under the layers of paper – I was sick again. I totally broke, in a dusty alley in the 'beautiful and mysterious' Beijing.

A miserable, miserable moment in my life.

Mountains of tissues, baby wipes and antibacterial hand wash gel later I still don't feel even semi clean, but I know I need to get to the school so I can get some water, wash my face, wash my leg again and try to compose myself. I scurry there in tears. No longer 'I'm going to throw up' tears, but instead 'I'm so done with this' tears. I felt as dirty as the man who did this to me, and probably found my lowest ebb since I got here, many very long days ago.

The school was my haven for a while. After being ill on my way there, I swung in and out of hot and cold sweats, I got a pounding headache and fell asleep with my head on a desk. I thought I was physically tired before but now I could barely lift my head. Amity and Aoife were there to make me a cheer-up cuppa but I don't think anyone could have pulled me out of my slump until I was ready. And I wasn't ready for a good while…there was too much misery pent up inside me for any sort of quick fix.

When I had pulled myself together and regained some semblance of normality and dignity, I was told that I had to venture back out on those vile streets to go apartment hunting with Noel, who had come in on his day off to help us. I sobbed pathetically for the next few minutes…I didn't want to go back to the streets.

Unable to defer to another time, and still acutely aware I needed a home, Noel and I headed off to an area that would prove to be our starting point for the house hunt. Noel was kind to me, told me 'you look like crap' and told me that he had never in his seven years here, heard that anyone had ever been spat on. True the Chinese just spat, carelessly in any direction, but he'd never met anyone who had actually had a landing. Lucky me. I've also heard I was the only person to have ever seen a man beat up a teenage girl on a subway, or have an underworld Chinese agent have me collect money from men for them at night whilst home alone, or been confined to a dingy room for days on end and had my passport taken from me. Clearly, I'm one unlucky person.

And the unlucky streak continues. To cut a long story short, I saw three apartments today. One terribly filthy although better than the ones Chinese Louise had arranged for me, one acceptable-at-a-push one, and one was a really great one. Western in style, so freshly painted the brushes were literally still out on the table, a new kitchen in the process of being fitted, in an okay area. The bathroom was shabby and the furniture not great, but essentially it was clean and bright. Two very rare things in Beijing.

Annoyingly, Noel and I had another foreign couple literally on our heels viewing the same apartments, so decisions to rent had to be made on the spot. After calling Aoife to run her through the details, she agreed we should offer and so we did. Noel was all for it too. As for deposit, Alfie had promised me the cash so all it would take was a call to the school to send the cash over, and Aoife and I were potentially laughing – and moving in tomorrow. So after just double checking with Alfie that this was okay to proceed with, and after him saying 'yes of course', Noel put in a call to the school to arrange a wire of the money.

But did I really think it would be that easy? Turns out, the Chinese female boss (Kyla) who runs the school for Alfie and holds the purse strings, went crazy at the agent's fees (that were standard) and refused to send any money over on principle. Point blank refused.

As soon as the foreign couple behind us see this place they're going to take it I just know it, and I lose the prospect of a new, bright, clean home, just because Kyla the renowned nasty Rottweiler that she is, wants everything for free.

Noel was violently cursing her name, so was Aoife over the phone when I called her. Agent fees are factored in to all rentals and Kyla knew it, she was clearly just having a bad day – that's left me homeless – again.

She knows nothing about bad days.

It's now gone seven in the evening by this point, it's dark, my stomach and head still don't feel right, the last time I even had a drink was six hours ago and so instead of heading to a party with the other teachers, I decide I can't face anything else but to make the hour and half trip back to the hotel, and just climb in to bed, and ignore the world. If I could have, I would have speeded up my journey by getting a taxi for the equivalent of 50p but I'm learning fast that taxi drivers here don't want to pick up Westerners, their basic Olympics English lessons are long forgotten, and my Mandarin so poor at this stage, that I could have ended up anywhere in China. So, the grueling and aggressive subway journey was my only, long, depressing option.

As I stroll up the dusty rubbish tip of a driveway to my hotel, I ponder on the name of it – 7 Days Inn. I've been here eight now, more than likely will be here for 10. I wonder if they would consider changing their name to '10 Days Inn' in honour of their longest staying guest?

I'd like to think I could leave a more permanent mark on Beijing than simply throwing up in their gutters.

THE WINDING PATH TO A HOME

The
Dawning

Today I was instructed to continue my hunt for a home. Aoife wasn't starting work until 4pm so we had a good few hours of searching together before she had to leave for the school. Luckily, Aussie Amity, who speaks Chinese very well, also had the day off and offered to come with us to help us out with agents and negotiate deposits and fees. Without her, Aoife and I would be relying on hand signals, our Pictionary standard drawing ability, and some well-timed grunts to try and get our requirements across.

We arranged to meet at a subway station in the area we had chosen to be our home: well positioned and easily accessible for both schools and the other teachers for a social life. By the time we had actually found each other, it was 11.30am and we decided that it was as good a time as any to get brunch/lunch and plan our attack on the housing corporations of Beijing. In Beijing, you have to visit housing agencies in the immediate vicinity of where you need to rent, and on our way to food we passed several offices so we figured the odds of finding somewhere who could help us were stacked in our favour. We decided eating wasn't a risk to our time.

Lunch/brunch/my first proper meal since my accidental gutter illness was a Chinese hotpot. This was my first experience of the delight of cooking our own food in a pot of soup-like boiling spicy seasoned oils over a gas ring in the centre of our table. We ordered plates of thin shavings of beef, pork and lamb and enough vegetables to hit our five-a-day in one sitting, and away we cooked. We emptied the plates of delicious looking raw food into the boiling oils, waited a few minutes for them to cook and then plucked them out of the communal pot, morsel by tasty morsel, with our chopsticks. Despite having a burning hunger for this amazing spread, I still hadn't mastered chopsticks well enough to get my fair share of the food but I certainly tried my best and was well rewarded with what little I could successfully fish out.

Once lunch was over, we were keen to get ourselves started on the hunt for a home and headed for our first agency. Amity expertly arranged us our first viewing in an apartment a two-minute walk from the agency – which was conveniently close to the subway too for our daily commute. It was also off the noisy main road and in a block with a lift – which isn't as common as you might think for multi-storey apartments here, so that was a good starting point.

Despite the typically dusty and depressing lobby of the block, we were led to a lovely, well kept, newly appointed, clean and very western style apartment. It was within the price range of the apartments I had viewed yesterday and had been approved by Alfie, so I was confident that my half of the rent would be covered. Frustratingly no-one had been able to give me a straight answer on exactly how much my allowance was to contribute to the rent

(Aoife would contribute the other half), but like I said, I was within the range that Noel and his ever-so-feminine hand bag had taken me to see the previous day – so one would assume today's apartment was going to be acceptable too. Wrong. Surprise!

Whilst we were in the apartment, as per yesterday, there was a chain of other house hunters following us and a quick decision was going to be necessary. And so, we placed the phone call to the school for permission to sign the lease and have the holding deposit (we had already negotiated a reduction for immediate occupation) wired over to the agency. Amity fielded the call and battled her way through the Chinese administration staff at the school, only to discover that they wished us to communicate through Noel who had been instructed, again, to help us. He would then be communicating with Alfie and Kyla for final sign-off. A long-winded route that certainly would not bring us a quick answer. Of which it didn't, of course.

What I noticed of Noel yesterday was that he was slow. Slow to walk, slow to talk, slow to do anything. I have yet to meet anyone here that's been in the country more than two years and who has retained a western style of efficiency (other than Amity of course). Noel was certainly not an exception. I let him off yesterday because it was his day off after all and he was trying to help, but today his inability to cooperate and communicate effectively was beyond frustrating.

From the moment we made the phone call to the school to ask them to agree the rental, and the moment of the final conclusion, took over three hours – which included awkwardly hanging around the prized apartment for half an hour with a stream of other viewers filtering past whilst we were desperately trying to get commitment from the school to sign the lease, another 45 minutes sitting awkwardly in the rental office waiting for return phone calls that never came, Amity and Aoife becoming more and more furious by the second, and myself getting quieter and quieter due to feeling a familiar sense of pending doom.

We spent the remainder of the three hours sitting in a coffee shop killing time, knowing that there was clearly something going on back at the school that no-one was bothering to share with us, and just hoping that the apartment wasn't being snapped up as we sipped our lattes and waited on useless China infected decision makers to come up with a plan.

We then finally received a phone-call from Noel detailing the money that London Linked School would be willing to send us, to cover my part of the rent and deposits. A result, one could assume. But something didn't quite add up in my mind and so I scribbled down the various values he dictated over the phone, and hung up whilst we double checked the sums. If this worked out properly, then we could formally negotiate with the agency in order to strike a deal to get the apartment. Finally! We had been given a straight answer. But - not the one we expected.

In the calculations, the rental allowance they had given me fell short of my share of the 50%, and on calling Noel back I discovered I would personally have to make up the shortfall (despite it being much cheaper than yesterday's apartment I viewed). Oh, and lo and behold – there was no money provided for the agency fee. So really, what had they offered us? Nothing of value - unless I wanted to pay a whole month's salary upfront as a non-refundable agency fee and lose a fifth of my measly monthly salary to rent.

Three hours of wasted time waiting for them to come up with a worse deal than yesterday. Yesterday they were willing to match the rent, today we found an apartment for less rent only to find that overnight they had decreased my allowance. So not just no agency fee this time, but now a lower rent for me too. Why on earth were they making us go through this entire rigmarole when there was clearly no intention to assist us in any way? And so, for yet another day, I cried in despair.

Amity got an angry rash. Aoife swore a lot in her gorgeous Irish drawl.

Then, to our surprise, at 4pm on yet another wasted and upsetting day, we got another phone call from the school.

Noel and his merry band of geniuses had decided that they would finally help us – and informed Aoife and I that we could move into the school's rented 2-bed apartment near the London Linked School and that they would evict the Chinese girls currently living there on our behalf. The very apartment they had evicted Aoife from last weekend, and the one I should have moved into when I stepped off the plane in Beijing all that time ago. Can you Adam and Eve it?

Every second of pain I've experienced since I got here was only to bring me right back to where I should have started, had they honoured my initial contract and not tried to flog me to the Chinese underworld. Every single horrible thing I had been through had been for nothing. Every day Aoife had slept on Amity's sofa because she had no home to go to, had been for nothing…There are not words strong enough to explain just how I felt at that moment.

The sting for Aoife came when I was told I could move into the apartment tonight if I wished, because although she had been evicted from there last weekend as they wanted to move more of their Chinese administration staff in instead, no-one had actually moved in to her room after all. Aoife left us for work in furious silence, late, but not caring a jot for the organisation that messes with people the way it had with us.

So that left Amity and me, slightly stunned by the turn of events. Me battle weary, and Amity, acknowledging with anger how I must have felt over the past few weeks, vowing to quit her job as soon as her contract was over and end her own personally dramatic association with this farce of an organisation.

That same night, I spent my last night in the hotel for hopefully the very final time. I'd already had to pay for the night earlier in the day so I lost nothing by doing so. It was also more appealing than staying the night in another un-sanitised apartment with strangers as it would be a few days yet until a new apartment would be found for them to move in to.

Staying in the hotel also meant I could at least have one more night of internet and contact with the outside world – my new home was not wired up for the internet and I would have to order a SIM card for my laptop which would take a few days. This felt like a real blow after the internet had become such a major crutch for me over the past few weeks - but beggars can't be choosers and I was grateful to be getting a place I could call home until my six months sentence was up, if I chose to last that long. Plus, when Amity and I called passed the apartment last night, I saw that I would have had to sleep in Aoife's old room with no bedding and that wouldn't have been a wise option for anyone in the currently freezing Beijing.

Thankfully yesterday, Amity had been kind enough not only to waste her day off on us and our wild goose chase, but then her evening on me too. She obviously decided I needed some picking up, and had trudged all the way back to my hotel with me to help me move the bulk of my luggage into my new apartment (and then took me back to hers for a commiseratory drink, food and a DVD) so today's moving in day should not be too tough.

And so, at long last, this morning I checked out of my hotel which was still inaccurately called the 7 Days Inn, waving goodbye to the filthy litter ridden driveway, the prostitutes and its nicotine stained confines that had housed me for so much longer than the name described.

I was meeting Aoife at London Linked School at 1pm so we could both head over to the apartment and figure out what the state of affairs was, and Aoife also wanted to confirm that she would not be evicted again and could settle there and make it her home again too.

She and I were assured that the apartment was strictly ours for six months and that to demonstrate their commitment to us, they ordered me a double mattress (as my room, despite being shared by three Chinese girls, did not have one) and told us they were on their way out of the door, right that second, to view apartments to move the staff in to.

The signs were as positive as they could be, so we made the short walk to our new pad, to devise a shopping list of essentials we would need to get it shipshape as soon as possible. Aoife had the next two days off so even if she couldn't move back in just yet, we could at least prepare it for ourselves as far as possible.

Life in Beijing

SETTLING DOWN

Life in Beijing

Our apartment block was in a highly residential area in the south east suburbs of Beijing. There were two main areas of these 30+ storey tower blocks either side of a main dual carriageway running north to south. Our apartment was situated on the west side of the road and the South East School, which was nestled amongst the tower blocks on the east side a 15-minute walk away. This meant a mad dash across the chaotic road on our future walks to and from the school.

The southern end of our road met the South East Subway station and a multi lane highway that took you into the lower end of the city, right past Tiananmen Square on the south side and the Forbidden City on the north side. It was a permanent traffic jam. Heading north, the road met an equally wide feeder road into the north of the city centre. Another permanent traffic jam.

The noise was horrendous. Not a second goes by in Beijing when you don't hear aggressive tooting of car horns. That and the spitting noises everywhere you go, pretty much summarises the soundtrack of daily life here.

The tower blocks were gloomy and where they were once white, were now a grey/brown colour from all the pollution. Windows were murky and there was little point cleaning them due to the constant smog. From our window we could see factories to the south of us billowing out black clouds of smoke day and night, although no-one seemed to know what the factories were for, nor did they question what the fumes were.

Due to the pollution, the sky was often hazy, imitating a thick fog at its worst, and often during the daytime, we could only just make out the blocks across the road – and what lay beyond them remained a mystery.

Where you might have expected to see open balconies on these tower blocks, they were instead fully enclosed in glass. Giving the effect of narrow greenhouses. Again, due to the pollution, no-one would benefit from outside space and besides, balconies were wasted space when instead they could convert this to a makeshift sleeping area and house another person, or two, in the apartments.

Washing was often hung on extended poles out of windows, due to the lack of space inside the overpopulated apartments. Although it seemed strange to me that people would hang clean washing out to dry in such visibly dirty air. It also struck me as strange that clothes didn't blow off in the high winds as you never saw any lost laundry on the ground. Either it didn't fall off, or it was nicked the second it floated into grabbing distance.

The heights of the towers gave me anxiety to live in one. At home I didn't even like staying in high rise hotels because I was obsessively concerned about fire risks, despite the only risk being a dysfunctional hair dryer or a kettle. Here, where people lived full-on lives at this crazy height with kitchens and a multitude of electronics, worried me. I have to say though, that fear eased on one of my flat hunting trips before now. I viewed an apartment in a tower block that had experienced a flat fire. What reassured me was that the unfortunate apartment had just burned a hole in the building, the surrounding apartments did not seem to be affected and it simply looked like someone had removed a Jenga block out of the pile. That single view alone made me feel a little more trusting of living in a high-rise.

There were courtyards at the base of the tower blocks where there would sometimes be a play area for the children, a bench or two for the elders to take a rest or play Mahjong, a ping pong table if you were lucky, and reasonably well manicured lawns. It was currently winter so everywhere looked especially dull and lifeless, if not wholly depressing.

No matter where you went, and no matter what time of day, you were bound to see an elderly man or woman practising their slow-motion kung fu, or in the evenings the occasional group dance session. An attempt to get people out and about and moving around. With the pollution being so bad you never saw people exercising hard on the streets. But gentle exercise was encouraged and well organised.

The entrance hall to our apartment block was dark and dusty. Almost like a deserted forgotten building that didn't really see hundreds of residents traipsing through every day. We were lucky to have lifts as often the shorter blocks don't.

The lifts were in stark contrast to the neglected foyers and hallways. They had plasma screens in them advertising anything and everything and regularly updated advertisement posters to entice the captive audience. As the lift stops at each floor you can see the front doors of other apartments, all adorned with red New Year banners and stickers. It was considered unlucky to remove them before the year had finished so you had to make sure they were well stuck on. Some of them had clearly been there many years and were looking tired, but nonetheless, still holding on.

I've mentioned it before, but in a lot of these buildings, you would often not see a 4th floor – the death number for the Chinese due to the way the Number four could be mispronounced to sound like the word 'death'. It made me chuckle. Just because they had omitted the death floor number, surely it just made the number 15 the new number 14? It wasn't like there was just dead space where a floor should be – which actually would seem fitting.

Our apartment itself was considered large for two people. It could easily have housed six or eight sharing the two large bedrooms rooms and sleeping on the floors of the communal spaces, as was often done to keep housing costs down for the individual.

We knew we were lucky. And had the apartment been kept in good shape it could have been quite a palatial place to be.

As you walked through the front door, you came face to face with a small galley kitchen. It included a hob, a sink and cupboards. There was no room for an oven, which was rare in Chinese homes anyway, and the fridge was in the living room. At the far end of the galley kitchen was a narrow, enclosed glass balcony that offered extra storage for mops and brushes and such like, but also offered light into the kitchen. As with all the 'balconies' they were reinforced with waist height metal bars that made you feel like you were in an adult playpen or a prison for short people.

As you turned right from the front door, before you lay a wide-open space stretching down to the windows on your left that couples as a living room and an eating area. At the far end, another glass enclosed balcony type extension to the room, with the waist height metal bars.

Straight ahead is the sink for the bathroom. Unusually it was outside of the central bathroom and in the open space which is something I had not seen anywhere else. To its left was a large double bedroom with built in wardrobes, a double bed, and a glass balcony at the end for light. And to the right, down a short corridor, was the second double bedroom which overlooked the courtyard below. The bathroom, whilst still being a wet-room, was very un-Chinese in as much as the shower did not stand over the toilet and it was big enough to house a washing machine too.

Another luxury we had were air con units which meant we could both heat and cool our rooms and not risk our lungs by having to open windows to regulate temperatures.

All in all, not a bad place. Just in a state of disrepair and filthy. The walls, the ceilings, the windows, just needed a good jet wash. But as long as you didn't brush yourselves along the sides you would be fine. If we kept on top of clean floors then we could maintain some level of cleanliness against the dust and pollution that would inevitably creep its way in. I assumed that this was why everywhere you went in Beijing, electronic equipment was covered in thin plastic or retained the protective sleeves they were delivered in.

As you can imagine, despite the apartment having huge potential, we saw a huge cleaning task ahead of us, so we bit the bullet early, now we knew it would be ours, and made a visit to the local hypermarket to buy supplies. We spent a Chinese fortune on cleaning materials, buckets, mops, rubber gloves and the like, and carted them the half-hour walk back to our new home.

A quick visit to the local market before we began our cleaning task and the markets closed was to buy me some brand-new bedding. A couple of pillows, a duvet and a mattress cover/cushion thingy that they all have out here to soften the mat like mattresses. I had no bedcovers to put on them, but until I managed to get those, these would certainly be fine on their own. Plus, the sooner I could sleep in my own clean bedding the better, even if it was in Aoife's old bed for the time being.

It was about 5pm-ish when we returned to the apartment and with all cleaning avoidance errands run, we made a start. After I had changed into my spat-on leggings for the task as I didn't care about ruining those with the gallons of bleach we would be using (which I later vowed to ceremoniously burn). We had until 8.30pm when the Chinese admin girls came home from work and we wanted to be done and gone for dinner by the time they appeared. One of the girls, Jenny, was given the apartment to make her permanent home after London Linked School decided they could not afford to give her a pay rise.

She had moved in the day Aoife had been evicted but for some reason moved herself into the shared room with the other girls, instead of Aoife's. Sadly, she had her entire life either unpacked into the many cupboards in the apartment and her room, or still piled high in the living area. She had also filled the fridge to bursting with her food (that smelled like parts of a decomposing human body) and the kitchen with her cooking stuff.

We felt sad for her being messed around like this as we all knew how that felt – and embarrassed that we were the ones that were doing it to her. Hopefully London Linked School will honour her the promise of a home and find her a new apartment – otherwise she will be returning home to her cramped living quarters with her family which consisted of one large room shared with seven people.

Cleaning around her stuff was going to be difficult and pointless till it had all been removed so we decided on scrubbing the kitchen and the bathroom. The two hardest rooms, and the ones where we would disturb the least amount of her belongings.

Suffice to say the filth was incredible and it took us much longer than we thought it would. Thankfully Jenny was late home as she had headed out for food with the other staff, because we didn't want to offend her or them with the depth of cleaning and levels of filth we were getting stuck in to.

I have heard several times that if Asians marry across culture, they check there is no occurrences of mental health in our families. If you could see Aoife's and my herculean efforts on the cleaning and the microscopic degree to which we were scrubbing - I would have said we justified that mental health check quite easily. Certainly, the way Aoife was getting stuck in made even me question it.

The problem with this apartment is that it had never really been any one person's permanent home. Yes, Aoife had been here for six months, but due to the volume of ever-changing staff filtering through the apartment doors, no-one had ever taken on any level of real cleaning for possibly years. I guess no-one had ever felt any homely pride in it. That would certainly explain why we discovered in the kitchen that the taps were bright shiny aluminium, the cooker hood wasn't made of frosted glass as Aoife had always believed, and the floor was actually pale grey tiles, not black slabs. It is such a lovely apartment that when we are done cleaning every available surface, it's genuinely going to be the best apartment out of everyone we know. And that's what we were working towards.

The oil and grime dripped black off the walls like dollops of filthy bird excrement and the litres of water we had to go through just so we didn't spread the filth would have drained the River Thames. It stank – and even Mr. Muscle was pressed to his limits.

We thought we would get both rooms done in the same evening, but we had barely finished the kitchen before the fumes and the hunger nearly finished us off. So, we had a quick change of clothes and headed to the BBQ restaurant around the corner for dinner at gone 10pm. This is now officially my most frequented venue since I had arrived - barring the 7(10) Days Inn, the School and various branches of KFC – and even the odd sanity trips out into the wilds with Mitch or the girls.

As per usual, the food was flawless, cheap (at the equivalent of £2.20 each) including beers, the company (Ms. Aoife) was priceless and we two exhausted scrubbers were finally done for the day.

I took myself back to the apartment and Aoife returned to Amity's sofa across town. I crept into the shower before diving into my wonderful new bedding in another temporary bed and looked forward to a nice long sleep in. It didn't worry me that by 2am I still wasn't asleep because I knew I had until midmorning at least before Aoife came over for round two of Project Grime. And besides, despite the hard work ahead of us, I was content knowing that I was in my soon-to-be-beautiful new home and finally feel settled.

13

THE BITTER TASTE OF THE WEST

Life in
Beijing

OK, smugness of new home aside, my lie in didn't happen. I was so close to experiencing my first night of unbroken, and plentiful sleep, that I was more than a little disappointed to have someone knocking on my bedroom door (and entering without invite).

It appears Jenny had enlisted help in the form of Rottweiler Kyla before her shift at work to help pack up her belongings ready for moving into her new place - and they felt the need to let me know the details. At 7.30am. After several weeks of no proper sleep. The only reason I tolerated it was that her going meant we were a step closer to having our apartment to ourselves, so I kept out of their way until the coast became clear.

By 9am the packing team had left – not taking anything with them, but making a hell of a racket and stacking a good majority of their things in high piles in the free space in the living area. But thankfully they had emptied my room so I could finally move in. There is still no sign of a mattress though so I will still have to sleep in Aoife's room for now, which means she will have to stay on Amity's sofa another night, but I hope for its arrival pretty soon.

As I was up, and I had heard word from Aoife that she would not be over till mid-afternoon, there was nothing else for me to do than get to work again on the battle against the grime.

I begin re-cleaning the kitchen. The first attempt yesterday had been to remove the worst of the filth, so this morning I cleaned it again and was pleasantly surprised at how little dirt was left. I got on my hands and knees with a pan scrub and scrubbed every inch of the kitchen floor and when I was satisfied, I started on the bathroom. Luckily this is a wet room so once the walls, floor and toilet were scrubbed and bleached, I simply hosed down the entire room and it sparkled. The only downside was the fact that the shower plug-hole was so blocked with hair and goodness knows what else, that I was left wading in a pool of water with the contents of the drains backing up all over my newly polished floor. At least I had uncovered the source of the smell that had been seeping through the apartment and a bottle of drain cleaner would hopefully clear it.

Aoife's arrival by 3pm saw the separate sink area outside of the bathroom scrubbed till you could eat off it and a start on sweeping each of our bedrooms. A swift shower for each of us (and a short wade out of the stinking quagmire the blocked drains left behind), had us ready to leave our cleaning for another day and head out to join the others for food and drink for the early part of the evening. Fingers crossed this was my last night of camping in someone else's room, and into my permanent resting space for the remainder of my six months. I had been informed the mattress was coming tomorrow so bearing that in mind, I also had a new roommate to look forward to as well because Aoife could have her own room back.

Aoife and I were meeting our little gang in an area in Beijing called Sanlitun, which centres around 'The Village' shopping centre (international brands, the official Apple store etc.) and is the renowned Westerner/ex-pat area of Beijing. I have now had several experiences of this area, through lunches in French cafes or American diners with my friends, to bars and pubs of Western style providing more Western food and Western drinks. Stepping outside of the local BBQ restaurant experiences.

I must say though that my visits have been purely to experience the 'new' places my friends take me to, and not because I wanted to eat familiar foods or drink familiar drinks - because each and every time, I didn't really enjoy it nor need it, as such.

In comparison to Chinese food (which is not as you would taste in Chinese restaurants and takeaways back at home, but a whole lot better), Western food is heavy, bland and feels unhealthy by comparison. Western prices on a Chinese salary are also not possible to keep up – so I'm pretty thankful I have no cravings for it. Being here in China and eating native food has started to make me feel all-round healthier. The loss of bread and other complex and manufactured foods from my diet has made me feel significantly less bloated, my stomach isn't as sensitive as it was back home and my skin is pure and spotless (I'm weighing up whether it's worth it against the loss of lung function from the country itself though). But why wouldn't I stick to my newfound diet?

The drinks in Western bars are also clichéd cocktails with Western prices, or poorly brewed foreign beers, and they don't even do them well enough to warrant the price tag either. I literally choose the cheap local beer every time now – despite the fact it is rumoured to contain traces of formaldehyde. But at least my internal organs will stay perfectly preserved.

The reason the food out here (Beijing's biggest positive, in my opinion so far) is not found in England is because this food is typical of Northern China. It is rare (previously impossible) and very difficult for the Northern Chinese to leave China without jumping red tape, anecdotally having something like the equivalent of £70,000 in the bank and a formal invitation to visit another country, therefore it is highly unlikely that you will find a Beijing style Chinese restaurant anywhere in the world... the Chinese foods we eat at home are mainly of Cantonese origin, from where the Southern Chinese folk were able to travel in a freer fashion due to colonisation by the British Empire. So you really shouldn't judge your home takeaway against the delights we get to enjoy here. Still not a strong enough reason to stay in this country for a long time, but I'm trying to find positives.

Food aside though, the 'taste of home' is not as good or as comforting as you would be forgiven for believing. Another hugely negative thing about this Western hub – is that I feel repelled and ashamed by some of the Westerners abroad.

Just from this one evening, my experience so far of Sanlitun, is that they are clearly pick up joints for very drunk male Westerners, who are a long way from home and behave like kids in a sweetshop when they realise the abundance of Chinese ladies vying for their attention. Also, the number of new Western male friends they can meet and drink with, reminisce about home, and share their being treated like Kings in the Eastern world is in abundance. There are very few white women to be seen.

With over 20 million people in this city, you can spend an entire day here, and never see another white face. So, you can imagine the air of desperation in these honey pots for proximity to more familiar races.

I've traveled a lot in my time, but have never experienced quite the intimidating cheapness there is in those bars - not even in the party capitals of the world for teenagers, and we all know what those are like. Sure, there's no-one half-dressed (but then it has been pretty cold here) drunk girls dancing on the bars and pulling strange men on the beach, but instead there are adults with less innocent agendas, and more power than a pubescent boy. It's not something I feel comfortable with.

It's lecherous, and hot, and we even had a Western guy come past our table in one bar just to ask us shamelessly if anyone had any condoms on them as he needed them ASAP. It was worse than back home at 2am in the morning. I hated it at home anyway, but seeing as this is worse, I hate it in these bars even more. And the occurrence of falling-over-drunk white girls increased ten-fold in this area – I wonder if they're trying to mask – or drink through - the difficulty of being a white woman in these countries. It's embarrassing to be Western sometimes. No class, whatsoever.

In such a short space of time I find it hard to believe I have gone from craving familiar food and company – only to be faced with it and feel repelled. I have no idea where I belong anymore. How quickly the tables have turned.

Needless to say I won't be returning here in a hurry. I decided to leave everyone to it and find my own way home, still mentally and physically exhausted. This would be my first taxi ride unaccompanied and was proud to say I successfully guided the taxi driver, paid and exited, to the doorstep of my tower block. This alone was my proudest moment so far.

14

ATTEMPTING THE LANGUAGE ... OF LOVE, PERHAPS?

Life in Beijing

Another lie-in foiled as I groggily awake at 9am to the sounds of more banging in the apartment. There's me thinking I had the place to myself. On venturing out in my pyjamas I find Jenny and her mother unpacking and repacking her things in the living room.

Another good sign that we are soon to be free of any more random unannounced visitors and other people's things littering the floor that we desperately want to clean. But I wish they'd knock before they invited themselves in. I don't like the thought of strangers coming and going whenever they fancied. I wondered how many other people had keys.

I shower and dress and appear again to an army of Chinese folk (the moving team I suspect) and make my excuses to leave the apartment on a quest for more cleaning supplies. Drain cleaner, more gloves and more bleach. All finished or wrecked in the frenzy of the last couple of days.

By the time I've made my two hour round trip to the supermarket on foot, I find the army laden with bags and boxes making their move towards the door and a man holding a brand new double mattress. It's definitely looking good. And in a flash the apartment is cleared, my mattress is on the bed and we finally have something resembling a home of only two people, not half the working population of the school.

The only bad side of all of the belongings being moved out is that the living area looks like a bomb has hit it and exploded debris and dust as far as the eye could see highlighting yet another epic cleaning task ahead of us. It also showed up the state of disrepair the apartment was in. But I didn't care. The end was in sight.

The only downside was that Jenny had informed me that their new apartment didn't have a bridge (I assume she meant fridge) so our fridge was still jam packed with stinking food. So although we could clean the dirt from the apartment, the lingering smell of decomposition would remain with us for a while yet.

I texted Aoife the news that we finally had the apartment back and she planned to move back in tonight after work. In the meantime, I relished the task of washing my room from floor to ceiling, disinfecting every surface, every drawer, every handle – and finally unpacking my bags after living out of them since I had arrived in China. It felt like I was going shopping, seeing all the 'new' things I had brought with me that I had not yet unearthed. It was also weird seeing the range of things I had brought with me. I knew within a matter of weeks the temperature would be going from below freezing to sweltering hot so the thick woollen tights stored next to the flipflops was a strange sight to see.

Plus, once this was done I could actually do some washing and dry it in a clean(ish) and dust free(ish) environment. It's the small things you have no idea that you miss that make you feel more settled - even if the washing machine was covered in Chinese symbols and I had no idea how to use it, it would surely be better than my handwashing efforts using shower gel since I got here.

Unpacking once the room was clean was a great feeling. It was like I was finally laying down some safe roots in this crazy unfamiliar city. I didn't even let the fact that all the coat hangers had been nicked get me down.

The thing that made me smile the most though was the little notes I found wedged between my belongings, lovingly placed there by my Mum. They brought a tear to my eye as realised I wouldn't get to see her for a good while yet, and upset at how she must be feeling about all the traumas I had been relaying home since I'd been here. I still didn't have a way of contacting them regularly so it was harder still. We had no internet in the apartment and phone signal was hit and miss. Mostly miss.

By the time Aoife had finished work and collected her belongings from Amity's, I was half way through the sweeping and mopping and wiping of every surface in the living room and gathering up a pile of rubbish that had obviously been stored in the apartment for years.

We had collected for the bin: discarded Western sized clothing (that must have been there for years as Aoife had never known another Westerner to live here), shoes, broken umbrellas, life-sized posters of Princess Diana and Shakespeare, filthy old brooms, buckets and mops, broken door frames, broken rice cookers and literally hundreds of empty recyclable beer bottles which had built up over Aoife's six months of residency and could be exchanged for crates upon crates of fresh bottles.

This was a nice little bonus so we kept them to one side and decided to recycle them at intervals when our beer stocks were low. In the meantime, we each took shifts in heading down in the lift to drop the rest of the junk in the bins at the foot of the apartment. They were full to overflowing and our apartment was considerably emptier.

We even put the old TV (complete with its plastic protective wrap) into a cupboard to hide it away. The channels were all in Chinese, we didn't have a DVD player to play the many knock off DVD's sold on the streets, so there was no point in it taking up unnecessary space in the room. Plus, we had such limited amounts of useable furniture that somewhere to put down our tea cups would be handy. We had to make this squat work for us.

In our search and clean of the apartment we also discovered a small fold out bed complete with a straw mattress lurking in the corners of Aoife's bedroom (that she had never even noticed was there). We decided we would fashion another sofa out of this as we only had one tiny two -seater between us and so put it to one side in the living area with the intention to set up later. It was filthy and decrepit but we figured we could cover it and make it work for the time being. We also moved the table and chairs from being the first thing you walk into when you enter the apartment, against the inside wall, over to the balcony area so that Aoife and our guests could smoke directly under open windows and we could have a view of sorts when we sit there.

As we picked up the trusty table, a leg dropped off, our hands stuck to the grime on the surface and the chairbacks came off in our hands. Aoife's hobby of peeling off the sticky tape encrusted all over them whilst she sat there in the past drinking endless cups of tea had removed their only means of remaining intact.

Once we had completed our task we were ready to relax. Aoife made the tea and we settled at our rickety table and precarious chairs in the balcony. We scanned the room...it was a damn sight better that it had been but where the floors were now spotless and all the junk had been removed, the filth on the walls was blindingly obvious, the couch had seen much better days, the frame of the balcony area had fallen off in our hands and paint and plaster regularly coated our clean floor as the building moved. It was by no means perfect, but it was ours for the foreseeable. So, with that in mind, we started making plans for an IKEA trip and to purchase essential living items in the safest and most familiar place we knew. The market would do for the rest.

Extra strong sticky tape to remedy the chair situation was on the list as well as some sort of table covering, as were throws for our manky stained sofa and our makeshift sofa-cum-bed. When we had erected it, it was like sitting on a cold concrete park bench so we figured a couple of pillows would be useful or someone was either going to get piles or a bad back – or both. I still didn't own any bedding, only the bare duvet and pillow cases I had purchased from the market; we needed coat hangers and crockery.

We owned a few stolen pub glasses and two chipped tea mugs but beyond that the rest had to be thrown away for hygiene purposes. Therefore, our shopping trips were promoted to the top of our apartment TO DO list. We also desperately needed drain cleaner and a shower head because not only did the bathroom daily turn into a putrid swamp of gunk but the shower went from ice cold to 3rd-degree-burns-heat in a dangerously frequent cycle. In England that usually happened because of hard water and due to the weak flow of water once the head was attached, we figured that was the cause of our issues so put that on our list too.

With lists of shopping as long as our arms now written and a little flame of hope that our home could actually be homely, we headed out for a celebratory dinner at the local BBQ restaurant – for a change.

On our way out, past the bins that were once overflowing with our filthy and broken cast offs, we noticed Princess Diana and Shakespeare were the only remaining evidence of our clear out. The rest had been swiped... On our way home, Lady Di and Shakespeare had also apparently found new homes.

The following day, Aoife had classes so disappeared off early. And I still wasn't starting my formal 'working' of shadowing teachers until tomorrow so I had one last day of reprieve. I didn't hear her leave. I was finally dead to the world, in my own room, on a brand-new mattress, and calm at last. The thing that woke me was a text message from Rob.

When I had first met him, we had exchanged numbers on the promise of him teaching me basic survival Mandarin but I hadn't thought anything of it. Many good intentions go unfulfilled. But here now was a text message asking if I would be free if he popped by after he had finished his lessons that day. I accepted of course...glad of the company and the thought of nurturing new friendships. Plus, we had got along pretty well and it would be nice to see him.

A couple of hours later he's ringing on the intercom and I let him up. I'm greeted with a warm hug and kiss on the cheek and his eyes are dancing like he's excited to be sharing his knowledge or something. He amuses me. His light is also infectious.

I pop the tea on and after a long chat about our respective last few days he instructs me to get out a pen and paper. Chat now over, we were beginning our lesson.

We decided to stick to basic formalities and survival language. He began with writing down pinyin words and teaching me the four main tones, and one neutral tone, of pronunciation, saying the words aloud and having me repeat them back to him parrot fashion. I was always pretty okay learning languages of the

European variety but this Mandarin lark was a whole new ball game. You have to use your throat differently, do stuff with your lips that doesn't feel natural, and get the tones just right or the word you're trying to say could be misconstrued as being one of its four or five other meanings that use the alternative tones and made the words sound subtly different.

It was this nuance of the language that had led to the number four being an unlucky number – because if the wrong tone was used it was heard as 'death'. I now knew officially why it was the death number. Another good example Rob informed me of was Amity, when she was still new to learning the language, went into a bar and asked for four arseholes instead of four beers. I was also instructed never to say the English words of shabby, or newbie – as they meant something pretty offensive that I daren't type here.

On the subject of being offensive, I asked him why the Chinese thought it was okay to say nigger every second word. Everywhere I went that word rung out around my ears and I'd gone from feeling 'how dare they' to 'what does it really mean?' realising that foreigners were so rare that insulting them so regularly made no sense. Turns out it's an unfortunate sounding term they use as a sentence filler, the same way we would use the word 'like'. I would need to remember not to get mad the next time I heard it.

Over the course of the lesson I learned basic shopping words: counting, thank you, hello, chicken, beef, pork (hoping my pronunciation didn't mean I unwittingly ordered dog or cat) and secretly hoping I could survive on pointing because I sounded like a twit. Numbers were an unexpected toughie – if only because they were often accompanied, or replaced, by hand signals instead - which were not at all sensical in my mind. In England (and everywhere else in the world so I thought) we use a finger to denote one, two fingers to denote two and so on. In China, they count to ten on one hand. Past the number five they contort their hands into what could be universally interpreted to be the signs of greeting for gang members. And if you give them the double thumbs up then you have probably multiplied your order by several thousand. Sheesh.

I figured I would also need to learn the phrase 'I don't understand' as I was pretty sure that would be the most common phrase I dared to utter. If you deign to shrug your shoulders at a Chinese person, you're showing them disdain. I'm panicking at my pending faux pas and mortified at the offences I had already committed.

I also learned that their sentence structure was very abrupt. In a shop and you're looking for something you say: 'have, don't have?' to enquire after something or you hear 'want, don't want' if you're asked if you want a bag or something in a supermarket. I learned ten shopping bags sounds like 'do you want a sugar daddy' and giggled like a child. I think my reaction confused Rob, but he had no idea how long it had been since I'd been able to have a sense of a humour. But to be fair even I was surprised at my childishness. He laughed at me, not with me. Learning this language was a serious business for him.

I also learned taxi instructions: turn left, turn right, stop here, straight on. Bearing in mind I didn't know my own address I figured this would be useful.

I also learned: 'you're welcome' and 'I'm sorry' – at my insistence to want to be able to apologise for myself or be gracious – obviously the English politeness in me coming out and I also hoped it would endear me to some of the cold faces I came across in my daily life. Rob laughed, told me it was unnecessary to be that level of polite here, but he taught me anyway.

I basically spent the lesson blushing, gurning and bouncing my head along with the tones in order to master them and felt like I was singing the words, not just saying them. I imagined this was what it would be like to give a bad audition for the X-factor that was guaranteed to be on 'the most embarrassing' segment, but Rob was so sweet about my novice attempts that we ended up laughing at my shame. It was easy to be his pupil and I found myself wanting to be a good one.

We sat at the sticky and rickety table for a good two hours drinking tea, gossiping and learning this strange language in such a fun manner that when he said it was time to leave, I felt disappointed. I hadn't been ready to part from his company...he was fun, we were on the same wavelength and it had been a long time since I'd spent any good amount of time with anyone here (except Mitch, Aoife and Amity) that I didn't want it to end. Plus, I realised I loved how his whole face smiled and how he was naturally a very tactile person. I'd missed human touch and kindness for so long.

Luckily, he wasn't leaving without me and announced it was time to put my learnings to immediate use and that he was taking me to the nearby food market to buy him his shopping. I was mortified but he was clearly not going to stand for my shirking putting into practice his well taught Mandarin. No matter how mortified I was at the thought, one look at his earnest face I knew I didn't want to disappoint this guy by not going.

I donned my jacket, my woolly hat and mittens-on-a-string and exited the building into the freezing Beijing afternoon, Rob on my arm and nerves rising...I suspected for more than one reason.

The market he took me to was the one Aoife and I had been to when we bought my emergency bedding. The market was on the way to the subway which I had learned well enough on my treks, past the little old man who sat on a moth-eaten couch on the dusty street corner next to his bicycle cart adorned with a sewing machine and shoe fixing tools. Just passed him was another bicycle cart with a woman selling budgies in cages, small rabbits and turtles. Hopefully being sold as pets and not food.

If Aoife and I had dared to venture further into the market we would have seen the glory of the stalls upon stalls of highly packed fresh and vibrantly coloured vegetables, fresh meat and live fish and other water creatures in tanks that would be killed and gutted on demand of hungry shoppers. It was like walking into the pages of a story book with rainbows of bunting draped from the dirty, but still somehow vaguely transparent, ceilings and people buzzing around. I felt like Alice in Wonderland looking at the leeks that reached up to my knees, the carrots as big as my forearm and potatoes as big as my head, suspiciously looking like they had been grown using huge amounts of steroids but still managing to look yummy.

On sharing my awe and surprise, Rob informed me it wasn't steroids, but MSG. They weren't that brightly coloured or clean looking without bleach washes. But what the heck - they were just so vibrantly attractive I'd risk it. Plus, the monstrous veg, along with the meat, would give you the best-looking dinner for less than the cost of a postage stamp, so again, I was willing to risk it.

However, it only managed to distract me momentarily from the pending task of actually speaking to the stallholders and buying something I had only just learned to say. My first experience of real communication in a country I had become accustomed to being the equivalent of deaf and mute in.

Rob had clearly been here many times before and the stallholders he gave his regular custom to greeted him with familiarity. He translated that they asked him if I was his girlfriend, which he laughed off (disappointingly earnestly) and then pushed me forward and reeled off his shopping list to me in English. First up: he needed 500 grams of beef. Looking at him helpless didn't plead my case any and he stood there in silence next to me with his eyes dancing in amusement as he saw the blush washing over my face and my stammering start. 'Jin niurou' fell out of my mouth.

The stallholder grabbed a slab of the reddest meat I could see, hacked me off a section, and using his bare hands grabbed the meat and thrust it into a small bag, tied the top and threw it at me. I felt partially relieved that I had managed to order 'something', concerned that it may have been part of a kitten due to my bad pronunciation and mortified at the thought that there was raw meat and bacteria on the outside of the plastic bag he had given me. How quickly I was distracted from my accomplishment. Rob looked proud, rubbed my shoulder in congratulations and barked out his next request. He was the most pleasant taskmaster I had ever encountered.

When it was all over and dusk was upon us, he walked me back to my apartment and carried on his journey to his own place, just across the river. Not without a full body hug and a heartfelt kiss on the cheek. My face was burning as I made my way upstairs... what an unexpectedly lovely day....and how too quickly it had ended. I think he might be trouble for me.

15

THEY'RE JUST ANOTHER BRICK IN THE (GREAT COMMUNIST) WALL

Life in Beijing

Although I am still writing my diaries, I'm sure you do not need to hear a day-by-day, blow by blow account of what I am up to – especially as there are no 'exciting' dramas to report any more that require live updates. Instead I have come to expect a level of 'surprise' to my days and shall summarise as and when the stream of constant, more minor, but equally irritating and interesting Chinese dramas occur.

I'm now two and a half weeks into a more 'normal' routine, just how things should have begun several weeks ago on my arrival. It feels like I've already been here for several months based on the volume of my experiences to date, but alas, I'm still only a small portion of my way through the entire experience. Don't get me wrong, those weeks haven't been all bad and I do thoroughly enjoy some aspects of my life here, but there are some things that I will be happy to walk away from as soon as the six months are over… if not sooner.

My thoughts and plans are currently up in the air as to my leaving date, but you can be sure I will not be spending a minute longer in China than I'm contracted for, or as is necessary. I hesitated to write that as it sounds incredibly negative and that I'm trapped here – I'm not of course, but my purpose for being here has not gone away and there are some things out here that resemble the quality of life that I didn't have the luxury of at home.

Although I'm not feeling totally settled just yet and still lack a stable routine, I definitely feel like things are slowly coming together. Or, more accurately, I'm gaining a level of acceptance to the constant state of flux I now live in.

So where to start on explaining the strange new world I reside in? The best way to do this, I think, will be to split my thoughts and experiences into some key areas. They are all inextricably linked so it may be tough to get across a true and clear picture - but please bear with me. They will be coming piecemeal over the length of this tale.

Now that I have formally begun my teacher training and shadowing of colleagues at the City School to prepare me for taking my own classes, I guess the best place to start is the Chinese educational regime – and my part in it.

This has to be the single biggest thing to tell you about and not least the most relevant seeing as this is the reason I am here.

My teaching schedule is full (not necessarily of teaching per se but I am required to be somewhere during my working hours). It's ever changing and it's proving very hard to plan my time off in the evenings and days off too far in advance for several reasons that I will explain as this update progresses.

A bit of background to the London Linked School set-up may help before I begin my tales of the school I've been wedged in to.

There are two schools here owned and run by the international (alleged) criminal Alfie, both falling under the umbrella of the

"London Linked School" brand. One is called City School (named after the street in the centre of Beijing where it is located on the 7th floor of an office block) and the South East School, which is located in another block on the south-eastern outskirts of the city. A 10-minute walk from where I live, and a twenty-minute walk from the hotel where I spent a great deal of time holed up during those early weeks.

The London Linked School is an international reaching English Language school which was set up by the mastermind Dodgy Alfie and his wife. They are both strict Catholics from Ireland (clearly the 'though shalt not defraud others' morality code is non-existent in his version of the faith).

The London Linked School in London is controlled by his wife and is a shining example of how TEFL training and private foreign language schools should and could be run apparently (although, I doubt this now). Their reputation precedes them and is equally strong in other countries over which she has control. The China school's are an anomaly in the portfolio and very much seem to be a playground for her allegedly dodgy husband and all his weird and mixed-up cronies, who are mostly outcasts from society and would not fit in back in their home countries, thus is the reason I suspect they congregate here.

I have since learned without a doubt, that all of the internet acclaim they have is manufactured. Idiot William of TEFL 'X' is now permanently employed to pose as an internet blogger making up imaginative stories of how great his experience is as a 'fake' intern and to debunk any bad press they receive, that is apparently quite high. He is paid to police the reputation and lie, basically.

It turns out that, Alfie (via further allegations from my contacts out here) has an allegedly devious and criminal past of defrauding investors for building foreign schools that then never happened, defrauding foreign governments for educational grants – then leaving the country etc. He's a slippery fish that to your face is weak and meek and very grandfatherly in his nature (although this is an insult to my own wonderful Grandfather), but clearly uses this to his advantage where money is concerned.

China is one of the few countries that he can apparently live in without fearing the government or lynch mobs. He is also only skilled at extracting money on an allegedly illegal basis and not on a business level. His business skills are utterly terrible (I have seen far too much of his ridiculous ideas to disprove this claim), and his early financial successes were due to his wife being financially savvy and by the nature of their marriage, sharing the successes. Bearing in mind my previous edit as to the morally reprehensible nature of how they got their cash, she appears to be just as dodgy.

China is only kept running as it is the only country that apparently does not make any money in their questionable business portfolio; it does not have a reputation to ruin, keeps Alfie from meddling in the successful ventures and allows monetary losses made here to be shared to reduce tax bills in other countries. As the gossip here would have me believe.

Of the two schools running here, South East is seven months old and has only two full time teachers. Scottish Holly and a sacked Pete. ('Sacked' will be explained shortly – and is the latest major drama that will potentially screw up my time here). They have very few students, tiny classes, and work 12-8pm on weekdays and 9-6pm on weekends.

Being based at the South East School means they have to work where the TEFL 'X' Offices are, and where the head honchos: Dodgy Alfie and Rottweiler Kyla, are based. They also have two Directors of Studies to oversee them: Pathetic Noel and Pervy

Jim. I get the strong impression that life is not great for them. Holly is degraded and preyed on every day by Pervy Jim and Pete gets to work in an environment which clearly does not make him happy, especially as he is one of life's lovely good guys.

They spend much of their time hanging about the teacher's office, hiding from society's social misfits and surfing the limited web – before teaching the very occasional class on a weekday, and working solidly on their weekends. The only saving grace for Pete working there is that his equally lovely girlfriend is one of the hundreds of London Linked School admin staff also based there. Two teachers, very few students, two directors, and hundreds of admin staff surely indicates a costly and loss-making enterprise, no? To you and me this is clearly absurd….and this is what they are finally realising, especially now that they have two surplus teachers (Mitch and me) they have to find salaries for.

Now, the story of Sacked Pete. Although it is not written into their contracts, recently scorned-by-a-Western-man Chinese Rottweiler Kyla verbally informed all teachers and staff some months ago that inter-office relationships were banned. Pathetic Noel who will here on in be referred to as Mole Noel, got wind of Sacked Pete and admin girl Honey being in a relationship since Christmas and in his usual style (the history here is long) fed the information to the powers that be and both Pete and Honey were summarily dismissed last week. Sacked Pete's salary is twice what mine and Mitchell's is as trainees (laughably intimating that there is training of any sort) so they found a way of making their money back in one foul swoop. Sack one; afford the two that you are scared of and that have enough dirt on you to report you. Nice move London Linked School, what remains of your integrity is further smashed.

They soon realised however that the knock on effect of this

sacking meant a shortage of teachers at South East and the resultant effect of having to steal a teacher from City would upset too many of the fee paying parents based over there.

With the inconsistencies of teaching staff for both sets of schools, they have temporarily revoked the sacking, but put a cat among the pigeons for the rest of us, that will mean big changes for some poor soul having now to move permanently to the living nightmare that is South East, so that if (when) this happens again in the future, they have a permanent member of staff ready to step into the breach with minimal disruption and cover their backs should they next want to sack someone again.

So, who's the mug that currently has no classes to disrupt at City which would upset the money givers, who lives near the school, and who is free to start observing and getting their face known at South East at short notice? Enter: me. Pervy Jim, Mole Noel, Rottweiler Kyla and Criminal Alfie are looking likely to be my new playmates. And I thought my first few weeks in Beijing were bad.

But again, I digress from my telling of the tale of how messed up the educational system is here – even without the meddling of the incompetents listed above.

All children of school age in China endure a gruelling and harsh regime with regards to schooling. They are expected to attend school from 7am every morning dressed in their school uniforms of tracksuits (mostly white in colour – which is a bizarre choice in this filthy country).

They have to run two kilometres every morning (in said tracksuits, with no showers available and in a country that doesn't sell deodorant and is about to hit 30 degrees in a matter of weeks) before beginning lessons (sporting ability is 30% of their entry grade for higher level schooling and failure to gain entry to the appropriate prestigious school has been known to cause family suicides caused by the shame) and they often have to run again twice after school when it finishes around 4.30pm. On top of this they will sit weekly exams in key subjects. Mathematics being one of them, where they are almost five years ahead of their British peers.

Homework is usually set to cover four hours of their time once they return home from school. That is of course if their parents haven't decided to pay ridiculous sums of money for them to attend a foreign language school (where they will demand their child is given more homework) such as those which London Linked School provide and for which we are 'teachers'. I use this term loosely as the standard of teaching is variable and unimpressive from some, despite the Cambridge qualifications held by a lot of them. Oh, and if the teacher doesn't have one, the parents are lied to in order to make them think the educational standard is worth the price.

So basically, my fellow teachers and I are just another painful experience to these children, on top of an already long day, just so that they can become highly programmed robots to fit in to their still highly communist country. The parents see nothing wrong in robbing their kids of all the blessings and freedom of a childhood and use the foreign language schools as a tool by which they can gloat to their friends about how much they are paying for their kids' education and how well their children are doing academically. Which is all this society cares about…. too bad they invariably lack common sense, manners, and personal hygiene – at least they can add up and run for hours. But who are we to judge? They probably think Westerners are their half-wit relatives.

School holidays are then four hours a day of set homework from their official school and holiday camps of long gruelling days at a foreign language institution. I pity these children. But I also cannot warm to many of them in the slightest... this I will also come on to.

The quality of teaching, from what I have observed so far during the past two and a half weeks, ranges greatly in quality. Doing a TEFL course gets you these jobs abroad, but it doesn't have any bearing on your real-life teaching ability or even your ability to interact with pupils. I have no idea whether I'm having a bad experience of TEFL (you have to admit my track record of experience so far isn't great) but I think it's a bit of a joke. It's a great way to work and travel the world but you have to have more than just a functional interest in teaching to be worth much to these children.

Arguably this is the same anywhere in the world though, at any level of qualification. Some people are naturally going to have a passion and flair for their roles in society and be very good at it. Others will be appalling. Good teachers and bad teachers are everywhere, sadly, I just feel there is more of a risk of terrible ones amongst pretty much unregulated travellers, whose only positive is that they can speak English at all. And unfortunately, I can see it with my own eyes.

This is not to say that I personally would be any better or worse than those that I have observed so far (amongst which are people who have become my friends), but a bit of self-pride and personal standards should surely set me above the most ineffectual - one would hope. But if you're just using TEFL to travel and don't care about the kids? You're on to a winner. It's not hard work and no one is measuring you...you can suck as much as you like, get paid for it, and move on – conscience clear.

16

A SEMBLANCE OF A NORMAL LIFE

Life in
Beijing

A **semblance of a normal life**

Aside from my initial teaching observations (there are plenty more tales to come on this subject as my learnings grow), I am managing to establish a settled and enjoyable life outside the classroom in my new home.

I'm slowly adjusting to the noise of the roads and car horns at night, and I am now sleeping better. Thanks to light pollution, I haven't seen a star since I left England, and I feel like I'm living in a permanent hazy daylight. I'm having to wear extra layers of clothing to bed at night though, because it's so cold and I have no heating. The air-con unit has decided to spit out lumps of ice instead of warmth so I've had to stop using it. I'm already wondering what the summer will be like in 30 degree heat with nothing to cool me. There's no chance I'm opening my window or I'll have nightmares that I'm sleeping in the middle of the road, even from twelve storeys up.

Plus, some days, from the crack of dawn, the sound of fireworks in the streets below makes me legitimately believe I could be in a warzone. When I arrived in Beijing it was Chinese New Year and the fireworks went on for days. Now, they still happen, but for other celebratory reasons instead. I've stopped trying to risk walking the streets when a local wedding is happening because of the risk of being hit in the face by a firecracker. Some days when I walk to school, l I turn up smelling like a bonfire with watering eyes because I got caught up in something else. It's a wonder there aren't more funerals in this city than the number of weddings I seem to be experiencing, what with one health hazard or another.

Now I have to trek daily to the City School, an hour each way, I'm starting to really notice other Westerners, which is very rare. Some will nod at you quietly from across the road, or from our height vantage point on the subway trains, as if to say 'I got you', or 'this is crazy isn't it?'. Others stare you down as if to say 'I'm the only foreigner here, this is my town'. It feels almost 50/50 as to whether you will find a quiet foe or a sympathetic friend.

What I have noticed from other Westerners I have spoken to is a corresponding 50/50 attitude to the country we are living in. Many hate it, seeing out their time and rolling with the punches, but others have such a fierce allegiance to the country we are residing in. These people mostly have committed a lot of their Western lives studying the Chinese culture, or the language, or the history, (without ever previously visiting) that it's like they feel compelled to support or turn a blind eye to the bad behavior, the atrocities, the frauds, the bad treatment, because otherwise their life studies would have been wasted. Alternatively, they found a role in society out here that they couldn't get back home, so are forcing it to fit their ideal through their words. Excusing the negatives to fit their version of what they would like to be true.

Also I'm finding that women are struggling harder much harder to get by out here than men. The white man is respected, a white woman is disrespected, a threat to taking the white man - and we are not obedient in nature, we are brash, and we are virtually Amazonian in size to the locals. We are just a hard sell out here. Also, when a female has freckles out here it is seen as a lower class trait and a sign of our impurities. At 5'7", blonde, freckly and outspoken, I can see why I've struggled to fit in.

Aside from my more general learnings, Aoife and I are turning into a great little team. We take it in turns to cook in our miniature kitchen most evenings. I've now been shopping successfully many times in the local market that Rob introduced me to and we have been cooking up regular feasts. I've only had one mishap where I got cocky and suspect I ended up with snake – it was gross, boney, gristly and quickly binned.

We are now so settled with our Eastern food that despite having easy access to knives and forks, we naturally now always grab chopsticks to eat with.

As an aside, we have discovered that it's not just England that you can't buy a good wok in. You know how they never, ever truly get clean again after that first use? They don't here either. You'd think the Chinese would have figured something out by now, bearing in mind it is their kitchen weapon of choice, but no.

As well as mine and Aoife's evening routines of eating and drinking tea, it is very rare that an evening would exist of just the two of us. If Rob wasn't swinging by, it would be Scottish Holly, Pete, and invariably our practically 3rd housemate, Amity. She even had her own toothbrush at our sink.

Without a TV and reliable internet, we often had to make our own entertainment. We would steal paper from the school and play Pictionary, play cards, eat, drink, but mainly dance around our apartment to classic 80's tunes. Amongst us we had such an eclectic taste in music it was the only collection of music we could all stomach. Plus something inside of me did not want to ruin my favourite tunes from home, lest they be tarnished with anything negative out here.

Amity also employed her self-professed talents as a hairdresser when anyone needed a trim. It was notoriously difficult to find a hairdresser in Beijing that either we could communicate with effectively, or who knew how to cut Caucasian hair. For this reason, and the fact that we didn't much care what we looked like out here, we let her loose. Not all results were positively received, but all were hilarious to witness. Hairdresser she was not.

Our home was becoming quite the social hub so we decided we needed to change its stark interior to be a bit more homely. Since we had done our massive clean-up, we still had not bought proper bedding, couldn't offer more than two cups of tea at a time, the pop up bed we had fashioned into another sofa still looked and felt like a park bench, so we decided we needed to go shopping. Where else, other than IKEA? Plus, once it was a homely home, we could hold an official housewarming party, for all our teaching friends to attend.

The following day, after another insightful day of trailing around shadowing my colleagues at various schools across Beijing and Aoife putting in her hours torturing children, we decide that we must start fulfilling our to-do list of making our now semi-acceptable apartment more respectable and make the trip out to IKEA.

I finished an hour earlier than Aoife so I figured I would go on ahead and meet her there. I envisaged a nice quiet coffee and a mooch around familiarity before she arrived. I confirmed with my more Mandarin versed colleagues the translation Rob had given me for IKEA so I could get a taxi to the door, rather than risk the subway all the way to the outskirts of town in rush hour. I was too far from the bus stop that Rob had recommended I use instead and could not see any matching Chinese characters on any of the passing buses to be sure I would get the right one to where I needed to be.

My plan almost went well as I was dropped within viewing distance of the familiar blue and yellow warehouse some time later. The challenge only came when I realised I had been dropped the wrong side of a busy intersection with no direct and safe route to my final destination. I had been foiled. And conned out of an extortionately large amount of RMB for the pleasure. I felt little surprise at the newly presented difficulties and set about surmounting them, kicking myself for being so constantly vulnerable in this country.

By the time I had circuited the major junction in one gratifying piece, the hour leeway I'd had before Aoife arrived had disappeared and we met on the steps, ready to pick up some home comforts.

It was a weirdly nostalgic shopping trip as we waltzed around very Western styled displays of furniture and soft furnishings. At every turn I saw a reminder of home…the patterns of the material I had used to make the curtains in my home in England, the odd piece of furniture my parents had in their beautiful little country home, the kitchenware my brother was so obsessed with. It was the first time I had actually felt a pang of regret and longing to just be home, to be safe and to be comforted by the familiarity of all I had left behind. I felt more desolate in that familiar store than when I discovered I had been sold in an alien Asian country.

This sadness may also be the reason we comfort ate as much as we did. We shared a portion of chicken wings and supersized our

Swedish meatball intake mid-shop. We topped off our long and expensive (by Chinese standards) excursion with a hotdog and a stock of IKEA's finest frozen meatballs (should we ever fancy a rare Western pick me up) for our freezer – that incidentally is no longer smelled of rotting human flesh, which was nice.

The only thing to halt our excitement from our comfort-shop was that we were too exhausted to unpack our wares after an extended and typically difficult trip home. Still… we looked forward to the long-awaited transformation of our living space.

When Aoife and I finally got round to unpacking our IKEA purchases for the communal area, it was a whole two days after we had obtained them. I had refused to empty the communal stuff until the living room floor had been mopped to within an inch of its life. We had previously been unable to do this thanks to the Chinese girls having left piles of their belongings at one end and delaying emptying the fridge of dripping and stinking body parts.

We had so many visitors that we simply hadn't found the time. Aoife had lost her wind for cleaning and as I had done the lion share of the previous clean up, I was feeling petty and had deliberately not done it. I think she sensed my frustration and when I got home from a long day at school at 10.30pm one night, I walked in to a sparkling floor, her having taken up the whole of her day off doing it.

As neither of us had school until 2pm the following day, we grabbed a beer and unpacked.

We had bought a vibrant red throw to cover the stained and filthy sofa, a matching one to cover a single pop-up bed we had found in her room and fashioned a sofa out of, and coupled with additional throw cushions it looked and felt less like a park bench due its straw mattress. That gave us both places to lounge on. She always won the sofa so I was glad I had somewhere now to rest. It also gave us a proper bed for our sleepover guests. Amity was growing tired of sharing a bed with Aoife and her smelly feet, so that solved that problem.

We had also bought ourselves a kids set of brightly coloured plastic bowls. plates and cups. We did not have enough in the apartment if we both wished to eat and drink at the same time from un-chipped crockery. We stored it on the living room shelves which brightened up the corner.

We had also splurged on rolls and rolls of white wallpaper. Our intention was to stick it on the walls and cover the stains, chips and the shades of grey the whitewashed walls had turned. On one wall, we decided that it would be our guest book and that people would sign it when they came round. The second wall we used as a message board, shopping list and to-do list. The third wall was a blank sheet.

We had found a discarded copy of 'The Beijinger' one of the local Beijing news publications, in the school staff room. It was a type of 'what's on' guide to the Northern Capital. It detailed events that were happening over the coming months, recipes, journalistic articles of tourist spots and information for expats living in Beijing. It was usually a good read and being one of the few English publications, it was our view into the China we were living in. An article had specifically piqued our interest, though. It asked readers to describe Beijing in five words and whilst some of the entries were flattering – most were hilariously scathing of the country. We decided that it could be our ice-breaker for our housewarming party – that we could have now that the apartment was as finished and as habitable as it could be.

17

ST PADDY'S DAY

Life in Beijing

Today I had no lessons that couldn't be skipped for any better reason than the legal requirement to register my existence and residence at the local police station in this fine country, to avoid being an illegal alien. I'd had enough close shaves to know I did not want to risk not doing this within the specified grace period for foreign visitors. Being considered an illegal alien would land me in a deep pile of poop with immigration. Although I was accustomed to poop by now, there was no need to exacerbate the situation.

On that note, I roll into work at 9am and announce my legal requirements for the day. It seems like if I am not on the ball, no one else cares. Thankfully 'they' understand my priority is not teaching the little brats I have to torture out of a childhood on a daily basis, but my legal capacity here, and I am reluctantly provided a guardian for the day, a very sweet girl from the admin staff named Seven, who will escort me to the local police station to be registered. I am informed at 12.30pm she will begin the escort and the owner of the apartment I now live in will meet us there to countersign my declaration of accommodation.

It's an easy morning which I kill reading the painfully patronising kids text books and the awful American butchering of the English language. But whatever. This is the world I now live in.

When it comes to the allotted time I seek out Seven, who has the lowest level of mastery of the English language amongst the admin girls, (coupled with my poor Mandarin, I accept that it's going to be a non-chatty excursion), we seek out a taxi to take us to the police station.

The meeting time of 1pm at the station, having been designated by the school, turns out to be the beginning of the police station's lunch period, therefore, on arrival, myself, Seven and the poor landlady who had arrived promptly, have nothing else to do whilst we wait the hour and half but to pace the forecourt and wait for the police station to reopen after its lunch period. It's a freezing and bitter winded March afternoon, none of us are able to communicate with each other or even make small talk to pass the time so as the wait stretches before us, we all get increasingly annoyed that the plan had not been thought through.

Although I had learned well enough the biting cold of Beijing, I had not dressed for loitering outside in the open air for 90 minutes and immediately regretted my lack of thermals and head wear. I thankfully did still have my mittens on a string attached to my jacket (like a toddler) and through pacing like a mad woman the length of the carpark and back several times, I did manage to sustain blood flow to my extremities. My fingers and toes coped but my butt cheeks were chafing on my trousers and I became concerned about whether there would be any skin left by the time I had reason to stop. It became a mental choice between sacrificing the skin on my arse or losing my phalanges - and my fingers and toes won. After all, who would be seeing my bare arse in China?

The police station was south of the murky river of scum and other godforsaken levels of pollution that we could see from our apartment window on a clear day. It was exposed from the banks due to a remarkable absence of high rise buildings in this super industrialised area and the only passing fare were old men cycling rickshaws of recyclables past the isolated building on its dusty byway, or police cars pulling up for a spot of lunch. I got to see a stream of Beijing's finest law enforcement officers and there was not a single one of the short and lean men that exited the vehicles that I reckoned I couldn't take in a fight if needs must. A good feeling towards protection during my stay was not felt.

But regardless, I was grateful of not having to suffer being in the damned school of money grabbers and con artists that even clocking up the miles on the soles of my well insulated Ugg boots was beyond concern.

When the police station finally opened for me to present my passport and sign the landlady's declaration of my legal address (a ridiculously laboured process), enough time had been killed to warrant my going home rather than going back to school, which I was glad about. In addition, to save walking home the entire way, the landlady pitied our blue appearance and took us half the distance home.

Getting home early from the school was doubly exciting for me. Today was St. Patrick's Day, and as Aoife was the only Irish contingent amongst us, myself and the other teachers in our little gang had grand plans to celebrate the Western tradition with her. And knowing today was her day off, I was excited to get home to her so we could design suitable Irish fare to adorn ourselves with for the occasion and get in the mood by listening to Irish music.

I get home to find Aoife, chain smoking (judging by the full ashtray) frantically colouring in green paper ribbons we could all wear to show our affinity to Ireland and the word Saleinte had been scrawled in celebration on our sketchpad paper wall, next to a four leaf clover. Although it was written in Gaelic green it was spelt wrong…it should have been Slainte but who was I to judge an Irish English teacher who was so happy to have a reason to celebrate anything in the depressing country of China.

Ignoring the spelling faux pas we both got girlie-typical about what we would wear, we both sought out our green coloured clothing and did our hair. Aoife even wore makeup for the first time that I had ever seen. She looked fab. It was fun and reminiscent of time spent with my girlfriends at home who I often felt a pang of nostalgia for.

Aoife and I were the only ones who would not be teaching for the rest of the day/evening so we snuffled down some dumplings and ran out the door to get an early start on our celebrations. It also meant we were guaranteed a seat in one of the few Irish bars in the Western area of the city we were looking to spend our night at and that we expected to probably be heaving with other Westerners.

We weren't wrong. The bar was packed and it was still early. We had at least two hours before the others arrived but it was nice to be out in a place with a jovial atmosphere and we relaxed into our evening with Guinness (or at least I did – Aoife insists she wouldn't stoop so low as to drink Guinness anywhere other than Ireland so she stuck with her old friend Voddie) and gossiped as per usual until the others rolled in. We were expecting a full turnout of the gang, but disappointingly not Rob who had other plans. I'm not going to lie and say I wasn't disappointed. I'd been really enjoying his company recently and so looked forward to his presence at any given opportunity.

I was to be pleasantly surprised though. He turned up before the others arrived on his way to his dinner plans. And that's when something totally unexpected happened. I felt my stomach actually flip as I saw him walk through the door. No matter what I told myself out loud about how I wasn't looking for any romance, and that I couldn't possibly fancy someone who I had initially written off as 'not my type'…my heart was clearly in a different place. Who knew?! It was confusing. And I tried to ignore it. But I hadn't had enough to drink at that stage to blame the alcohol and the feeling was so rare that I was stunned into silence to experience it so apparently out of the blue.

Then, to make matters even more confusing, I found myself feeling jealous that he had prearranged his arrival with Aoife and she knew he was on his way, but that I didn't. I felt left out of the loop, outside of the friendship circle…even after all the time we had spent in each other's company the last couple of weeks. My mind was having a thousand strange thoughts in a matter of milliseconds. I hated that my heart was fluttering for someone who had no inkling of my existence and that my butterflies had taken flight for no reciprocated reason. When he greeted us with his kiss, his full hug and his twinkling eyes, I wondered if I would go crazy. Where had these feelings suddenly come from? Was I out of control of my tiny mind?

Then the night felt weirder. The three of us managed to fit in a drink before the others arrived and the conversation mainly focussed between Aoife and Rob and I felt like a third wheel for the first time. He didn't even sit next to me. Why was I noticing these things? What did it matter? We were all friends… seriously... why, oh why, was this bothering me? Maybe I shouldn't have touched the non-Irish brewed Guinness after all. There were clearly some mind altering drugs in the two pints I had consumed.

When the others rolled in I was relieved to have people to talk to and take my mind off what was an unexpectedly confusing situation. It took Amity less than one sip to spill her Guinness down the front of her light coloured jumper and I felt glad some things at least were reassuringly normal. Because my mind certainly wasn't.

By the time the sluttily dressed Guinness promotional girls tottered by handing out their branded chopsticks (only in China), the Paddy's day celebrations were in full swing and the gang was united to the tune of Irish jigs and merry shouts of 'Slainte' all round. It was as the party was rising that Rob began to make his exit. He said goodbye to Aoife first and slowly worked his way round the table with his pecks on the cheeks for the girls and farewell handshakes to the boys. My heart sunk when he reversed his farewell circle round the table just as he was about to get to me. My paranoia quadrupled. And I was disappointed not feel his face pressed up against my cheek and to have an eye sparkle just for me.

I felt embarrassed. Acutely aware of something weird going on, I whisper as well as I can in a bar of rowdy revellers to Aoife, that I feel like Rob is awkward around me, and that he has barely spoken with me so far tonight, and how strange it was, have I done anything wrong etc. In her now stronger (drunker) Irish accent she brushes me off and raises her 17th vodka of the night to my partly drunk pint of nastiness and tells me to 'fecking snap out of it'. I gulp down the remains of my drink and try to ignore the guy who was having this inexplicable effect on me, and who was about to leave our evening and who hadn't even said goodbye to me.

A few drinks later we are all ready to leave the frivolity of the Irish bar, which is now full of Western men leering over local girls who have seen their chance to snag a husband, and head to one of the other ropey bars, still within the confines of the Western area. Clubs in China do not exist beyond the realms of foreign territory as drinking and dancing is our thing, their thing is Karaoke bars - and none of us had the stomach or patience for that.

The night is bitingly cold as we take our walk (verging on a stagger) to a well frequented bar called the Stumble Inn. Appropriately named judging by the state of our gang. It's full to the brim of hot, sweaty and vulgar, inebriated Westerners but the vibe is uplifting. As my spirits lift with the din of the music and the partying crowd, more drinks are ordered and I try to distract my mind from Rob.

I seem to have hit a wall with my drinking capacity. I am not managing to get as drunk as I wish I could and the liquid levels in my bladder have caused me a bloated belly that jiggles with every wiggle I make to the party tunes I haven't heard since I got to China. It's fun. It's hot, and whilst surrounded by the gang, we girls are protected from the lecherous drunken gropes of the strangers around us. Aoife, who has a tolerance for alcohol her Irish brethren would be proud of, is propping up the bar with Amity, who is not handling the volumes particularly well.

Fortunately the increasing stains of alcohol spillage on her top have grown to look like a pattern on her plain jumper and her dribbling is disguised by the sweat the bar is producing on us all. We have stripped off as many clothes as possibly decent in the body heat of the bar and the floor is littered in discarded scarves, gloves and ski jackets which will provide a soft landing for Amity when her legs give way...which I'm pretty sure is not a long way off.

And then He arrives. The first I realise of Rob's re-emergence into our night out is when I get a poke in the ribs by Amity and a slurred observation that the gang is complete again and that she is raising a glass to it. I look up and sure enough, I am staring into Rob's face as he makes his way through the crowd of revellers. And he's looking straight at me. His eyes shining and a smile is lighting up his face as only his could. He wends his way through the crowd as other members of our party scream their greetings at his unexpected entrance.

Amidst drunken man-hugs and sloppy kisses from the girls, I realise he has not once taken his eyes off me – and is headed in my direction. If I wasn't already pink with the heat I would have been furiously blushing…and I grip tightly onto my jumper in one hand and my empty glass in the other like they're going to afford me some protection from whatever it is I can feel might be about to happen. But before I can take flight, or recover myself, he is stood in front of me. He's looking so deep into my eyes that I feel like he's cast a spell on me. He raises his hands, gently grabs my face and lingeringly kisses me fully on the lips. I realise that somewhere in my head I had imagined kissing him would be perfect and when it finally registers that it is actually really happening, it's even more perfect than I thought it could be.

It wasn't a long kiss, but it was breath-taking. When he pulled away he kept his face close to mine and whispered for only us to hear: "that's all I've thought about doing all night. I just had to come back to do that. I'm sorry."

I'm speechless. All I can muster is a dumbstruck smile in response. My hands are both full so I can't pull him back to me, show him that no apology is necessary – they just kind of hang in space, useless. I don't even know if I have any power left in me to do that anyway. I feel like I'm in some sort of cliched romance novel and am weak at the knees at how unscripted and dreamy the last few seconds of my existence were. And for something my conscience didn't even register wanting when I woke up that morning.

I stand there in stunned silence as the bar around us comes back into focus and we become aware of the close proximity of our friends and how awkward this must be for them: two of their members crossing lines so blatantly, the embarrassment of something so intimate happening literally underneath their noses. But his apology wasn't to them, he showed no thought for them and nor did I care. It was to me alone. Like he didn't even know if he had permission to do what he just did. He had no idea that I had unknowingly been waiting for that moment to happen since the day he made me buy beef.

Luckily for the others, unluckily for us, the moment of tension that hung in the air between us was broken by the inevitable fall from Amity. She was now on her hands and knees, doggy style, with her head pressed up against the underside of the bar where she had slumped in a drunken stupor. Aoife was grumbling angrily for her to get up and Samuel was passing glances at his new Canadian girlfriend in apology for the embarrassingly drunken behaviour of his flatmate.

It was clear once we had scooped her off the ground that the night was done for us. Samuel made it clear she was my and Aoife's responsibility as he had grand seduction plans for him and his girlfriend later that night that didn't allow room for someone who had passed out and would need watching. So we made moves to leave and take her home, gathering up our discarded cold-weather clothing and saying our goodbyes.

Coming over all self-conscious, I went to say goodbye to Rob, who had now joined his other friends at the bar whilst the rest of us got our things together, and offered him an awkward peck on the cheek. His eyes smiled at me and I think he realised this time to kiss me so blatantly in front of two separate audiences would have not been appropriate. I felt sad and wished I had the courage he had shown shortly before, but I was too shy. And so sadly I turned to leave with the others.

As we stepped outside into the bitter air, we realised that the sky's glow around us was a mixture of the yellow of the street lights and their reflection on gently falling snowflakes that had already settled an inch deep on the ground. It was snowing in Beijing. A rare and unseen sight for many months. It seemed fitting that it chose today to come and that the clouds that had hovered for days, had finally let themselves go.

Amity was so drunk, Samuel scooped her off the ground and carried her in his arms down the wooden stairway to the pavement from the Stumble Inn (which after midnight should be called the Carry Out) and on towards the taxi rank. It wasn't until we were almost at the point of the roadway that I realised he was not wearing his jumper. He claimed he couldn't find it with the rest of our belongings when we left so he had abandoned hope of seeing it again. There were no taxis at the rank and he was wearing only a thin shirt in the freezing weather…so I offered to run back to the bar and double check if it was there.

I made it back to the bar in double time, knowing I had no idea what his jumper even looked like, but just knowing I had a chance to see Rob for another fleeting minute.

He was on his own at the bar. I was glad. I told him that I had come back for Samuel's jumper. He smiled. He pulled me tightly to him, and he kissed me, with no audience and no self-consciousness.

And when it was over, I reluctantly left. Again. With no thought for missing clothes or freezing friends, but consumed with excitement and nervousness of what had just happened…and what I barely dared to hope would begin to happen.

HOUSEWARMING

Life in
Beijing

Aoife and I now had days to actually pull together our housewarming party. Aoife applied her artistic streak to the design and printing of our official housewarming invites, devoid of an address so that we didn't have any strays or unwanted guests arriving. That was our excuse anyway. We still didn't know our own address and Amity and Rob who knew it well enough to speak it to order our breakfast or dinner takeaways, were unable to spell it.

We had made it a weekday so we could get maximum attendance. Weekends were off limits as everyone had to work those as they were the biggest money spinners for Alfie and his cohorts. It also meant that 80% of the people attending, if they had to work at all the next day, would not be due in until 2pm. We had planned to kick the party off at 6pm and Aoife, I, or another regular to our apartment would be available to escort the others here safely.

The party had been kept under close wraps for the last couple of weeks with only our trusted friends coming and was probably the first time all of the teachers had gathered in one place. I think everyone was looking forward to it. It was already forecast to be a mass therapy session where everyone could bitch to their hearts content about the failings of the school and the gossip we had all gathered over our times there, and also the frustrations of Beijing. No-one gets a smooth ride here and I had the unending need to hear other people's pity stories so I didn't feel so inept out here.

Aoife and I had counted the empty beer bottles in the apartment during our mass clean-up operation and what with the 'return six empty beer bottles, get one free' situation at our local mini market, we calculated we could pretty much hydrate the entire party for two weeks. All we asked was that when the beer ran out in the fridge, volunteers would carry a few crates of the empties down to the shop to swap for new refrigerated ones. Simple.

For food, as we lacked an oven, we took a trip to the local supermarket to pick up nibbles – and dumplings, the quick and easy hot food we could wok in a few minutes. The supermarket, the one which sold live terrapins in the food section, served us well enough and fairly cheaply so we were all set.

When the day of the house warming rolled around, we very quickly had a full house. Unfortunately a couple of the guests were on the late shift and didn't arrive until 10.30pm but the party was still in full swing. We had totally underestimated food consumption and Rob and Amity between them had to navigate the local pizza joints to get round two of food.

The wall hangings Aoife and I had put up were a gift that kept on giving. 'Beijing in five words' had to get an extension of paper as people teetered very close to drawing on the actual walls with their pent up frustrations at the city. I daren't repeat what was written but it was in equal parts horrifyingly true, all the way to ridiculously hilarious.

They had also adopted our shopping list wall and had drawn lewd pictures and vented further about the school and the world. If anyone of any status saw the output, we would have been sacked from our jobs and probably detained by the Chinese government for defecting and seeing through the propaganda. I took extensive photographs to remember it all by, knowing that the paper would have to be burned ASAP. We would also have to return the 'borrowed' board markers before we got done for theft too.

It was a great evening all round. But it was also the first time I had seen Rob since St Patrick's Day three days ago and I was a little nervous in his company – as was he. He had strategically arrived late and a little tipsy, by which point I was too…Dutch courage at its most useful. He was as friendly as ever with his beautiful shiny eyes and attentiveness was second to none. But 'the kiss' was like an elephant in the room.

Word had got round, adults will still be childish on such topics and there were more than a few awkward moments. But still, the butterflies were flying and I couldn't wait to get time alone with him. Other than an awkward moment in the lift on a beer run, both armed with crates of empties and a gooseberry called Samuel, we had barely spoken. And it wasn't until the party was winding up that we got our moment of privacy.

Knowing Aoife's aversion to being tidy, and knowing she was at work tomorrow and I would be responsible for the clean up of the mess the 20+ guests had created, I began it as the last few guests straggled. Rob was also quite obviously hanging on…he had cancelled his Mandarin lessons the next day, which I had overheard in conversation to someone else and I was hopeful that we could spend the early hours together once everyone had gone and Aoife had gone to bed. I suspected he had the same thoughts and helped me gather plates, glasses and rubbish – a not so subtle nudge to the hangers on to leave and end the party, so we could be alone.

They didn't leave as quickly as I had hoped so I began the mountain of washing up we had accumulated in the tiny kitchen. On hearing the taps running, Rob appeared at the door. He smiled his eye glinting smile and said a nervous 'Hi'. He'd been at the party for hours, and we had spoken, but it was the first time that he had addressed me and me alone. My stomach did a flip as he reached around my waist and gave me another incredible kiss.

No sooner had it started, it had sadly ended though, as we were interrupted by Aoife demanding her pre-bed time cuppa for her and the two remaining party goers who were dribbling in the living room. Whilst this was disappointing, without even speaking, Rob and I knew we were getting close to it being just us two, with no prying eyes or gossipers hanging on our every move.

We spoke for many more hours. He spent the night. We ordered in breakfast. He only left minutes before Aoife got home from school so as to avoid a grilling that might take away from our sparkle. It was utterly perfect.

Until Aoife got home from school, asked why Rob's shoes and backpack had been at the door when she left that morning and demanded to know EVERYTHING.

19

SHOPPING DATE AND A REAL DATE

Life in
Beijing

Two days after the housewarming, I had a 2pm start and for some reason Amity and Lana were keen to see me. Gossip hunting I could only assume.

However there was another reason they were in touch – we had agreed that they would take me to the famous Silk markets in the Chaoyang district and today was the day.

I got up early, had a weirdly consistent temperature shower that didn't flood and headed to the Yong'anli subway station where I was to meet them. Despite it only snowing in Beijing less than a week ago, the weather had drastically warmed up and we needed to clothe ourselves for the pending heat wave. Also we had decided to take up badminton with our fellow teachers and the school admin staff and needed trainers and racquets for the job.

The silk markets are immense. 1500+ stalls of (allegedly) fake branded items across floors and floors of a high rise. Your bargaining game had to be strong but I was well prepared for it – and excited about it. I had brought with me so many winter clothes that I had planned to wear and discard whilst out here, that

I hadn't had much room for summer clothes, or even practical items, and I was tired of muddling by.

After we had a quick snack, we ventured into the markets so I could kit myself out with the necessities of trainers, work shoes (to replace my winter boots), a work bag and a dressing gown through the horrible system of aggressive bartering. The dressing gown was to be my frivolous purchase of the day because once you've lived on your own for as long as I have, modesty isn't of great importance, but now I was sharing a home, I felt the need to comfortably cover up, so a Chinese silk robe was purchased. Cheaply, of course. Fake silk, of course.

The market was little like I had imagined. It wasn't street stalls or market stalls, but instead a well-structured set of clean orderly concessions within a building the size of a department store with many floors. It was packed to the rafters with fake goods and some great replicas, others were poor tacky substitutes of everything you could ever wish for, and sold by Chinese staff in silk waistcoats with excellent English skills.

The prices they gave were Western prices initially but after strong bargaining (of which I feel I am now a master), the ultimate prices were probably only a fraction of the initial price given. It's possible to get them to under 10% of what they started at and telling them you are not a tourist and actually live and work here in Beijing allows you to get away with a little more than the short term visitors can. Once they are aware you know their game, they actually give in quite easily.

They also assume you could be repeat trade if they are good to you. It's embarrassing and particularly tough for us to be so hard in our bargaining when you're not really arguing over a great deal of money, but that is their way. And by the end of my experience I held no prisoners and felt no remorse at bargaining to reasonable rates knowing how many other unsuspecting foreigners they have fleeced and will make their money from.

But don't be fooled – although the goods are very cheap and if chosen well are passable as originals, it is not as dirt cheap as you might think, seeing as they are probably all made in local sweat shops for a few pence. But hey – you can only improve on prices with experience and I was pretty proud of my first attempt – as were Lana and Amity who have asked to employ my services on their next shopping trip, or at least come and watch me again on my next trip for the spectacle. I definitely think my first few weeks in this country have made me into a tough little lady who will take no-one in this nation a prisoner.

Shopping done, we headed to a French café for a coffee where Aoife, after finishing her own errands on her day off, joined us. And then they took me to sample a Fragrant Hotpot for my lunch before I sloped off to work. They all knew I have visitors coming in May so they vowed to show me as many great places as possible before then so I can wow them (or at least fake it) when they arrive.

Fragrant Hotpot is different from the other hotpots I've tried where you cook the food yourself in a vat of boiling oil-like soup at your table, but instead is where you select various dishes of meat and vegetables for the chefs to cook and throw into a large vat of chillies and spices and then serve up like a cauldron of goodness you communally pick from. Once again, the food did not disappoint, and the bowl was reduced to chillies within no time. Which was lucky because I had to get off to class. Oh, and did I tell you I also had an official first date with Rob tonight?

After the housewarming, his impromptu sleepover and day of company afterwards, he formally asked me if I would like to go on an official date with him and I could not be more excited. It would be our first time out for dinner just the two of us.

School strangely flew by, even though on the occasions you have something to look forward to after work they usually drag. In fact I managed to knock off a little early thanks to being re-routed to an out-reach school nearer home.

However, I still didn't get home in time to shower and change before I met Rob, thanks to the standard horrendous transport situation here, but it was more important to see him sooner than have my second shower of the day.

I met him at the base of his tower block at the agreed time. He had planned to walk me north to a huge shopping mall whose entire top four storeys were a deluge of restaurants. He had in mind a duck restaurant to take me to, but in case I wasn't keen, he wanted to take me somewhere that had choices, which I felt was really thoughtful.

Unfortunately, nothing went exactly to plan. By the time I had managed to meet him, and we had walked north (unable to get a taxi to speed up the process) it was verging on 9.30pm and the mall was closing shortly. We knew we would have to run to make it to any restaurant at all before last service so that's what we did. Luckily, neither of us took ourselves too seriously so we could do this with no embarrassment, but we still got stumped.

The mall was HUGE. So many escalators, so many lifts, none that took you a direct route to wherever you needed to go. We were going up and down in this mall like yo-yo's. It was like a real life game of snakes and ladders. We tried in vain to reach the upper floors, suffering static shocks on every escalator we climbed on, laughing ourselves to tears when the other person squealed in fright at minor electrocutions…all the while, the lights were slowly being turned off in this crazy vertical maze and we finally realised it wasn't going to work out.

Once the giggling had stopped and the realisation set in, we gave up and strolled back towards his apartment in good spirits, but achingly hungry. We instead opted for his local BBQ restaurant, the sister restaurant to the one Aoife, the gang and I usually frequented, and got our standard fare. Not the fancy date restaurant he had hoped to treat me to, but the random adventure we had just had was worth his embarrassment.

All considered it was a brilliant night. I stayed at his and there was no shame in my walk home the following morning.

20

THE TASTE OF A SLOW DEATH

Life in
Beijing

The second instalment of schooling and the rest of my stories can wait for now – the overwhelming pollution situation needs to be talked about, it's haunting my existence here and requires a monologue of its own. If only I could have made it chapter four or 14 for 'death' then it would have been so fitting.

I'm prompted to write this now because we are currently going through the absolute worst times I've experienced since I got here. Walking to school today for my 2pm shift, I decided to get an ice-lolly to cool myself down on my walk. It dripped on my hand, and rather than waste it, I licked it off. Only to find, after only having been out of my apartment for ten minutes, that I had licked my hand clean. Not just clean of the lolly drips, but CLEAN of everything else that was on my skin. In the minutes it had taken me to leave my apartment and get to the local shop, the pollution had visibly coated my skin in a fine powder – and I'd just ingested it.

You now think you know something vague about the pollution in Beijing? You've read the other media horror stories? But do you know what? You don't. And thankfully you won't – unless you choose to live in China. And I would recommend that you never do, this being only one of the reasons

I don't even know how adequately to explain this to the rest of the world.

It's no secret that Beijing is the most dangerously polluted city in the world, but to really 'appreciate' it, you have to experience it – and if you don't want to lick your hand to experience it, try reading on to get some sense of it.

I've been taking daily pictures from my apartment window to document the changes in visibility from day to day. Sometimes it looks like a cloudy day, but really, it's just the haze of the pollution stopping you from seeing more than 100 metres. Low hanging, dark, angry looking rainclouds are actually the pollution blanket wrapping you up. It doesn't rain much here although you end up begging for it to come, just to clear the air. At night when the street lamps are on, they illuminate the polluted air particles and dust floating around you and you wonder how you can breathe at all.

It's no wonder that living in Beijing is reportedly the equivalent of smoking 20 cigarettes a day. I always thought the surgical-face-mask-wearers were just a little precious about catching germs, but I have learned that wearing a facemask has been clinically proven to reduce the risks of respiratory diseases caused by air pollution. I'm buying one – if it's not already too late to save my lungs.

So, you understand now that the pollution is so bad here that it is visible to the naked eye, right? Well that's not the only one of your senses that gets assaulted by it.

The only way I can explain the horror of the pollution on

particularly bad days, in a way that non-China visitors can appreciate, is to get you to imagine something.

Imagine you have been given the task to sweep out a deserted building piled high with dust and filth that has not been cleaned for many, many years. It smells sulphurous and it gets cemented into your nostrils when you breathe. You are given a sweeping brush and nothing else. No dust mask, no gloves, no water. Its arid dry. You get to work with your brush and you keep going, with fast brush strokes, so that the dust and filth do not have time to settle and your vision gets blurred by the clouds of muck you're disturbing.

Your eyes start to sting and you have to squint, and you daren't open your mouth because you know the muck will get in. But it's already in you. It's snuck in through your nose. You panic when you feel the need to cough or sneeze because you know it's going to force your body to inhale gulps of this toxic waste. Opening the windows just brings in the dust from outside and the wind makes the dust you're disturbing swirl even harder.

There's no way to beat it. You make the mistake of accidentally licking your lips and you can taste the filth on your tongue and no matter how hard you swallow, you call still feel the dust in your mouth. You dare not grit your teeth because there's already grit on them from simply breathing in the air and you worry you will break them or grind them down with the friction. Your mouth is insatiably dry. And you feel dirty. Your fingernails are black. Your bogies are black. Your hair feels like the sweeping brush you're using. Your skin is itching. Your eyes are watering. Your nose is blocked. And you have no choice but to keep going. You have no idea how long this is going to last. There is no escape. There is no fresh air. You can barely breathe…and in reality, there is no brush, or dusty room. They only exist in your imagination. This is the city. This is you going about your daily life. This is a dusty and dirty lung destroying hell.

Welcome to Beijing.

21

WHERE IS THE LOVE?

Life in Beijing

Not here (Rob excluded for obvious reasons). I've learned so much recently about this aspect of existing out here, and it is so alien to me I just need to share it.

The single child policy which was implemented in China in the late 70's for population control has led to a ridiculous ratio of something like 6:1 of men to women, at my time of writing. Obviously if you are only allowed to have one child, the age-old preference would be for a boy. They will have a greater earning capacity, carry on the family name and so on. What the government did not foresee was that a nation cannot survive without continued procreation for which you obviously need one of each sex.

Despite their intense and (in my opinion) inhumane schooling levels, they really don't know much about life, clearly. The shortsighted plan of population control is going to seriously damage their fiercely guarded culture and nation in future generations. And in a country that reportedly makes up 30% of the entire world's suicide numbers, they really need to have good think about this mess.

But anyway, due to the severe lack of women in this country, the women demand more of their suitor in the selection phase, and they can exert it, because they are they are the choosers, not the beggars here. What a formal sounding sentence…but what a formal approach to 'relationships' they have. They don't talk of love, or happily ever after's, or even liking their husbands. The selection criteria are the amount of money the man has, the car they drive and the size of their apartment. If a guy has none of the above, they will never get a look in with girls. The relationships are so transactional that women do not care if the men seek comfort elsewhere in the bedroom department – that is not what they are in this 'relationship' for. Sex doesn't buy them handbags or designer gear for their ratty dogs, so why would they put themselves out for it?

It is well known that there are tower blocks of mistresses and prostitutes on the borders of this city, and many other cities in China, where a successful man will pay for the pleasure of the company of another woman. The only concern from the wives is that the mistress does not get pregnant and become entitled to a share of their marital money.

In these marriages, 'face' is the most important thing. And this involves status - money, children and education. There is no room for this 'love' that you speak of. Apparently, there is no shame in your husband turning to a hooker, but there is family shame in getting divorced, in not spawning a genius and not being able to afford wearing Gucci.

As a Westerner, the thought of a living a life devoid of love and having money as a single motivation for existence, makes a huge part of the romantic in me die. And what about those rare Chinese who have broken out of China and experienced the Western culture? From those that I have come to know well, they feel this too and it makes them incredibly sad. But it will not change their underlying culture and they know that their offspring are the most valuable thing to them – not just because it's their flesh and blood, but because the child dictates the mothers own place in society.

Often, the mothers will stay with their children in Beijing, where the education is considered top class, and the men will work elsewhere for months at a time supplying money. It's not that there is no work in Beijing, its more that the men seem care about their own monetary status above family, and the women care more about not losing face by having a merely averagely educated child.

When I first came here, my heart was warmed by the number of men I saw dropping kids off at school, picking them up afterwards, and getting food with them etc. I thought it was lovely to see a society where men were able to be so involved with their children. But silly me, these men are not fathers, they are the drivers, running kid related errands whilst the mothers are probably getting manicures or are too busy boasting about their child's grades to bother to spend time with them.

This feels like such a passionless, loveless, society. I even witnessed a salsa dancing lesson here not so long ago and it looked like a group of rigid stick people vaguely moving in time to a beat. They didn't even look to be having fun doing one of the most flirtatious dances on the planet. No smiling, no laughing, no unnecessary bodily contact – God forbid.

(Talking of God – they are not particularly religious here. I wonder if that's because the government have replaced Him…)

Western men are also hated by the Chinese men, understandably. To have white skin means you are rich. Therefore, you are immediately more attractive to a Chinese girl and you are also a ticket out. They are short enough on girls here that they can't afford leakage to foreigners. But although the local men hate Western men, they are not aggressive or threatening to them - they just quietly give up and accept the situation - which is pretty sad. They don't even try their luck with the Western girls because they've been so degraded by their own women that they have zero confidence in themselves to risk further shame. Plus, Western women are deemed to be far too independent and strong willed to fit the ideal mould of the obedient wife. (Oh, and we are fat and over-grown – but that's another story.)

But there is real trouble to be had from the girls who date the Westerners...

I work with a few guys here who regularly date Chinese girls. They enjoy it because they feel like Kings and are apparently appreciated more (they are deemed rich and apparently have comparatively larger 'appendages' than the Chinese males – not that I would know, but stereotypes prevail for many reasons). The Western guys admit the conversation isn't great, but when your ego is being stroked so well, what does talk matter? But the boys pay a price for taking the risk of delving into 'relationships' with those ladies of a completely different culture and one which they haven't bothered to fully understand.

The ladies of course have very little experience of Western culture either – heavy censorship by the government means they don't even get the vast exposure to the Western films and TV to learn from (they have some carefully picked or heavily censored ones, but not all). Regardless though, that still doesn't justify the crazy behavior I'm hearing about. Granted every nation has its quota of what you would deem crazy people, but even in my small sample set, the occurrences are way too high to be a coincidence.

One of my friends, who shall remain nameless, ended a four month relationship with his girlfriend. She smashed a bottle and threatened to slash her wrists with it before locking herself in his bathroom with a kitchen knife. It took a while, but she calmed down and she eventually left his apartment.

A couple of days later, he returns to his apartment and as he is opening his door, she springs from a hiding place in the stairwell and forces her way into the apartment, hanging off his back. Shortly followed by her attacking him, ripping his shirt off, punching, kicking and scratching him and begging for him to have her back before he manages to physically drag her out of the apartment. At which point she calls the police and he is on the verge of being arrested for assault. As a foreigner it could have been very messy but he was lucky in that he had Chinese friends to call in as translators and back up. The case was eventually closed days later and his imminent deportation taken off the table as she did not have a scratch on her and he was bruised and bleeding. I think he may have gone off dating Chinese girls.

Another example, this friend too shall remain nameless, had a regular fling with one of the Chinese girls who hunt the Westerner bar strips for a husband. (If you reach your late twenties here and haven't settled down, you need to prowl for men so you don't disappoint or embarrass your families further). It wasn't a relationship, it was just physical – and it was easy.

Sadly, Western style in its physical-only approach – not necessarily something we Westerners should be proud of, I admit. Until one evening, after half a dozen or so bed-time encounters, she turns up on his doorstep with her life in a bag, expecting to move in. Out of the blue. Not discussed. Just assumed because they had been 'together', and therefore they were destined for marriage apparently. He panicked, got her out of the apartment and shut the door in her face in a messy exchange of tears and heated words. Her response to the rejection? She pooped on his doormat.

And then there are my female friends who are actively online dating here. A girl has needs, and Western females are not the first choice out here, so they have to actively seek it out. We are renowned for being too independent, too tall, too unfeminine, and basically unattractive in the main, but apparently there are guys who like to taste it.

Lana has been doing private language lessons on the side and has used it as a way to meet guys. Which she has done, very successfully. But dating them has not been so successful. Sex aside, the courtships are very staid, awkward even. Not growing in tactility as a relationship progresses, but almost businesslike. 'Dates' are scheduled affairs with a start and end time, they do not involve dinner, or drinks to grow a relationship such as we are used to in the Western world.

Her experience so far has been scheduled meetings in a park, for a 30-minute walk and should both parties agree to something further, it's a trip back home, to formally undress (individually), and get down to business. No passion, no hugs, no hand holding, just a functional meeting of bodies. And she still won't give up – not least because it's pretty much the only physical contact a Western female out here can hope to expect.

Scottish Holly on the other hand is shamelessly and dangerously embracing it. She advertises herself on Craigslist and whilst we all have begged her not to do it, for her own safety, gets regularly used by random and short-term visitors looking to relieve themselves with a female that finally takes notice of them and they don't have to compete for.

If it wasn't for Rob, I'd have lost all hope in love right now.

HYGIENE? ANYONE...?

Life in Beijing

Short answer? No hygiene detected. Please do not continue reading if you have recently/or still are, eating.

I have to keep reminding myself that this is a developing country and my Western expectations are too high. But really, so was Swaziland where I lived in a tent for three months, but they had good reason to have poor hygiene – no running water, no education, and no jobs for money to buy hygiene essentials. China has no excuse. Beijing is the city with the largest number of billionaires in China and a far lesser number of its population living below the poverty line than in African countries.

The education system is massive too – so what is their excuse? The Olympics boosting the economy and the government knocking down hundreds of old apartment blocks and replacing them with sky-high tower blocks with full drainage and running water leads me to believe the majority are just plain lazy or too accepting of the state of the country and thinking they can get away with it. Because even when I've seen that it exists, it is not adequately used.

Tell me this: What is the logic behind someone washing their hands before going to the toilet, and then leaving without doing so again? I can't see it. The school I work in is next door to an eye surgery unit and we share bathrooms. The white-coated staff never wash their hands. And I mean never. There is no excuse for this, especially when dealing with delicate body parts. There is a sink there – why not use it?

Talking of bathrooms, I have never seen a city with so many public restrooms which is a good thing if you have a bladder problem. But you would never want to use them. I tried to use one on a subway the other day (which I thought was a safe move because the subways are very modern indeed) but as I rounded the corner of the toilet, I saw no cubicles, just a random collection of open holes in the ground, a lot of bare bums squatting and women wiping their legs and feet free of pee with their bare hands before exiting.

Clean your trousers before you leave of course, but don't clean your hands? Use tissue instead, maybe? It's handed out like sweets on the streets and in subway stations after all. Suffice to say I didn't use it. By all means squat in a hole in a public restroom if that's your culture, I'm not a prude, but when given the opportunity to be clean – why are they not making better choices?

If you do find a Western-style toilet, even with a carefully constructed toilet paper seat, you may not want to use them.

The Chinese are used to the hover approach and a Western toilet just seems to be an obstacle for them that does not allow them to squat properly, and results in the rear wall and the area surrounding the bowl of the toilet being sprayed with all manner of bodily excretions. Word of advice? If you do need to use them, never let your trouser legs touch the floor and do not touch a thing. Don't expect to breathe and not retch either.

Also, don't be surprised to see footprints on the seats, or cracked seats – because despite the growing occurrence of Western style toilets, some people still like to squat and will climb up on the toilets to do so, damaging and messing them in the process. I accept that the squat is a natural toileting position but don't vandalise the places that don't offer you a hole.

The men's bathrooms also just have holes in the ground for number twos but where they are not so practiced at hovering as us ladies who are veritable experts, the trauma is avoided at all costs by Westerners. Good old little Mitch point blank refuses to learn to squat. He's terrified of accidentally dropping his business in his lowered trousers and will do anything he can to hold it in till he's in a safe area – which is some feat bearing in mind he's poisoned himself with his own cooking on several occasions. He explained his worries to me at length which is why they are added here. If I have to have this mental image, so do you. Read it and weep softly to yourself. Then laugh – because you don't have to live it.

I term us ladies as hover experts but Amity cannot be included in this. She is notorious at leaning on the badly made doors of the cubicles (if she is lucky enough to have found one with privacy partitions) to balance her squat and has on more than one occasion fallen out, trousers still round her ankles. In communal toilets of all places. No wonder the Chinese think us Westerners are weird. She's really not giving a good impression of us.

When you really have to go and are forced to make do with the communal squat rooms, if you are a Westerner, expect to have all eyes on you when you do your business. Your fellow toilet buddies will not be able to control their curiosity and will stare at you and your bits throughout the entire performance. It's like being the main attraction in a zoo except the only non-humans in these rancid environments are the cockroaches and no-ones paying them a blind bit of notice.

The worst place for being rudely ogled at is apparently in changing rooms at sports centres. One of my friends, Lana, following her first gym session, was drying herself post her shower and attracted quite a following whilst she dried and dressed. Apparently, the show wasn't as interesting as it first seemed to one of the crowd though, who was clearly bored of staring at the weird naked white girl, so proceeded to take a pee and change her sanitary towel in the drain of the changing room. Metres away from the toilet I might add, and not bothering to use a bin for her used towel. Needless to say, I never entered the changing areas or toilets in these buildings and do not plan to.

The only remaining option for relieving yourself is to take the alternative, but oh too common approach, of just dropping your pants in the street and taking a number one or two, whichever you need, whenever you need. And please don't worry about finding a gutter or an out-of-the-way patch of ground to do it on – the pavement is apparently more than acceptable. And if it's in the flow of vehicle or pedestrian traffic, who cares. When you gotta go, you gotta go. That's what they learned as kids (split pants are a real thing you need to look up) so that's what they continue to do as adults. That reminds me – watch out for the kids doing the toilet-anywhere thing. They will indiscriminately spray and splash and I assure you, you WILL get hit.

What else can I say about hygiene (or lack of it?) We are now all aware of the spitting issue and for the sake of my gag reflex I do not wish to talk about this any further. Except to say that if you ever come here, it's not safe to lean on anything in public because the bit of phlegm or spit that doesn't detach on the first spit or nose-blow gets wiped onto the nearest tree, fence post, bus stop, bench…TOUCH NOTHING.

Deodorant? Can't get it anywhere other than few and far between Western-style pharmacies – at a steep price. Can't wait to smell this country in the summer… but by which time my already fading sense of smell should protect me. Also I'm hoping that the rumour that Asians sweat less is true. In which case, I take the above back – but only time will tell.

Cleanliness at home? I think I've covered that one before too. I've seen enough of these homes to know I'm going to check the box that says 'no apparent discernable efforts'.

Cleanliness of clothes? Doesn't appear too bad. Although their sense of style is very different out here, people generally look typically work smart in the City areas. But the lack of mirrors out here really makes me wonder how? Trying to find one for our apartment was nigh on impossible.

I don't think I can go on discussing this any further. It's now making me question the food and I'll be dammed if I'm going to ruin my favourite thing about this country.

23

BACK TO SCHOOL

Life in
Beijing

As my lesson shadowing continues, and I begin to teach a handful of lessons on my own, I continue to learn more and more about the state and approach of the educational system out here in Beijing.

As well as the London Linked School offering farcical 'superior' private schools for English Language, they also contract us out to local schools – termed Outreach Schools, where the children are forced to take 'optional' classes (non-examinable) to improve their English. So again, we are the inflictors of more misery there too. I gave up my job as an auditor in the accountancy world early on in my career because I hated being a necessary evil to people – and I've gone and wound up in exactly the same position, but this time to poor defenceless minors.

The external school visits have however, been fascinating in regards to learning more about the regime and lifestyle these children experience.

The schools are basically institutions. They demand nine hours of acute attention each day. They 'officially' run from Monday to Friday, as it is illegal to run classes at weekends, (unless you are a specific private foreign language school like ours). This, as you would have guessed, is a rule that is not followed by the schools and students are expected to pay for and attend full days on Saturdays and Sundays too – a seriously lucrative and somewhat undercover operation. The only exception to this is when government officials are in town and the schools will close without notice to avoid detection of their extra-curricular money-making schemes.

Even specifically government run schools break the law by running weekend classes, the only difference being that they do not allow foreign English teachers to be a part of this, so they can take all of the money for themselves whilst cashing in on the constant battle for child excellence fought for by the parents.

There is corruption all round China and using children to make money is big business. It is rare to find a child that doesn't school for seven days a week. Literally the only exception I've come across are three 13- year-old girls, who I teach at my own school, whose parents are as rare as rocking horse dung, and insist that they do not go to school at the weekend and actually have a break.

The sad thing is that this upsets the girls because they don't get to see their friends and are trying to persuade their parents to let them go to school instead – just so they are not outsiders. They could have been free to actually enjoy their childhood but meanwhile the rest of the Chinese society screw that hopeless dream up for them. Be the best – or be nothing.

All these hours of intense schooling, as you can imagine, has a severe effect on the children's personal development. These kids are so sheltered that they are very 'young' for their age. The naivety is incredible here and the freedom to have a childhood is robbed from them at every turn. There is no room in their lives for it. One university student I taught, whilst discussing dreaming and sleep, announced that dreams, and the escapism afforded by them, were of no use to him. Neither contributed to his studies and therefore were considered a waste of time. A world without dreams, to me, is a hollow one.

On the flipside, due to being so busy and dedicated to education, there are very few drug problems, teenage pregnancies, and crime… there's an interesting debate to be had right there. But I'm not sure this extreme works either.

Any sort of dream children may have in this country, is related to education – what a surprise! It is not uncommon for parents to have dragged their precious single child around Harvard, Princeton, Yale, Oxford and Cambridge at the age of eight to get them to choose their ultimate educational destination. At first I was pleasantly surprised to hear the children were given freedom of choice, but really?

The child is too young to realise the ramifications of such a high bar. Ask any child here what they want to do in a few years and they will robotically tell you which high ranking institution they wish to attend…never mind what they would like their career to be. A racing driver, a singer, an actor – common responses from English kids. But, the Chinese?

Learn. Learn. Learn. And learn some more. They don't have the vision to see beyond this and into the rest of their lives. But bearing in mind they do not have time to get jobs until they have completed their education, not even part time pocket money jobs, I guess the concept of careers and working is alien to them and too many years of hard academia ahead of them. Their only vision is that of their parents – to be the very best academically. It's just a pity that only one child will be able to be top of the class.

Just because they learn, however, does not automatically mean they have an iota of common sense, or what we might consider, decency to other human beings. They walk round in these weird bubbles, spitting on people, creating their own pollution by farting and burping whenever they like (and no I'm not just talking about guys – smartly dressed business women do it too whilst they totter down the street in their ridiculously high platform heels and dangle fake bling handbags from their expensively adorned wrists), picking their nose and wiping it on trees or fences as they pass, barging through crowds, no polite sidestepping through narrow areas to let people through, no holding of doors open for the person hot on your heels: they are ignorant of those behaviours we have brought from the Western world.

I wondered if it was because a lot of the population grew up without siblings that they have not learnt to share, or be kind, or considerate. But that doesn't explain an entire nation devoid of manners to their fellow humans. Plus they are very respectful of their elders in their family so they do know how to be nice and polite – it's just not a transferrable skill to the outside world apparently.

That brings me on to the weird bubble they live in.

In one class we were discussing global, life-changing events. One would imagine 9/11 would be mentioned (seeing as they love the Americans), the war in Afghanistan and the countless lives lost to it etc. But, no. Top answer? Michael Jordan, the famous basketball player, becoming the face of Nike in 1985 (they all want to be famous basketball players – but no-one's told them they may have a height issue). Followed closely by the globally life changing event of Princess Diana dying in 1997 and Michael Jackson dying in 2009. All of which rocked nations, granted – but life changing…? Questionable answers for the rest of the world or those fighting for peace in it.

As for the American influence, despite them having no clue about the country itself, they learn American style English and it irritates me, as a person proudly brought up to learn the Queen's English. To add insult to injury, the books they learn from and from which we have to teach, are the Cambridge Interchange series that is published and printed by Cambridge University Press UK, which teaches them words such as gee, trash, closet, dollars, candy, leash and American spellings with z's and ou's dropped out of words.

And whilst we are at it, why don't I highlight pronunciations of words they learn from us 'English' speakers, which are just as bad. Amongst our teaching team we have Serbian, broad Irish, broad Scottish, Canadian, Australian, American and English, all speaking different versions of words. The pronunciation of the number 33 is a great example. This manifests itself as thirty three, dirty tree, thurrty threeee, furty free, terty tree. Good luck with that one kiddos. When they're learning the basics, do so many variations really help at this stage? No wonder the overall quality of spoken English in China is so low.

Don't even get me started on Amity's lesson that I shadowed on the apartheid. Did you know it's pronounced apper-thyde? Not apart-eyed. Apparently. When western speakers can't consistently grasp the English language, these children have no hope.

Once again I've ranted my way off-topic. The outreach schools – my opportunity to have witnessed the official schooling system of China, continues to fascinate me.

Traditional Chinese schools are hard to explain. On visiting them, more often than not, they are in old style traditional Chinese looking buildings, quaint exteriors of picture book quality...but beyond the walls, another world exists entirely.

Classrooms are shoddy. I am unclear if this is to do with the fact that China is a developing nation or whether or not the 24/7 use of the facilities have taken their toll on an otherwise acceptable building. Either way, the school buildings are multi storey, big wide corridors, stinking squat-hole bathrooms whose smell drifts down the corridors, and old school speakers affixed to every wall. The curtains hang off the broken rails against the windows, the 40+ desks regimentally rammed into each average sized classroom are rickety and graffitied and the chairs are splinteringly broken.

The presence of graffiti I find an interesting contradiction to the un-opinionated and conforming students I have met. I find this a fascinatingly 'normal' expression of school age children. Granted much of the hieroglyphics are in Mandarin and I can't be sure what they say, but there are often English phrases too, depicting mal-formed blasphemous phrases and filthy language.

Knowing what I know about their institutionalised and suffocating lives I find this weirdly reassuring and heart-warming, rather than chavvy as I would in England. It's a reflection of kids being kids. Pity it's confined to etchings on a desk and not in their free will outside of the confines of education. It confirms to me that these kids have it in them to be kids if only they were allowed to be.

Every morning as school begins, after their exercise regime, they are ushered into classrooms to begin their days, to the sound of 30 seconds of xylophone music, which repeats between every class. At intervals throughout the day, there will sound, over the PA system, two minutes of an eerie voice counting to ten, over and over, at which point the children will stop what they are doing, close their eyes and massage their heads and temples. To encourage learning, apparently. At the end of the formal day, more eerie sounds play through the speakers to instruct students to get out their homework.

It may sound like the school bell in England signifying events – but for every sound played, there is a different demanded action for them. It's not a sound of reprieve. Ever.

I mentioned to a fellow teacher, who was American, how weird I find this and that I felt like it was a type of brainwashing. Interestingly, they responded that it was not so different from American schools where they pledge allegiance every morning, which really made me think that perhaps this was not that odd after all and that the UK was just more relaxed. But it didn't make me feel any more comfortable about it.

Before every class we have to do a roll call. Which should be straight forward, but it never has been. For an English class, the children are allowed to go by their 'English' name. One which they have assigned to themselves, but which annoyingly changes on a daily basis. "Is Vampire here?". No. today she has called herself 'Orange'. Often when a child is looking for an English name they will tell us their name in Chinese and we will give them a similar sounding English one. But they will not accept it until we have described the meaning of the name and they are happy with it. Invariably the next day they will change it so I wonder if our efforts are pointless. Buy hey, I'm just glad they are being creative, so I play along.

It is not uncommon for the kids or students in any of these 'optional' classes not to have completed their homework, something the school and parents demand we give to them.

Responses to the question "have you done your homework" are met with: "I did my real homework until midnight and then I was too tired". Can't really argue with that. I have also noticed during my shadowing, especially in the schools of younger children during the optional classes, if a child looks to be physically exhausted, the English teachers will permit them to put their heads on the desk and sleep through the lesson – no questions asked. This is one action I completely support, despite knowing back home this would have been a detention waiting to happen.

They also often forget their textbooks, don't bother bringing a pen, or a notebook. The optional English classes which they have only taken to please their parents are tough to manage sometimes. Mostly because it is very hard to be strict in these lessons. We foreign teachers are not authorised to discipline the children, as we are discouraged from causing a situation that that may have to be reported to the school board and it subsequently end up being detailed to officials – and how dare we shame the schools.

One of my fellow teachers told me how he was sick of a troublesome student in his class, and as per Western schools, got them to write lines of 'I will not talk while the teacher is talking'. The child complained and as a result, the teacher in question had to write his own essay as to why he would punish a child in this manner, in order to keep his job.

So basically, whilst I have always admired the intelligence of the Chinese nation – I also now realise it did not come without pain, significant amounts of money, and irreparable cost to childhoods.

In the meantime, life at the London Linked School continues as before. Challenging, farcical, and money grabbing.

Their latest ruse is that they will be charging parents for lessons that fall on public holidays and therefore will not be fulfilled. Which of course, the parents are complaining about.

Meanwhile, we teachers are also livid about it. If one of our scheduled teaching days falls on a Monday, we have to reschedule everything to a Tuesday and cram just as many weekly hours in to catch up. We don't get paid for public holidays like the rest of the world (and that our contracts state we should) but have to do double the work for a day a month – whilst the school gets paid double for doing nothing. They just don't stop at conning anyone.

In the meantime, feelings at both the City and South East Schools are becoming unnervingly sour.

Scottish Holly is so bored with her lack of teaching schedule that she has taken to reading during her office hours, mostly in a bid to avoid talking with Pervy Jim. She had always wanted to read the Quran but apparently that was too expensive so she's resorted to the Bible.

Pervy Jim has taken on a whole new level of perversions recently that everyone is on the verge of being violent about, as there is nothing else they can do to stop it.

His favourite words are now n****r and c**t. He asked Mole Noel (who is in fact gay), in public, 'how much cock' he reckoned he could take, he asked Samuel and Pete their opinions on one of his 12-year-old student's developing breasts, asked Holly where she stood on 'big cocks', and constantly discusses his idol Ron Jeremy, the porn actor.

There's so much more to him and his ways that I could vent here but I feel sick even putting any more of it in black and white. And this is a guy the school is paying to work there.

An English man working for this allegedly world-renowned chain of English Language schools. I did not think I could be anymore disgusted with this whole set up until I heard these stories. And there was literally nothing we could do about it, or anyone to report it to. The only thing I could personally do was insist on shadowing his classes when he had them, in order to guard the children.

24

LIFE CONTINUES

Life in
Beijing

In China, it is actually illegal to be homeless, so beggars are very rarely seen on the streets, nor are piles of blankets in nooks and crannies of the city serving as homes for those of no-fixed-abode. The only exception to the beggar story of course came from Mitch, who I still have the pleasure of crossing paths with occasionally. On his regular jaunt to work he passes the same old lady everyday sitting on her favourite step and rocking backwards and forwards muttering, in Chinese, "Mummy, Daddy, Mummy, Daddy".

He has fondly named her 'Vegetable Eye Garden' because apparently she has only one eye and growing out the socket of where the other should be, is something that resembles a cauliflower floret...but I digress; there are virtually no street people here.

This could be because they are all currently serving time in some ghastly prison somewhere, but I sincerely doubt it as the police here are ineffective (the road behaviour that is allowed to happen here is a perfect example of the effect of their absence) and invisible – you rarely see them, but thankfully, other than for traffic reasons, their presence is virtually unnecessary. Crime here is low. Very, very, low.

None of my friends have ever heard of anyone being the subject of a crime, not even a petty theft, or witnessing any sign of criminal or dangerous activity. It appears my subway experience of the girl-beater was a one-off. Lucky me.

Thankfully I have not seen a repeat of this, but the subways are still ridiculous and I wish I didn't have to use them every day. There have been several occasions when Aoife and I have been physically forced off a train we tried to enter because of the violent crowds trying to steal our spots – but we have come to find it amusing and film it as a reminder to ourselves and our families just how crazy it is to travel anywhere here.

Anyway, Mitch. He's surviving well and is convinced the mother of one of his highest paying students fancies him, so he is over-performing at every turn and the school are pleased with him. Plus, no one yet has noticed he is dyslexic or his academic certificates are forgeries of mine.

His only current concern is that for some reason his apartment hasn't had water for three days and he's starting to stink. As he is regaling me with his woes about lack of washing, he takes a chug from his bottle of Coke and instantly recoils. He thrusts it under my nose and asks me if it has 'gone off'. Having never known this was possible, I sniff it out of curiosity and smell nothing strange. It's only then that he realises it's his hands that stink and vows to wash them before he handles more textbooks and kids workbooks. As gross as he can be, he is still an addiction of mine.

For different reasons, so is Rob. His language school is a few floors below ours at the City School and he often pops by after lessons to say 'hi' and spend a bit of time with me between my own lessons. He is still always popping over in the evenings too, so is Amity, and life is good fun in that respect. We still dance every night, we still play games and drink cheap beer regularly as a gang, we still graffiti our walls and have had to change the wall paper several times... we've found our happy existence in this otherwise crazy country... and these people make me smile.

The
Beginning
of the End

THE FINAL COUNTDOWN – THE GOOD

The Beginning of the End

Well, well, well…where do I start? There's been good, there's been bad and there have been some seriously ugly happenings over the last few weeks. The only part I think you will be surprised about in that list is the 'good' part. So, let's start with that. You can wait for the bad – and the ugly isn't over – so I can't finish this tale yet…because I'm still in China.

Since my last schooling update, where I was mostly observing classes, teaching a few, and easing into teaching on the internship as planned, everything appeared to be ticking along nicely. Cue Pervy Jim.

He appears at the school one day and takes, myself, Aoife and Mitchell to one side separately and discusses with each of us that he would like to put us on the CELTA course for the month of April (in three days' time). We are the only three 'teachers' at the London Linked Schools who have yet to study and qualify as Cambridge University accredited foreign language teachers, so the 'offer' makes sense for the London Linked School as they would then have an enlarged base of teachers they can contract out to external schools for lots of money. (There are other sneaky benefits for them too, which I will cover in due course.)

The CELTA course was also a great option for us and something we were all planning to complete anyway – it's the only really valuable thing that the London Linked School could offer us for our future. The month-long intensive course is conducted by external tutors and administered by Cambridge University – therefore it was also untouchable by our school. All they do is provide a centre for the training and recruit people on to the course. This was also a qualification we could take anywhere in the world and command higher salaries with. A no brainer for us and was actually Mitch and my favoured option to our dilemma all those weeks ago.

So, it sounds simple, right? We go on the course, get qualified, and live happily ever after. Wrong.

As usual, there's more to this than meets the eye – and surprise, surprise, the London Linked School haven't just turned into wonderful upstanding members of the community before our eyes.

To get on to the CELTA course, you must undergo a thorough assessment of your ability and knowledge of the construction and interpretation of the English language through lengthy interviews and written assessments. After which, you are either accepted or denied entry to the course. Once accepted, there is a lengthy 50-page pre-course task you must complete (that can take several days to do), required pre-reading and an expected level of pre-requisite knowledge.

We were being offered a CELTA course that began in three days' time.

Why? Because they were surplus two teachers thanks to Mitchell and my arriving, therefore they were carrying the cost of two unexpected salaries, were undersubscribed on the CELTA course for April and needed a minimum of two more people for it to breakeven, they wouldn't have to pay us a salary while we did it (so double win for them – not only would we not be being paid during the month, but also we would have to pay a considerable sum ourselves to do the course) and finally, it would take us out of circulation (existing staff would absorb our classes), therefore we were not guaranteed a job at the end of it.

So, they squeeze the last drops of money out of us whilst we are still here, find a way to claw back the extra cost Mitchell and I am to them, and then potentially turf us out afterwards. They saw a winning situation here.

So, Aoife, Mitchell and I had a decision to make.

Aoife was initially offered a slight discount on the course so Aoife snapped it up (not thinking through the consequences of doing so) as she was desperate to save money for her Europe travels in September and was booked to do it later in the year anyway. Her reasoning was that it's cheaper for her to do it now, and means her last month in China (when she planned to do the CELTA course) wouldn't be full of studying and could instead be spent partying.

Mitchell turned it down. Being severely dyslexic he was worried about not having had time to prepare for it and subsequently spending a lot of money just to fail the course, plus he doesn't have the money to do it yet. And also, by him not doing it, he knew he would be in a perfect position to take on Aoife's classes and secure himself a job.

Myself? Not so clear cut. Do it and I potentially have no job in a month, don't do it and I have nothing formal to take away from my Asian disaster.

We didn't have long to weigh up the options – having to make a decision that day. As far I was concerned, emotionally I was pretty drained thanks to the last couple of months so, really? If I didn't have a job at the end of it, no big deal. Probably a blessing. I saw this as a way out of the China mess with a valuable qualification in my hand so that my time in China wasn't entirely wasted. So, on that front, I was all for it.

However, I was angry at them for expecting me to line their pockets with £1,250 for the honour of getting the qualification after having paid for a traineeship already, I was angry that they would be getting away with not paying my salary for a month, and angry that they would think they had 'won'. Stupid pride I know – but it worked in this instance.

The CELTA course can cost anything from £1,500 upwards if you do it anywhere else in the world, China is one of the cheapest countries to do it in so it's a very popular scheme to do here. But no matter where you choose to do it, you have to cover the additional costs of your accommodation, subsistence, and daily travel to and from the course – which makes it a costly undertaking for most.

Realising that the benefits of me accepting a place were greater for them, I knew I was in a position to negotiate – and so I did. I had nothing to lose after all.

I pointed out to Pervy Jim that there was no benefit in me doing the course – in that I had a job, I was being paid to do it (a meager half wage at that, but an income nonetheless), I had already paid to be here so why would I pay again, and it appeared to me that the benefit is all theirs. So, what were they going to do to make it worth my while?

He looked like a rabbit caught in headlights and flustered over saying that maybe he hadn't thought it through and that he had thought he was doing me a favour by offering it to me. (Regardless of the fact I could have done it anywhere in the world if I so chose and not line these cheaters pockets any further.) I did ask him to clarify what classified it as a favour and after a moment he blurted out that he would make sure my accommodation costs were covered as a sweetener. I told him that wasn't good enough and left the room.

He later tracked me down and tried to persuade me again, so I told him that if he wasn't going to pay my salary, then I wanted a further discount, to the same value, taken off the course fee.

I later received a text message from him saying that they couldn't stretch to discounting me that far, but that they would compromise on discounting my salary, less £50. Funny really. They didn't want to look like they'd succumbed, and instead kept £50 of pride back. Idiots. What a bargain for me. I was in. I get an international qualification, for now nearly half price, plus my accommodation covered, and leave China with something other than an incredibly bad story to tell. I was also aware that my job here was not safe, the internship was still a sham despite constant battles and I did not trust them not to just turf me out, leaving me with nothing of value to offer to my next position elsewhere in the world.

He also requested I don't tell Aoife what price I got it for. But I did. And she got the cheap price too. Ha.

And so, Aoife and I were signed up for the CELTA course and now had a weekend to prepare for a Monday morning start.

Needless to say, despite being given the answers (!) to the pre-course 50-pager task, we had limited sleep swatting up on the course material and began the course on the Monday with coffees in hand and matchsticks holding our eyes open. Not the best start to an intensive and extremely hard course admittedly, but it was worth the pain. We were nowhere near prepared in comparison to our six fellow students, but the course was brilliant. From beginning to end – it was brilliant.

The tutors were the best teachers I've experienced during many years of studying, our classmates were an interesting and varied bunch who we laughed away the 20-hour working days with and bemoaned together the severe sleep deprivation we all suffered during the month. The Chinese adults who dutifully turned up every day as guinea pig classes for us to practice teach on were amusing, gracious and supportive and completed the experience nicely. I became fond of everyone involved in the whole process.

No doubt it was one of the hardest and time-consuming courses I had ever undertaken. Over a period of seven days during the toughest part of the course, Aoife and I got less than 20 hours sleep. We were hailing taxis home at 4am from central Beijing after planning lessons and writing assignments with our classmates, and getting up again at 7am to get to school to print and submit our work.

One night we got home at 9pm, were so exhausted by 11pm we planned a power nap till midnight so we could continue semi-refreshed. Obviously so exhausted, we both slept through our alarms and awoke in a blind panic at gone 4am. The sun was rising and we still had hours of work left – so we started our day at 4am that day. Weekends were just as torturous. No time for luxurious sleep of more than four hours. I could only dream of the days when I could lie in. Granted our intravenous coffee drips might have contributed.

We often had our classmates over for study sessions (they were hostel based so studying and eating was not easy for them without internet or a kitchen) and regularly worked collectively till 6am on the weekend, only to have a brief sleep to continue again. One of them even had his own toothbrush here and the sofa had his name written on it.

But you know what? It was fun. I wouldn't have changed a second of it. Working as a team with some great people, hysteria through sleep deprivation, and constant assessments and written assignments made me feel finally weirdly content. I loved learning, I loved teaching - and the experience was making me love Beijing. This last part was the biggest surprise. I was definitely confusing being happy, with the country I was in, but either way... life was good.

THE MIXED

The Beginning of the End

Although I loved the CELTA course, the people I met and the fulfilment it gave me, it was also an eventful month in other ways too.

My older brother and his wife announced that they would be visiting Beijing for the weekend from Singapore, where they both lived and worked. I was ridiculously grateful to be seeing family and sharing the madness of China and for the moral support they might give me. I was quite surprised that they were coming after having sent them my candid stories so far but then I realised that my presence and experience of Beijing also afforded them an in-country tour guide of a place they might not have otherwise visited. But whatever their reasoning for coming, it would offer a reprieve for me and I was looking forward to it.

I had also heard word that my extreme emails home had caused a level of doubt in the minds of my readers that surely things couldn't be as bad as I was saying they were and perhaps I was over dramatising the whole experience. I will admit that there was a big part of me that wanted independent witnesses of some of the horrors and that the doubt had made me a little angry.

My brother was due to arrive the Friday of my first week of CELTA. My tutors got wind of the visit and told me to make the most of it because there would be absolutely NO free time for the following weekends – and I was reminded I still had an assignment to hand in on the Monday, so it couldn't be all play anyway. I was okay with that. I could at least squeeze in one day trip over the weekend and have room for dinners with them. My sister-in-law spoke a small amount of Mandarin so I was sure they would manage without me for some of the time.

Despite my looking forward to their arrival, I also heard the news I was dreading. Rob had some success at his job interviews for his next steps after China, and would be leaving Beijing to start his real life again in the Philippines. And he would be leaving on the Saturday of my second weekend of CELTA. Due to my family visiting, there was very little opportunity of quality time left we could spend together just the two of us…and I was devastated. There would be no time to laze together and picnic in the sun at my favourite park as we had planned…no more long and leisurely breakfasts…no more putting the world to rights over dinner or drinking tea in bed in the mornings before school. I was torn…I just wanted to steal every last second I could with Rob while I still had him…and now I couldn't. My time was not 'ours', we had to share.

My brother and his wife arrived Friday afternoon and the second my classes finished I dashed off to see them in their hotel only a five-minute walk from the City School where I was training.

As I walked into the grand foyer of their 5* hotel the doorman courteously held the door for me and said 'Welcome back Madam'. My immediate thought was that he had mistaken me for a regular prostitute. I quickly shook that idea off when I realised that I was worth nothing in this country. How laughable. Instead I took with me the shock that someone had not slammed a door in my face and that it was the first and only time in my weeks of being here that someone had shown manners. I wanted to shout and point to the people on the street that 'this is how it's done!' but I bit my tongue and raced to see my brother.

I found them upstairs in the business lounge sipping gin and tonics, with their i-pad strategically leant against their glasses and a sign on it saying 'Welcome Gemma'. I could have cried right there and then for the familiar faces and the welcome they gave me. I could have cried even more when I looked around and saw cleanliness, carpets, polished mirrors and alcohol that didn't contain chemicals used to preserve dead bodies. Unfortunately, I also noticed that I stank. Aoife being a heavy smoker had not bothered me before – China had ruined my sense of smell, no-one even wears perfume here, but now I noticed it on myself. My feet were also filthy from padding around the streets of Beijing and I suddenly felt ashamed of myself. Thankfully I had my hair tied back so they couldn't see the amateur shaggy hairdo I now sported courtesy of Amity.

They both looked really well. All shiny and new in the city of madness. And they also looked relieved to see me in person to know that I was in fact okay and coping.

First thing was first, my sister-in-law handed me a bag of goodies and necessities I had requested. Knowing how much more developed Singapore was, I had put in a request for things I just could not get out here. Decent shampoo, deodorant, tampons, sun tan lotion that didn't have whitener in it, salt and vinegar crisps. I felt like a kid at Christmas. I never thought I would see the day that tampons became exciting but they were such a treat. When I asked the other girls if they desperately needed anything brought in, they all said tampons. No chocolate, no real alcohol. Tampons.

As soon as happy hour was over and I had devoured the gin cabinet and basked in the glory of being treated like a princess, we left the confines of the hotel and headed back towards a restaurant under the school where I knew I could successfully order us some really nice food and I could give them a brief tour whilst we were there. They were relatively impressed with the school and could see it wasn't a tin-pot joke of a place, but an actual functioning business and found it hard to believe the madness that was reported to go on there.

As we ate dinner, I had to confess to my real lack of time this weekend due to assignments needing completing. This did not faze them at all. My sister-in-law, although South Korean, had learned conversational Mandarin at school and she was confident that she could get them around the city safely on the Saturday whilst I worked. (Or at least to the designer shopping malls and back). I also knew my brother had his colouring on his side. He could adapt well to the 'white male is King' role and with a Mandarin speaker beside him, would not be a target for someone to take advantage of him.

We made plans to meet for dinner the following night and I headed home to work until the early hours on my assignment with the hopes of getting it done in time to be sure I could relax with them later the following day.

That night I wanted to 'treat' them to a real Beijing eatery. Of course, the BBQ restaurant we regularly frequented was about as real as it got here. It also meant I could show them my apartment as it was only a few minutes further along the road.

In honour of their attendance I gathered the troops so they could put names to faces from the tales they had heard so far.

I met them at the subway station and walked them the short five minutes through the hubbub of the lanes to the BBQ place – now nicknamed 'Little Fatties' by Aoife in honour of the owner's rather chubby son. The streets were alive with activity. It was dark and the lights were blazing, showing up the uneven dirt road and the hive of street sellers. The smells from roadside food carts was incredible and it was all I could do to stop them snacking on the way. We also passed a bike chained to a fence that Samuel had 'illegally' parked at the station some weeks ago that now had more parking tickets taped it than the price of the bike, so he'd duly abandoned it.

My brother and his wife were living in Singapore where cleanliness is next to Godliness and the actual law there. Fines and lashes were handed out freely to those who spat on the ground, dropped litter and caused a nuisance. This was a sight to behold for them as the phlegm production was high and my sister-in-law's expensive heels were not coping with the trashy obstacles.

We headed for the plume of BBQ smoke and the smell of freshly cooked meat to meet the others who were already drinking at the restaurant and began yet another feast.

My guests were amused by the fact that finished chicken bones were simply discarded on to the floor along with used napkins and skewers and joined in with gusto as Pete, Rob and Aoife led the ordering of food with their excellent Mandarin. My sister-in-law was a little nervous to use her Mandarin as it had apparently failed her today. They had taken a tri-taxi tour around the hutongs in central Beijing and instead of costing them 30 Yuan, it had cost them $30 which they had put down to a misunderstanding of the agreement. Unfortunately, it was a common scam here and they had obviously been caught out by it, which was a shame.

Our little table buzzed with chatter and stories and tales of the times we had all had in Beijing, the school, the challenges, the drama and so on. I was glad they were getting corroboration of my stories from others. I heard that my brother had mentioned to Mum and Dad that he had doubts about the truth behind some of my claims and the descriptions I had used…but this way he was getting independent confirmation from third parties, as well as experiencing some of it for himself. I felt like it was validation of myself. The only thing they weren't experiencing was bad pollution days. The sky was blue at the moment and although hazy, it looked like many other sunny days in cities across the world. Additionally, though the streets were grey, dusty and dirty, the flowers and tree blossoms had started to bloom with the change in the weather and there were now vibrant colours on the streets.

After we had finished our meals and the tour of the apartment was complete, Rob put my brother and his wife into a taxi to get them safely back to their hotel. It was only around 10pm so Rob and Amity came back for more beers. It was the first time this week Aoife and I had really had time to catch up with anyone and we didn't envisage much time in the coming weeks to do so either as our CELTA workload increased. It was also the weekend before Rob was leaving us so time was precious with him too.

In our wisdom, after a few oversized bottles of our local cheap beer, we decided that as we had never done Karaoke with Rob, his favourite pastime apparently, we would head to the nearest bar to honour his time here.

Although karaoke is immensely popular here and there are karaoke bars on most street corners, we decided to head to a more commercial bar that we knew would be open at such a late hour. It is not unheard of for Chinese folk to pop to these bars fully sober on a free afternoon, just like a Westerner might go bowling or play pool. It was almost a rite of passage, but to find one that catered for the hardcore wannabe X-factor auditionees like Rob and Amity, you had to go further afield.

We ended up at the mall Rob and I had toured on our first date and had just as many troubles trying to find the bar and an escalator that would take us directly to the right floor and not lose us for the next four hours, or give us electric shocks.

On finding it, it was not as I had expected. It was not a jolly bar where there was one stage for performing to the crowds, but small soundproof rooms where you sang only to your immediate party. It was a little awkward to say the least, not having a particularly strong singing voice, but desperately wanting to participate. I needn't have worried, Aoife was tone deaf and for all the energy Amity put into her performances, she was still appalling. Luckily, the rooms were well serviced by bar girls who catered for our every drinking whim, and probably more had Rob not been in the company of three girls with their eagle eyes on him. The prices were extortionate and more akin to Western prices than we had experienced yet in the city.

The more we drank, the more we sang – to each other. Once you had got over the weirdness and lubricated the vocal cords, it actually became hilarious. If you were lucky enough to find a song you recognised from the pidgin English in the song brochures, you were well away. And if your voice was terrible, the amusement in watching the cheesy and fake unofficial Chinese versions of the music videos on a cinema sized screen in the tiny rooms was enough to distract you.

Little did we know that it was one of Rob's favourite past times because he was incredible. Karaoke was obviously his party piece and if you shut your eyes you could easily be under the impression Craig David was in the room with you.

By the time we got bored/drank too much/spent all our money, we decided to call it a day only to walk out of the building and find it was daylight. We had been singing to ourselves for almost five hours straight. Maybe the Chinese were on to something here.

The following morning – or in fact in five hours' time, Aoife and I were joining my brother on a trip to the Great Wall of China. Although Rob stayed with me that night, he left at the crack of dawn to begin his packing to leave. I was going to have to get used to him leaving me. Even the mornings were hard enough, how would I cope when he left the country?

The Great Wall adventure was via a tour operator hired from the hotel who was to drive us to the Wall and back, so whilst being a good couple of hours away, it was hassle free, and I was keen to tick a big item off my lifelong bucket list and add something major to my appalling lack of tourism so far. As was Aoife who hadn't seen it yet either, despite being here for eight months already.

We were finally going to walk The Wall!

The journey out there was in a style of comfort you naturally would expect from a tour organized by a 5* hotel in a private limousine. We wound our way out of the chaos of the city via parts I had not yet seen, and out of the north west corner of Beijing.

On our route, we swept past the desolate and decaying Birds Nest, the 2008 Olympic stadium. It was a rusted and derelict building now which was a shame bearing in mind the Beijing Olympics were rumoured to have cost more than any other Olympic site to date. I think the numbers came in at a staggering $250 billion dollars so it was no small affair. Of course, that was cheap for the Chinese to ensure a place on the world stage befitting of their opinions of themselves, but an expensive waste of money now the venues were not utilised.

It was because of the Olympics that Beijing stepped up its game in the green stakes too. The pollution index was more than six times that of London and firmly in the hazardous zone. Despite shutting down local factories and forcing cars off the roads during the games, the air was still the worst the athletes were likely to breathe in their entire careers. But hey, it looked pretty to the rest of the world through their TV screens.

Some of the oldest parts of the city and the traditional buildings were also razed to the ground in order to make way for apartment blocks and hotels (bearing little architectural resemblance to the roots of the historical dynasties of China) that raised the aesthetic profile of the city. A great example being the Parisian style monstrosity directly opposite my brother's hotel. Whilst becoming the back drop for many a beautiful wedding photo shoot, it did not belong here. China had lost its way, as many cities do across the decades.

Also, on the route, as the roads became less busy and the neighbourhoods less densely populated, we passed the old and abandoned Wonderland theme park whose central feature was reminiscent of the Disney Magic Kingdom. Having never even opened, it was a decaying and eerie blot on the landscape.

An hour and a half into the journey we began to spy the first sections of the Great Wall itself. From a distance it looked like a mountain path that joined the peaks of the hills together but closer up you could see it was very much a wall, several feet high, and broken up at intervals by large square watchtowers. As pretty as it was, and knowing that it was over 5000km long, it was hard to gauge its enormity or effectiveness at this stage. But the second you swing towards the Baddaling section, there is no question as to why it deserves the awe it receives.

Baddaling is one of the most touristy areas of the wall we could have picked. It was absolutely heaving with tourists, souvenir shops and street food vendors. The toilets were filthy retch inducing holes in the ground. The queues for the ticket office to allow access to the wall were long and slow moving. Mostly because at this section of the wall, it was so high that the only way to get up there without several hours of hiking, was the cable car, in which there was limited capacity at any one time.

The route along the wall itself was very narrow in places – and rammed with people. At its widest the wall was probably about six metres across. Every inch of space was filled with people. At times you could not even see your own feet it was that cramped with tourists. Luckily, my brother, Aoife and I were at least a head taller than the crowd so we couldn't lose each other and we got to take in uninterrupted views of the majesty of the Great Wall. For as far as the eye could see, the wall swept up and down through the hilly terrain, with the watchtowers standing ominously and tall at regular intervals. It was breath-taking. If it wasn't for the cacophony of spitting and hysteria from the thronging crowds around us it would have been a magical experience.

It was because of the crowds that we decided not to stay on the wall too long. Despite it being a gloriously sunny day, the wind was whipping us and the stress of making it up precariously steep sections of the wall with people glued to you on all sides was a little off-putting. As usual, in front of touring Chinese folk, we were treated like the celebrities that we had been told to expect to be in Asia, but that we hadn't been afforded when in the city. It's fair to say the numbers of photographs with strangers we were snapped in reached into the hundreds. We accepted the attention politely and held the obligatory peace sign as much as our fingers could handle. It was just a shame that our own memories of the wall included photo bombing strangers who hijacked our poses and couldn't afford us the uninterrupted group shots we would have liked. But I guess that's all part of the experience.

Slightly sunburned and tired, we headed back to the smog of the city and our final dinner together before I had to wave goodbye to the sanity and comfort of my family until I didn't know when. They'd only been here a weekend, but the tears came when they left. I felt lonely all over again. Abandoned in this scary place, and having to face an altogether different goodbye again the following weekend.

The week following my family's visit, the stress of the CELTA course really hit Aoife and me. There seemed no way there were enough hours in the day to achieve the assignments and lesson planning that we were expected to produce and be marked on. It didn't help that due to the short notice we had been given to start the course we were already on the back foot having not completed the pre-requisite reading or gathered the base knowledge we were expected to have had. Every assignment we had to complete, we first had to learn the principles and then write and teach about it, meaning our workload of an already intensely work heavy week was doubled. It was also a good representation of the cowboy outfit that were running the course, and who we were currently working for. We should never have been allowed to take the course in the first place.

Although I was glad to be on the course, and as ever, happy to be learning something new, I was gutted at the timing. Rob was leaving in a few days and the demands on my time were elsewhere. I had such mixed emotions that I found myself wanting to cry in frustration at the daily demands, when all I wanted to do was snuggle up to Rob, my favourite thing out here.

Since I had met him, he had promised to cook for us girls and he had asked if we could finally do it on the Wednesday before he left. Aoife and I reasoned that we had to eat, and if we just ate and ran we could still get our work done, but still spend time with him. It was a sad compromise.

We arrived at Rob's around 8.30pm to an apartment of steam and outrageous heat from the feast he had cooked up on his hob. He had upgraded our usual beer choice to the 50 pence version and had set the table Chinese-style for us. Tumbler glasses for the beer, side plates, main plates with bowls on top, napkins, chopsticks, the works. It smelt amazing and Rob, although red in the face from the heat, was excited to demonstrate his well learnt Chinese cooking skills.

We feasted on a range of dishes that you would be mistaken for thinking he had ordered from a take away had we not have watched him cook it fresh in front of us.

I wished we had done it sooner, back when he first offered and not in the lead up to his leaving and when I had to share his company with Aoife, as much as I loved her company too. Every time she went to the loo, which gratefully a lot, Rob kissed me, hugged me and we had our moments. Boy was I going to miss him. I felt so special in his company and when he talked, even in a crowd, I felt like I was the only person he could see. I had never felt this special in my life and couldn't believe he was leaving me here alone after what I thought we had found.

It was hard enough not to cry during dinner as I spied the partially packed cases and how impersonal the place was beginning to look in preparation for his going.

When Aoife was out of ear-shot he continuously begged me to stay over…but the student in me had to deny him as much as my heart wanted to stay. I had an incredible amount of work to do for the following morning that even the time I had spent eating had been a luxury. Aoife and I would have usually grabbed baked sweet potato from the street stand on our walk from the subway to save time, but tonight we had made allowances and accepted that there would be an hour less of precious sleep for this pleasure.

We left at a pitifully early time to get home and do our homework. Aoife subtly waited around the corner of the apartment door, at the lift block, so I could say a suitable goodbye to the man who made my heart both leap and cry at the same time. He had tears in his eyes already, as did I, and he still hadn't yet gone.

I don't know how I worked that night. I was already in physical pain with his impending departure, mental pain from not having a clue what I was doing and under immense pressure to secure options for my future.

Aoife and I researched until 1am when the internet seemed to have a habit of shutting down and continued our lesson planning until we both gave up around 4am. With three hours before we had to leave for school, we had to cut our losses and accept our performance in class may not be optimal. The price you pay for eating well and having a break I suppose. As it happened, I wasted another hour lying in bed, staring out of my window, listening to the honking of car horns and watching the sunrise on a life in which Rob soon would not feature.

The following day, eyes feeling gritty, we rolled into school and gave the performance of our lives on a marked teaching practice. Maybe sleep deprival was the key to success after all.

During our mid-morning break, Rob made an unexpected visit to the school. I was used to him visiting when he was at college here, a few floors below us, but today was a surprise. He had been to the Philippine embassy to pick up his passport and visa and had decided to stop in 'on the way home'. But it wasn't on the way. And I was grateful to have him there. For probably the last time.

That night, after staying behind at school to research our assignments, Aoife and I get home at gone 9pm. Exhausted, but ready to plough into today's assignment and prepare our lessons for the following day. Rob had been in text contact all day and having known when we would get home and that we had not yet had time to eat, had turned up unexpectedly at ours, bags of steaming food in hand. Knowing we did not have a microwave, he had heated up the previous night's leftovers and literally ran to our apartment to ensure they were hot when he arrived. My heart melted for him as his brief visit was over and he left us to our work and he headed out for his farewell drink with Samuel.

He spent that night out till the early hours saying farewell to the city at Tiananmen Square, watching the flags being raised as the sun rose. I laid in bed, wide awake wishing it was me that could have shared these last few hours with him.

AN EARLY GOODBYE

The
Beginning
of the End

Tonight was Rob's last night and he had saved it for just the two of us. He had spent his week saying goodbye to everyone else and I was flattered that he would want to spend his last hours in the city he had spent the last nine months in, with me. Although I would have been disappointed if he hadn't.

I was due to be at his for eight o'clock and as school had finished at half past four, I had some time to be sociable with my new CELTA friends, who even after only two weeks of knowing each other, had built a tight bond of mutual support and even friendship. They were planning a big dinner and drinks session before they sacrificed their entire weekends to study and lesson planning for the following week. The tutors were upping the ante and chances like this were few and far between.

That meant I had time to have a drink with them before hopping in a taxi home, to wash and change before seeing Rob for our very last night together till whoever knew when.

But tonight, of all crucial Friday nights, was the night I could not get a taxi. We had headed north to the hutongs for our post school drinks and my subway stop was now a 40-minute walk south. Bearing that in mind, once I had weaved my way out of the winding narrow streets to the main road, I decided to chance my luck and grab a cab. It would get me home an hour quicker if all went well, and meant that shower I so desperately craved before heading to Rob's was all the more possible. It was not to be. I took the gamble of staying by the roadside instead of wending my way to the subway and did not get lucky. Fleets of taxis flew past me, saw my white face, and anticipating the hassle of a foreigner with little common language, carried on by. Realising they could easily pick up an alternative fare on this busy Friday evening was a winner for them, and I was the loser.

An hour and half later, I finally hailed a taxi as the rush hour began to die down and I became as good a fare as any. I called Rob to explain my lateness and that I still wanted to head home and shower but he was insistent I went straight to his instead of waste time. So I do, I arrive at his, flustered and grotty feeling, but glad to see him. He had a beer ready for me, having not packed a couple of glasses especially for tonight. As we were waiting for our takeaway food to arrive, he let me take a shower, dried me and dressed me in his favourite comfy trousers and his big and soft grey hoody which was a staple of his wardrobe. It smelt of him, I smelled of him. I never wanted to wash again.

I don't remember what we ate, or if I ate at all. I probably didn't because I had no appetite. We had begun laughing and reminiscing about our times here, but as it became painfully clear that this was our last night together and that his leaving was at the forefront of both of our minds, the conversation died. I think this evening was the first time we ever experienced silence together.

What do you say to someone that you might be seeing for the last time? What we had was incredible, and special, but who knew what the future held? He was about to start a new life in the Philippines. He had planned never to return to England, and I knew I felt the exact opposite. Our lives were going in different directions. Despite having secretly researched teaching jobs in the Philippines, I knew I did not want to go there. But it was the best thing he could do for his career. And it was what he wanted to do. I wonder if we had met earlier, whether things would have been different... maybe we would have had more time to figure something out together? But it wasn't to be. Although we talked about me visiting him, we both knew we wouldn't make it long term. And it was devastating to accept.

That night we went to bed and laid in each other's arms, and just hugged in the dark, still not speaking. I'd been crying on and off all evening and was surprised to hear him doing the same.

The morning came too soon, but there was no stopping the clock moving forward. We couldn't put it on hold, nor rewind it as much as we wished we could.

I lay in his bed whilst I heard him shower and dress and pack up the very last of his belongings. He was leaving his bed as was, so I stayed in it, staring around at the place so many memories had been made and taking mental pictures. I felt sick. I wondered when the crying would stop. I wondered if I would be able to sound sincere when I wished him good luck in his new life...it was sincere, but I just wished I was a part of it.

I finally dragged myself up and dressed quickly when I heard the door buzzer go. Aoife had arrived to say her own goodbye. She was emotional too. She could barely get out a thank-you when he loaded her with his leftover food, crockery, towels and clothes that he couldn't take with him. By 10am he was ready to go. His suitcase zipped, his door locked and keys posted in the letter box. We traipsed down in the elevator and to the road a sorry trio. I crossed my fingers he would have the typical Westerner hassle to get a taxi but alas, as soon as they saw the suitcases, they couldn't stop quick enough sensing an airport run.

It was almost less painful for it to be over so quickly. My heart had been saying goodbye to him for days but these last few minutes were the most painful by far.

He hugged a teary Aoife goodbye and she turned her back to us as we said our final farewell. The last of his kisses that I might ever feel, the last of his amazing hugs.

He whispered to me 'Thank you'. That's all he needed to say. But then my heart broke into a thousand pieces when he told me he loved me.

I watched his taxi drive away until I could no longer see it anymore.

Turning strangers into friends on the other side the world creates bonds like no other. They are the only people who know, who understand, who experience alongside you what living and surviving in an alien culture is truly like, and the daily battles you face. They are your support network, your sanity, your closest confidantes, your cheerleaders, and your family. And when one leaves there is a gaping hole you will never truly fill.

I knew there would never be another Rob.

THE BAD

The
Beginning
of the End

During our last week of the CELTA course, Pervy Jim showed his face and asked for a word with myself and Aoife. Both of us had been dreading the day when we saw him again, not least because we can't stand to be in his presence, but because we knew he would be the messenger of our fate after us finishing the course.

During our studying, we had to put to one side the fact that we could both be exiting China early and that neither of us were ready to go just yet – we just had to concentrate on passing the course as best we could as it was possibly the only thing we would take away from our China experience. We had to make it all worthwhile. Aoife wanted to stay and needed the remaining three months money for her travels, and Amity, her travel buddy, wasn't finishing her contract until August – so the timing for her was not ideal by any means to be cut loose.

Myself, I'd been on a high for the last three and a half weeks and, faced with the actual prospect of leaving, didn't feel like I was ready either. I never thought that would be an issue for me after the constant battles I'd been through, but during my good times I felt sad at the prospect of not having given the country a chance thanks to a string of unfortunate events. Getting to know more and more people who loved China, I felt I must have missed something. In hindsight – this is ridiculous and I can't believe I just wrote that. I guess that's what sleep deprivation does to you.

Aoife had her meeting with Pervy Jim first. It didn't take long and she came out looking furious. My heart sank for her – I thought she was out on her ear. But, no. She had been told she could continue working for the London Linked School at the City School where we both worked prior to taking time out for the course. However, she was told she would not be getting her regular classes back as these would remain with Mitchell. (The parents who pay fat fees for their kids to be here don't like it when teachers change and for once, the London Linked School were listening to their wage payers.)

She was told there were no classes for her to take but that she could spend her time doing admin, tidying, filing etc. Pathetic - especially for a newly qualified teacher. It also came with the risk that she was highly expendable as she would no longer have the power of her relationships with fee payers to ensure herself an ongoing employment. No wonder she was depressed.

My meeting was fine however. I was offered a teaching post at South East with my own classes, salary doubled, working a 10-15 min stroll from my apartment – which I was also allowed to keep (with Aoife) until the end of my new contract which finished at the end of August. Plus, I could have the week following my course off as annual leave – as per my holiday application when I arrived in February. It was handed to me on a plate – no bargaining needed. It felt suspiciously odd.

Despite everyone warning me how horrible South East was, I was grateful I had a job, a pay rise, and no more hideous commuting to do. I had also heard an ex-CELTA tutor, Scottish Frank, had taken over managing South East and that people were hopeful about what he would bring to the school. This gave me hope that things there weren't going to be the stuff of nightmares that others had warned me about and that I would not get to experience first-hand why none of them would touch South East School with a bargepole. I decide to be positive about my next three months…it seemed an okay result for me. And if I decide upfront I'm going to like it, I might, right?

Well I would certainly try to be positive. So, now that my immediate future was agreed, I could focus on my next ten days in China actually being a tourist with a friendly face from home.

29

A FRIENDLY FACE

The
Beginning
of the End

After a sleep deprived month of hard slog on the CELTA course, I didn't get an opportunity to celebrate its end with my new friends, or passing the course in an appropriate fashion. Not only were we all exhausted, but I had a friend from home, Pip, arriving from England for a week's holiday, at an ungodly hour the following morning and I had to leave for the airport at an even worse hour to get there to meet him.

He had been a really close friend of mine in the months leading up to me leaving and I was looking forward to seeing him. I had planned to put together a survival bag of Beijing goodies to welcome him but due to CELTA, I hadn't had time to breathe let alone shop.

I had picked up the odd thing along the way and managed to cobble something together, but it was lame. I had found us both 'I <3 BJ' tourist t-shirts, a face mask so he fitted in, some dodgy Chinglish named sweets and some trainee chopsticks. That would have to do, although I was disappointed in my efforts that a friend was coming this far to visit little old me and I hadn't done my best to welcome him.

Our plans were that he would stay in our apartment for the first night, sleep off his jet lag, and the following day we would hit the silk markets and deck ourselves out with fake branded clothes. Beijing was now heavily (and very suddenly) into summer weather, so my winter clothes, which had taken up most of my packing space, were redundant and I was wearing the same things, day in day out. Then we would head for the sleeper train to Xi'an and spend some time visiting the Terracotta Warriors and various famous tombs, then fly back to Beijing and hit the tourist sites more locally. He had very kindly booked us an apartment in the centre of Beijing for five nights so we could spend some proper time together and not have to battle the subway that I had warned him about, or being ignored for taxis when we wanted to be home.

I had managed to get the time off work because during CELTA I had worked through two public holidays and Pervy Jim had promised them off in lieu to Aoife and me. There were also another two bank holidays due to Easter this week and I had some unused holiday to take as well. It had all worked out well. Except that the morning Pip left, I would have to head straight to work, which was not ideal, but I was glad of what time I could get to relax and finally tour this country.

I made it to the airport after a sluggish journey on the subway and totally underestimated the time it would take to battle the hordes of passengers on a weekend. I had taken one of my old white t-shirts that was now a brown/grey filthy colour and written on it 'Welcome to BJ, Pip' as he had mentioned no-one had ever held up a sign at an airport for him. I thought I would go one better and wear one but as it happened it did not have the effect I had hoped. By the time I got to the airport Pip had arrived and was standing waiting for me, and I still had my jumper on.

As soon as I saw him, instead of saying hello immediately, I whipped off my jumper and showed him the sign I had made. It lost its impact but the thought was there I suppose. Then I looked at his t shirt, and he had properly printed on his t-shirt 'Gemma is Awesome'. I had failed badly in comparison. But I sure was glad to see him. We hugged like long lost pals. I felt like I hadn't seen him in years after what I had been through since I had arrived. In reality it was only a matter of months.

We cheated on the way home and grabbed a cab. The poor guy was exhausted having not slept on the flight and being awake for almost 24 hours. The taxi ride was fine but the end location was off and we ended up having to walk for about 15 minutes, which I felt responsible for. I'm sure he expected to be safe and serviced by a China expert, but that wasn't me and I was already feeling the stress of trying to make this an easy and exciting trip for him. Although he had read my blogs and he knew how tough this place was, this was the first time I had felt relied upon to host proficiently.

On arrival at the apartment, Aoife was not around. She had stayed at Amity's last night in a boozy, sleepy haze of post CELTA relief and hadn't yet returned.

Whilst I had been in China, Pip had organised to send me a survival pack of goodies. Proper tea bags (because China – the land of tea, could not do a proper version of English tea), Marmite, chocolate, crisps, gravy, stuffing etc not knowing that I did not have an oven to cook most of the items. He was such a good friend that he had listened when I lamented the lack of home comforts and had done what he could to help me out.

He had now brought out with him bacon, sausages, proper cheese etc…the guy was a marvel. So I was able to make him a nice cuppa and a bacon sandwich as an arrival snack whilst we caught up on the last few weeks and I shared with him the plans I had made for his trip.

He was tucked up in my bed not long after, shattered, whilst I napped on the pop-up bed in the living room so as not to disturb him and to silence Aoife if she returned.

That evening, we did our ritual BBQ evening to introduce him to the food and 'real' local Beijing life. He loved it. The grottiness of the surroundings being a novelty to him, and meeting my friends who he had already read about, enlightening.

An early night saw us up at the crack of dawn, another bacon sandwich scoffed and a subway trip to the silk markets to shop. Pip's cases were roomy now that he had offloaded his smuggled food items and he was eager to buy knock-off items that were so real looking you could be mistaken for thinking they were genuine.

We did the rounds. Me as a tutor in effective bargaining, and left laden with Abercrombie and Fitch goodies, Louis Vuitton, all manner of labelled sporting wear with genuine price tags on and various other named items for a fraction of the price. We were now equipped for our planned trips.

Late afternoon we had packed overnight bags and headed for the sleeper train station for our trip to Xi'an. Finding the station was in itself a mission and once we arrived, finding our ticket booth was just as tough. The train station was overrun with people sleeping on the floor and huddled together like a refugee camp. It also smelt like one. The stench of people was overwhelming in the growing heat of Northern China, and coupled with the stinking fruit of choice, the Durian fruit, it was retch inducing. We were glad to finally find our private train compartment for the night.

We had made a picnic to take with us and had purchased alcohol at the station shops, and so we settled in for the night. We talked, ate, and drank, till the early hours from our bunk beds and as the sun rose, with the curtains open we watched China's landscape zip before our eyes. Pagodas, paddy fields, shacks and the like. The sky was also clearer and remnants of the first stars I had seen since I left England were apparent.

Arriving at the terminal at Xi'an was crazy, taxi touts and Terracotta Warrior tour touts were out in force, despite the excruciatingly early hour of our arrival in the town. Luckily, foreseeing the transport challenges, I had pre-booked us a transfer to our hotel and swept past the hordes to the safety of our driver and later, our hotel.

This was my first taste of luxury I had experienced since I had joined my brother and his wife at their hotel for drinks. The excitement I felt at sleeping in a lovely cotton sheeted bed was more than I could bear, and the presence of an amazing shower was just a tease. The only thing that disappointed me about the plush hotel room was the same as I had experienced at the 7 Days Inn during my early days, there was a window directly from the toilet into the bedroom.

I had thought it was an oddity of the prostitute ridden hotel I had stayed in, but seeing as this was a 4-star hotel and there were no ladies of the night crawling around it, I was confused. Was watching someone poop 'a thing' here? I wasn't down for that and the blind was firmly pulled down. Much to the relief of Pip who clearly didn't relish watching his friend's ablutions either.

The trip to Xi'an was for less than 24 hours, all that was advised to do by travellers was to whip round the sites and escape again as there was little else to see. So rather than tuck up in the inviting beds for a nap, we headed to reception to pick up our tour guide for the day who would take us via private minibus to the main sites: the Terracotta Warriors, the tombs, and the obligatory retail outlet for which the driver would receive commission on any purchases we made. We weren't in the mood for shopping but it made the trip cheaper so we swallowed it.

But regardless of the peripheral sites the guide needed to take us to in order to earn his commission, the Terracotta Warriors were worth the wasted time and our exhaustion from our intermittent rest on the sleeper train and our ridiculously early start. I can barely find the words to describe why, or how, or do the site any justice at all.

The site of the Terracotta Warriors is the largest underground military museum in the world. And my goodness it's a site to behold. Having only been first discovered in 1974, the sculptures that were hand crafted and positioned to protect the first emperor of China in his afterlife, less than a mile from his burial site, was breath-taking to see.

There have so far, been four main pits of the armies of Qin Shi Huang (the first emperor of China) excavated. There are presumed to be over 8,000 warriors of varying ranks, more than 100 chariots with over 500 horses, alongside over 150 cavalry horses and various other discoveries of officials, acrobats, strong-men and musicians in nearby pits. Imagine walking into a covered football stadium and looking down onto the pitch below you and seeing a sea of life-size men regimentally standing to attention and all staring forward.

Thousands of them. It's eerie, it's surreal, it's magnificent. And that's only one pit – three more are still being excavated and restored. The detail with which they have been sculpted, the precision in their uniform military layout according to rank, the differing facial expressions, their clothes, their stances…it's nothing short of incredible. I don't think Pip and I actually spoke for the entire two hours we were there. I'm definitely sure it was out of wonder, rather than tiredness.

We circled the pits again and again. Wrestling for photos up against the barriers in typically polite English fashion, battling against the crowds of tourists. Sadly between us we couldn't beat the throngs and get a clear view, but it was enough to simply witness the spectacle. If Mitch had made it here, he would have stood no chance of seeing a thing. I'd have had to pop him up on my shoulders. Luckily Pip brought with him some self-sufficient height.

The visit was over before we knew it and we were whisked off to tombs of people that didn't register in my tired brain, and Terracotta Warrior workshops that tried to sell us human sized replicas of what we had just seen that apparently would 'look great in my garden', but not in my hand luggage.

By the time we got back to central Xi'an, we had time for some well earned food and a tired stroll round some markets for Pip's benefit. But all I had in mind was a luxury bed.

We came 'home' from Xi'an via plane, exhausted but eager to grab our stuff from my apartment and move into the central apartment that Pip had rented for us for the next few days – and it was bliss, from the second we walked through the door. Modern, clean, and full of home comforts. No fag-burned sofa's, a second sofa that didn't feel like a park bench, a fully equipped kitchen, two Western style bathrooms, fluffy thick towels and robes, an actual balcony, and luxury bedrooms and bedding. For the next six nights we would be living home-from-Western-home.

We tucked up in bed that night early as we were eager to start fresh and bright in the morning on our Beijing focused tourism efforts. There was so much I had not yet seen or done that I was excited to be sharing it with one of my closest friends.

Due to our central position, Pip had ensured that we would be free of having to attempt the mainline subway from the south east, that I had previously had to suffer too many times, and we could instead visit most of the sites on foot. I was looking forward so much to stress free travel. He had no idea how unwittingly easy he had avoided that trauma.

Beginning our tour of Beijing felt quite personally stressful. I was used to getting myself around this challenging city and learning from my mistakes, but now I felt the pressure to perform, to use my language skills, and make this go smoothly. The truth was – I'd been muddling through every day since I arrived, I didn't know the sites we were about to visit, and I was scared I would let him down. It's also hard to explain to someone visiting Beijing that it will be nothing like they have expected in more ways than one. I'd already warned Pip about the spitting, the strange hygiene, the pooping in the streets etc. so I felt I had the hard stuff out of the way. But there were other things too, that I had never thought to bring up.

One thing that is strange for new people coming to China, especially Beijing I'm sure, is that it is not visually the China that you imagine it to be. Obviously being in a city, there are no paddy fields and workers in conical hats farming rice, like you might see in tourism magazines, nor majestic pagodas at every turn. Instead it is, very simply, a modern metropolis, and without heading off the beaten track of the commercial buildings and multi-lane highways, you will see very little specific to China here, and you could be in any other major city in the world.

Unfortunately a major part of China's political history explains why. The Ming dynasty beauty of the area (The Ming dynasty were the last Han Chinese rulers whose reign ended in the 17th century and whose size and power rivalled the Roman empire) was recklessly destroyed to make way for the modernist high-rise sprawl you see today. Some would claim it was an effort to show the world the progression and economic status of Beijing as a force to be reckoned with against the Western world, a result of Chairman Mao Zedong's reign of power and his quest to implement 'The Great Leap Forward' policies he dreamed up to put Beijing on the world wide stage. A vanity exercise that would see Beijing soar into the upper echelons of international production, manufacturing and industry.

This was an exercise that sadly destroyed the mystique and uniqueness of the picturesque China we once learned about in our school days. It also caused Beijing to become one of the most polluted cities in the world, with towering smokestacks and a rapid increase of road traffic on the new highways.

So extreme was the destruction, Beijing was denied World Heritage status in the early 2000's, and only then did those in charge finally started listening to what the world wished of them.

The Heritage denial and the fact that over half a million of hutong dwellers were displaced by their traditional streets and homes being torn down, finally led to preservation orders to come into place to preserve what little was left of the ancient architecture, and the razing of the beautiful architectural history finally slowed down. Almost too late though sadly, but it was eventually realised that part of Beijing's principle attraction to tourists to this Northern Capital was worth something valuable to the economy, alongside the commercial industry they wished to attract. Pockets of such beauty can still be found, but you sadly have to look hard.

Bearing this in mind, I think Pip was shocked that he'd had to jump through multiple visa hoops and pay an extortionate amount for an airfare to get here, just to 'not see' the Beijing as story books depicted.

However, we were determined to hunt out the 'old China' of which we had learned and seek out what we could find of the remaining Eastern majesty and history the city could provide.

What better place to start than with the iconic Tiananmen Square? A large paved area that Chairman Mao had installed to physically reflect the enormity of the Communist party – and thus his power. It was only a short stroll away, down through the commercial shopping streets of central Beijing close to our apartment.

Tiananmen Square is the world-renowned landmark of the 1989 uprising of students, intellectuals and labour activists, in support of basic human rights, freedom of speech, and against the communist-led Chinese government. They were protesting against all that they believed was wrong about the government and their own future prospects.

The protest began as a largely peaceful process by unarmed attendees, many undertaking a hunger strike to force their point. Their mass presence alone being televised to the world to send powerful messages out to an international audience of the oppression they were living under.

The government reacted badly to the loss of face internationally, banned all continuing media coverage and opened fire on the gathered students and civilians to dispel the crowds, causing a death toll that has never been truly revealed to the world at large. China declared hundreds of deaths, the world counted tens of thousands. But in-line with Chinese propaganda and constant denial of anything negative against their country, one will never truly know the final body count. The guy who faced up a tank, now known as 'tank-man' allegedly didn't actually get killed that day, but his fate and life beyond that day cannot be determined, so who really knows? Footage of the whole incident was unapproved and allegedly smuggled out to the world's news outlets.

Tank Man is still referred to via a code-name on China's own version of social media to avoid the risk of writers and reporters, who dare to discuss it, from being traced. But it just goes to further prove the level of cover-up applied to the entire situation – and country, and perfectly demonstrates the lack of openness of life in Beijing and sharing of news, about which the students were protesting.

Despite the gravity of the human destruction that day, Tiananmen Square, which is ironically named after 'The Gate of Heavenly Peace', is still a target of hundreds and thousands of foreigners and native Chinese tourists at any given time, where the abundance of smiling selfies being taken is appalling. It's a bleak, grey, concrete square of over 100 acres (one of the top ten largest squares in the world). But it's the site of a hideous massacre. There is nothing to smile about here and it was unnerving to see. Whether or not the massacres actually happened within the square itself is another unclear point in history, but what began benignly in this square, caused uncounted fatalities that should forever be in people's minds. The rest of the world know this, but the Chinese propaganda machine has kept it hidden from its own people through its internet restrictions. Do these smiling selfie takers even know the gravity of the history? You have to wonder.

To the south of the huge square, is a fully restored Chinese Qing dynasty style pedestrian Street - Qianmen Dajie. Located near one of the original and preserved gates to the Imperial City that avoided demolition. It looks as if it has come straight out of a film set, and judging by the reported amount spent on its overhaul and refurbishment, whilst stunning, one would be forgiven for wondering how true to life and authentic it really is. Irrespective, it is definitely more as you would imagine a Chinese city to truly look like. But Pip and I wanted the 'real' more than the show-'reel' so we didn't spend too much time there.

Also to the south of the square, is the memorial hall to Chairman Mao Zedong. Home to his embalmed body, laid out in a purportedly crystal coffin. The queues of well wishers wanting to pay their respects to their late leader was ridiculously long and to be honest, neither Pip or I thought viewing a dead body would enrich our visit in any way. No disrespect meant to those who wished to do otherwise – but it wasn't for us.

The east of the square houses the National Museum of China. Again, Pip and I had no interest in visiting such a place. Everyday for the last three months I had seen newspaper sellers on the street report the tragic death of a beautiful young female celebrity. In my whole time here she had died at least 11 times. Even the local papers couldn't get their truth together (who knew if she even existed?), so I doubted that the museum would be particularly faithful to facts, or truly honest about its country's past. I wasn't about to pay to witness further propaganda adorning the walls of a bleak grey building.

West of the square was the 'Great Hall of the People'. Another bleak, but more ostentatious-looking political building. We took pictures but moved swiftly on, seeing no need to view the place where ego and untruths thrived.

Our focus now was the Forbidden Palace, off the north side of the square, through the very grand Meridian Gate, adorned with a gigantic portrait of Mao himself. A portrait I could probably recreate from memory I had seen it that many times across the city

We had high hopes for the Forbidden City, as it was one of the biggest attractions of Beijing. It is a moated and walled city that was purpose built for imperial families and high-ranking officials (by invite only) and commoners were banned from entering. As the home to 24 emperors of China during the Ming and Qing dynasties, it is the best-preserved imperial palace complex in the world, and we were keen to experience its wonders.

Sadly, whilst the architecture was stunningly beautiful, the stuff of travel magazines, the buildings were internally largely bereft of artefacts and truly authentic style. 20th century lootings by the Japanese, shipping containers of relics carted off to Taiwan, the Cultural Revolution destroying much of what was left and regular fires in the highly flammable wooden City had left very little to study. Add that to the refurbishment and repainting carried out to cater for the incoming crowds expected for the Olympics, the authenticity of the one million square metres of palace to which we had limited access to, was a little disappointing.

Heading out north of the Forbidden City was also a shock to the system. Whilst homelessness is illegal in Beijing, beggars had found their perfect spot at the exit to this tourist attraction. I had not seen anything as distressing in my whole time here in the city that came anything close to this. Whilst Pip and I are used to London and its begging community, as well as in most major cities we had visited, this felt like more of an assault to the senses and the heartstrings. The sheer number of severely disabled beggars here was like nothing we had ever seen. We gave what we could in return for small hand-made crafts but felt uneasy about who or what situation we were donating too and moved swiftly on.

To the north of the Forbidden City lies a man-made hill called Jingshan Park. One of the very few contours in the landscape of

Beijing. It was constructed from all the mud and soil extracted for the establishment of the moat surrounding the City that kept intruders and commoners out. It was collected at the north to shield the emperors from the bad feng shui coming from that direction and it resulted in one of the most breath-taking views of Beijing that we were yet to see.

The steep hill takes 20-30 minutes to walk up, through winding paths of beautiful flora and fauna and ends in a magnificent pagoda at its peak. Below us, the orange rooftops of the Forbidden City lay out before us. It looked like the China of dreams. The sun was beginning to set which only made the sight more stunning. Regardless of the high-rise commercial buildings to the left of the view and the haze of the pollution in the sky, it still felt like we would never see anything quite so picturesque in our tour of the city.

As our first Beijing-centric day came to a close, we wandered home and relaxed over dinner at a restaurant local to our apartment and rested our feet for our next day of adventures. And although it had been snowing three months prior, we ended up having to nurse our sunburn, like typical Brits after their first glimpse of sun after many months of rain.

The following day we decided to do less walking than we had the previous day so opted for rickshaw travel to our next destination. Walking back to the foot of Jingshan Park we hopped on our transport and headed to Houhai, a lake to the north of the Forbidden City, renowned for its bars, traditional buildings, preserved hutongs and waterside views.

We arrived at the southern edge of the water to be confronted by an American coffee chain and throngs of tourists. Not exactly what we had hoped for but an experience in itself. There were locals perched on small stools offering head and neck massages that looked more like physical assaults than relaxation, boats on the water stuffed with unimpressed tourists and building works and scaffolding as far as the eye could see. The sound track to the day was the Chinese Zither, a plucked string instrument, played in various spots along the southern bank. Obviously this location was deemed to be an upcoming centre of attraction and was being commercialised accordingly. It wasn't unpleasant by any means, but we had no desire to hang around the masses.

We escaped the crowds and began a walk around the edges of the lake and were nicely surprised at what we saw beyond the initial hubbub. Despite the sheer number of modern and distinctly Western style bars, for the first time in weeks I saw that outside living was possible in this city and actually looked quite pleasant. Granted this was a low pollution day and the sky was more blue than grey, it was still a very pretty area to spend time in. The flowers were blooming, the roof terraces overlooking the water on one side, and the hutongs on the other side, were really worth the extra pence you had to pay for your food and drink to allow you to savour it. There were also less high-rise buildings and noise that it actually felt genuinely relaxing. We embraced the calm after our busy few days.

Authentic or not, it was a lovely taste of the China that again we thought we would be experiencing but had not yet really found outside of the large tourist sites. After kicking back with a beer, some food and absorbing the views, we wended our way behind the water of the lake into the hutongs which had been spared destruction. Low-rise, calm, traditional streets. Courtyard gardens, lanterns in trees, pagodas, manicured flower beds, rickshaws but no cars…peace and beauty.

Later we trekked on to more preserved hutongs in Nanluogu Xiang (meaning South Gong and Drum Alley) that had received a facelift in recent times with the addition of bars, eateries and tourist accommodation, but still represented the more traditional (less wealthy than Houhai) living streets of ancient times. Taking a climb up the Drum tower at one end of the street, where drums used to be beaten to mark the hours of the day, just like London's Big Ben, we took in the view of the greyer hutong roofs and had a glimpse of how cramped the living arrangements had probably been in the wider city. It felt more 'real' than the central Beijing where we were currently staying.

That said, due to having a big day still to come visiting the Great Wall, we unashamedly enjoyed the ease of the commercial street bars of central Beijing that evening. That way Pip got to experience the not-so-subtle way in which Chinese tourists tried to surreptitiously snap us in the backgrounds of their photographs, having probably never seen a white person before they visited Beijing – and to be fair, there were still very few of us in this metropolis that we were still novel, so we played along. We smiled, gave the obligatory peace signs, posed with their families if we were asked to, and let them touch our hair and skin. It was fun, and friendly, and people were very kind to us. Although we largely couldn't understand what they were saying, hopefully it was positive.

He also came to learn of the younger generation's habit of 'twinning' whereby you mark being in a relationship by wearing identical clothes to your other half. Whilst the girls looked cute, the guys looked awkward wearing matching 'Hello Kitty' t-shirts and pink trainers. Pip could not be persuaded to join in with that behaviour despite me promising we could pick something a little more masculine to twin with.

The following morning brought with it a tour guide and a day trip to a lesser-frequented part of the Great Wall of China. I had visited the heavily overcrowded Baddaling with my brother, his wife and Aoife, and did not relish the thought of doing that route again. Instead Pip had planned an escorted trip to hike up the Jiankou section of the wall, stroll along the wall itself to Mutianyu and then head down again. It would take approximately four hours and would begin at a rugged and unrestored area of the wall requiring a hike and a rock-climb up to the first Great Wall tower, 1000 metres above sea level, a hike along the rough wall into a restored area of the wall where we could then get a toboggan down from the wall to the pick-up zone. I had looked forward to it until I saw the steaming hot weather forecast and began to panic.

Luckily our escort took our bags from us and we only had to carry water and our cameras for the duration of the hike because, whilst absolutely out-of-this-world stunning, it was also exhausting and dangerous. Pretty sure health and safety in England would not have allowed such a hairy trek.

It was also very different from my Baddaling experience. Baddaling was overflowing with people along a well-restored section of the wall after a comfortable cable car ride up - whilst our hike was bereft of people, involved collapsed ruins and was almost completely swallowed by nature in parts. Photographs we took included no-one in the backgrounds; there weren't even apparent paths. We scuffed our knees and got blisters on our hands climbing sheer and crumbling rock faces. It was exhilarating. The sheer size and scope of this incredible piece of construction really hit home during this visit. The views of the Great Wall spread for miles, the many towers dotted along the wall now fully visible, the snaking length and height in places made us both speechless. But quite honestly, so did the exertion required to get there. Worth every bead of sweat, however. We earned our sleep that night, for sure.

The following couple of days I dragged Pip round the commercial streets of Beijing, introduced him to the sights and smells of Wanfujing Snack Street where he understandably denied himself the opportunity to sample scorpions on sticks, snake snacks and starfish. He was tempted by the seahorses and cicadas but after threatening him with the likelihood I would vomit watching him do so, he relented.

We toured temples with heady and overwhelming levels of burning incense such as the Lama Temple (a huge Tibetan Buddhist temple which to my disappointment was not home to any actual Llamas). We visited tea houses, dodged the art sellers who wanted to lure us into their galleries and charge us a mortgage for the drinks they would provide for us. We ran from one legged beggars who accused us of taking pictures of them when we were only trying to capture sights in which they were accidentally visible, drank more beer on the streets, picked up freshly cooked gourmet snacks from the local 7/11's and watched brides-to-be posing with their future husbands outside all the weird non-traditional landmarks you could shake a stick at, but that would look great in images hung on their walls.

We also visited the world-renowned Summer Palace, a gigantic and well-preserved royal park, which, I'm sure, would have been a stunning trip had it not torrentially rained on us, were unable to get a taxi home and ended up walking miles back to civilisation.

Our days were exhausting, enlightening, hilarious and full. For the first time in weeks I felt I had truly experienced what tourists to the city had experienced, enjoyed, and regaled to their friends back home. It was worlds apart from my experience of trying to 'live' here, which had been challenging to say the least. I can also very realistically understand that people who have visited for a short while and loved the place would never, ever, understand the truth of attempting to exist here if they had only followed the visitor agenda whilst boarding in smart hotels. The two worlds I have experienced in my time here are like chalk and cheese.

Pip and I celebrated our last night of his visit, and my last night of freedom before I started my teaching contract the following day, at a famous duck restaurant. The ambience was incredible, his company was perfect, food tasted amazing. A perfect end, to a perfect adventure.

Until two hours later when he was tucked up in bed sleeping and I was vomiting all over our second bathroom.

30

LEAVE YOUR DREAMS AT THE DOOR

The
Beginning
of the End

After a hectic and exhausting week off finally being a tourist in the country I had been living in for all this time, I started work bright and early the following morning. Not a great start to the day having spent the previous night, until the early hours, being violently sick due to dodgy duck, but there was no way I was going to call in sick on my very first day. I had to make a good impression if I was to make this work. Before I left the city-based apartment Pip and I had enjoyed for the last few days, I had bid him an emotional goodbye as he set off in his taxi to the airport and I then headed back to my apartment on the east side with my cases, in order to get to school on time.

The day begun with Scottish Frank sitting Aoife and myself down in a staff meeting to drill us with rules and regulations about our new workplace.

Yes, Aoife and myself...Didn't I tell you? In their usual 'guess what's coming next' style, they had, during my week off, told her that she would instead be joining me at South East where she wouldn't have any classes of her own (still) but would be running freebie classes for drop-in students and doing demonstration classes to prospective students, sales pitch style to let them test-drive our teaching before signing up to courses.

She wasn't best pleased but at least she would be having contact with students and not simply emptying bins or tidying poorly photocopied textbooks at the City School (apparently there are no copyright laws in China and the tight wads of the London Linked School don't see fit to get their students legitimate books despite the astronomical fees they receive from them).

So, there we both are on our first day ready to be inducted. I won't bore you with the details laboriously delivered by Scottish Frank who is seemingly devoid of facial expression or personality. Instead I shall give you an overview of the prison we were in:

We were now working in Big Brother's den. There was a fingerprint recognition system in place to clock in and out on. We were to work nine hour days with an unpaid lunch break taken at a time of the schools choosing, even when we had no scheduled classes that day to work around. There were CCTV cameras in every classroom monitoring our activity and teaching.

The classrooms were like goldfish bowls and whilst we were teaching, the parents are permitted to stand on the other side of the glass watching us like hawks or viewing us on CCTV along with management should they choose to watch too. Poor performance giving a demo class that results in too low a sign-up rate immediately afterwards would be a disciplinary situation (despite being trained to teach, we were now also front-line sales people) and the depressing list goes on. It's entirely possible they modelled the school on George Orwell's literary masterpiece '1984'.

I've written a lot about just how bad the school was to work at prior to this experience, but I'm sure you don't need to be bored with the details of the unprofessionalism of the school. After all you've heard so far, I'm sure you will trust me when I say it was a sham.

In summary, I was scheduled for nine hour working days, five days a week, staggered two days off a week, and only one to two hours of teaching per day if I was lucky. The two hours being of bratty three-year-olds who we were expected to plonk at a desk and be taught and behave studiously, whilst being observed by their parents who were so rich and snotty that as a teacher you could never be good enough for their little prince or princess.

The children, who I might add, had clearly never been brought up with an ounce of discipline (I'm certain because of the one-child policy and gratitude by the parents of even being allowed a child) and at the age of three were the most spoilt, rude and horrible children I had ever had the displeasure to meet. I felt absolutely nothing positive for these children, I'm ashamed to say, but alongside an intense dislike was also sheer pity and despair for the educational regime they were growing into. They were such small children, it wasn't their fault at all.

The one child policy had a lot to answer for with regards to how doted on and lavished these kids were, but it also meant that these babies were on the first steps of a path to intolerable pressure and no childhood.

They were destined for the next 20 years of their lives to be studying 14 hours a day, seven days a week thanks to overbearing parents and a society that dictates that if you don't succeed in academia you are nothing, and your family is nothing. This is a society that ignores any disability too and children who need extra help don't get it – everyone acts like nothing is wrong. They are forced through their childhood with such high expectations so as not to put their parents in a position of 'losing face' that they become robots.

And here I was at the beginning of their miserable transformation. I did not want to be a part of this.

To annoy me further, my hours were predominantly 11-8pm or 1-10pm every day – not great for a social life and that ever sought-after work life balance. Plus, my days off were Tuesday's and Friday's – not even two days in a row, and none of my friends had the same days off as me so I was going to be pretty lonely. No social life, no job satisfaction, no desire even to be in this country, after all the positivity I had been determined to feel.

With the weight of Rob leaving and a great 'holiday' with my dear friend, reality really did start to set in when I formally began my contract to teach at the South East School. I wasn't filled with hope about how I would change the world child by child anymore; I just considered this a route to the next step, beyond China, away from this misery. It kept my options open for whatever else I would be doing in the world. Whether or not it was teaching I just didn't know, but I was loathed to waste the training I had just done, and deep in my heart I knew that if I gave up now I would probably go home and never leave England ever again after the traumatic experience I'd had to date. I saw this as a way of beating China, rather than it beating me.

On that note, I sucked it up and had every intention of making this work for the short time needed, to see out my planned six months here.

So, every day, 20-minutes before my designated teaching hours began, I used to trundle off to the South East School to work. And every day I had to experience the heart-wrenching trip past Rob's apartment to the institution where I worked.

As I came out of my apartment, I had to cross the four lane highway to get to the side of the street that held the school compound. After playing chicken on the road, I would be greeted by a huge fake neon rainbow that marked the entrance to the residential compound within which I worked.

To get into the compound I had to pass through a small gate in some iron railings demarcating the community. I used to smile to myself in bitterness every time I did this…'go past the rainbow and through the metal gates'…it felt like a metaphor for 'leave your dreams at the door'. And it could not be truer.

Once upon a time I used to do this walk to Rob's apartment block, and I never saw the metaphor, I never acknowledged my surroundings – I focused only on the destination. But now all I saw was the entrapment.

The school was, as the crow flies, the other side of Rob's apartment block, which meant that I either had to walk around, or through, the void under his apartment block.

I never walked around, always walking through. Mimicking the act of heading to the elevators to get upstairs to see him. Unfortunately, I had no reason to call the lift ever again, and as I walked past the call button my heart cried a little. I wasn't on my way to happiness; I was on my way to torture. For children, for myself.

The worst thing was, apart from Rob being gone, my job was the complete farce I had realised it to be on that first induction day with Scottish Frank. And as much as I hoped for my existence in this country to mean something – I'm pretty sure it didn't.

And to make matters worse, Scottish Frank – 'the saviour of the school' – was a pathetic and petty man, who clearly didn't like me.

I got called to have a word with him on several occasions:

I had apparently used more holiday than I was entitled. Pervy Jim had told both Aoife and I that two national holidays that fell during our CELTA course would be honoured. He was now denying having offered us this and now Frank was practically calling us liars and claiming we owed the school two days unpaid.

After requesting a last-minute day off because my parents had booked an equally last-minute visit to Beijing (to persuade me to leave) it was met with incredulity that I should dare ask for another one. It was then granted 'as a favour' and made clear I would not be given any more time off for the rest of the year. Yes, it was cheeky of me but if you don't ask you don't get, and let's face it, I wasn't feeling the love for my job and after almost four months of serious challenges, I wasn't going to sacrifice any of my time with my parents.

He also pulled me up for not finger printing in and out when I went home for my lunch break. This was not for any fire safety measures but simply because they were ready to pounce and dock your pay if you did less than 30 seconds under your scheduled hours – regardless of if you had to stay late or come in early. Therefore, finger printing your attendance to the school was essential for the tracking of your timeliness only.

I was already questioning at this stage whether I could face sticking out my newly signed contract. I hated the pettiness of the people running the place, I despised their patronising of all the staff - Chinese or otherwise, I was disgusted at their money grabbing approach and unethical teaching approach and the list goes on. Not least having to witness Pervy Jim's behaviour with small children he himself taught.

It is never appropriate to lock yourself in a toilet cubicle with a young child when they needed to pee, it wasn't funny the jokes he made about how easy it was to work in China without being police checked, it made me sick to my stomach when he gushed about how pretty or 'hot' some of the pre-school aged little girls were. It was DISGUSTING and deplorable. It just wasn't a pleasant, ethical or rewarding place to work. Plus, they didn't care about their staff one iota. So, I didn't care for them either.

The crunch point came however, when they expected me to work in the country illegally.

When I arrived in China, as per TEFL 'X', I was to be granted 'work permissions' in relation to my visa. This meant transferring me from the visa I arrived in the country with to one which meant I could legally be an employee and receive a salary in China. I'd come over on an internship visa, which meant although I could be in the country for business or training purposes, I was not allowed to be paid as an employee. This should have been upgraded upon my arrival in China but we all know what a screw up that was so it was no surprise they hadn't fixed it sooner.

Despite constant reminders over the past three months they still had done nothing to make me legal in China. Naturally this concerned me greatly. But it also confirmed my suspicions that for a long while they had had no intention of keeping me on. They had only given me a job now because they'd discovered 90% of the current teaching staff would not be returning in September and I would be useful in plugging a gap for them when the time came.

The day I began my new contract at the school, I had 12 days left on my existing visa. It was the first thing I mentioned at the staff meeting on my very first day formally starting at the school – that this needed to be fixed ASAP - and properly. Frank assured me he would look into it.

The same day he came back to me and told me I needed to provide a passport photo for Mr Qing (the 'official' owner of the school – aka the Chinese guy on all the schools paperwork who is a cover to the government for Dodgy Alfie) so that the paperwork could be processed. This was a pleasantly quick move by the otherwise lacklustre London Linked School so I was pleased that I wouldn't be having to rush out of the country when I wasn't yet prepared, or packed, my parents were coming and so forth.

My current visa also did not allow for re-entry, so if anything went wrong, my parents would have to be here alone. I questioned when I would find out about a date for my medical (to get the proper visa you have to pass all manner of physical tests) and again he said he would get back to me.

Days passed, my visa got closer and closer to expiry and all I was hearing was 'it'll get sorted'. Eventually I was told that I was to meet Mitchell and Mr Qing at the visa office in two days' time, three days before my visa officially ran out. I'd still had no medical and knew this would take time so I questioned what was happening about it. I received a curt response from Frank telling me that my old visa would be renewed 'as is' and not upgraded. My response regarding illegality of employment on that type of visa was met with: "Well, 12 days' notice didn't give us much choice did it?" i.e. it was my fault. I was furious – I'd given them three months of constant reminders and now they were blaming me for this situation?

It was the last straw. I knew I had to resign. The only thing stopping me from walking away there and then was the fact that my parents were due to visit in ten days' time and I didn't want to let them down (like I felt I had done since I arrived in China) - and I desperately wanted to see them and prove to them the craziness of this country. I figured if I renewed my visa then resigned, I then had plenty of time to see my parents and time to pack up and leave the country ASAP after they had gone home again. Otherwise, I was going to exit this damned country three days into their trip and leave them to fend for themselves which I absolutely would not do.

So, the day of the embassy visit arrived and I met Mr Qing as commanded, at the immigration office. Little Mitch was with him of which I was glad. I hadn't seen his familiar face in a while and it was reassuring to know once again there were at least two of us in the same almighty pile of manure.

Before we were led into the visa office, Mr Qing stopped us, literally on the pavement outside the main doors, and explained that getting visas at the moment was a very risky and scrutinised process and that we must get our stories straight before we went in.

The back story for this current challenge in visa processing was due to mobile phone video footage being spread around the internet of a man on a UK tourist visa sexually assaulting a woman in the expat area of Beijing. The tourist was then beaten to the ground by a gang of Chinese and the UK man was arrested. (Word on the street is that the guy was drugged up to the eyeballs and set up by the dealers who doubled as this girl's pimps – but that's a whole other theory).

Although the authorities do not claim this incident to be a direct factor in how they are currently treating visas, it has proved to be a great tool in drumming up hate for Westerners in their country and justifying the start of a 100-day clampdown on illegal aliens in Beijing for which all residents of Beijing are being asked to report the presence of foreigners in their communities for checks. The fact that the clampdown may be part of smoke and mirrors for current governmental change or political gain is neither here nor there – it was happening. And it had begun in earnest literally the day before we were stood outside the visa office.

And so, Mitchell and I were told to say, if questioned, that we were interns, we weren't getting paid in China, we were on a 'cultural awareness trip' and were being subsidised by the UK. If we didn't, then the school would get a slap on the wrists. So, in effect, it sounded like we were being asked to do the school a favour and that in fact it wasn't so much of a big of deal that I had come to believe.

It wasn't until we had handed over our passports for processing that the immigration and visa lady handed us both a press release detailing the nature of the 100-day crackdown, which clearly showed the illegal workers criteria, i.e. Mitchell and myself, to be the ones in trouble – not the employers. We personally could face fine, detention, deportation and a ban from China for the next five years. And there it was, in black and white. The severity of the 100-day clampdown meant that they were enforcing it harshly, in a very publicised manner, to hold Westerners up as examples.

I felt sick. I now didn't have my passport in my hand. It had already been whipped away for processing, ready for collection in seven days, so I couldn't even leave the country if I wanted to now.

And so here began the planning of my exit. I had to collect my visa in seven days' time and then within 24 hours I was legally required to re-register my residence at the local police station i.e. show up with passport, visa and initial residency certificate. I couldn't re-register alone (language barriers and landlord implications) so I needed the school's help to do this. If I resigned right now will I get the help I need or will they force me into a doubly bad situation of not only being illegally employed but being an illegal alien too?

I had to think carefully about how best to deal with this. I had the following day off and after a fitful night of sleep I had decided that my only way forward was to resign ASAP, but ensure the cooperation of the school to help me register at the police station. Although I knew many people who hadn't registered in a timely fashion before, I realised now was not the time to be taking chances and with my run of luck, I didn't feel like taking any chances at all. So that day, I started to pack up my things from the apartment. I wasn't planning to leave imminently if I didn't need to, but I wanted to feel prepared just in case.

The following day I went in to work as usual (already having packed my belongings and living out of a bag) with the plan to assess the likelihood of visa trouble. I spoke to my old buddy Frank about being angry that I was now in a risky situation and he scornfully replied "I've been here ten years and never once been stopped by the police. I never even carry my passport" (it's a legal requirement that you have your passport and valid visa on you at all times in Beijing in case of stop and search by the police – which is ridiculous seeing as the number one trouble of tourists is that their passport has been lost or stolen).

So basically, he told me I was overreacting and reminded me that it was my fault that they hadn't had time to get me a legitimate one. My fury was bubbling…

I went home that night and gave it more thought, read through my teaching contract and decided that I would resign tomorrow, but try my utmost to get guarantees of assistance from the school regarding my visa and the police station visit. From what I could see in my contract I also had to give four weeks' notice so as far as I was concerned, the sooner I could resign the better – the quicker this was over the safer I would feel. Another sleepless night and no appetite saw me going to school on the Saturday, letter in hand. Only to discover Frank wasn't in to give it to. I was reluctant to just drop the letter and run, or email it, without having talked my requirements through with him face to face – for what it was worth.

Luckily come Sunday afternoon Frank was in and I was able to hand over my resignation letter. It was no surprise to him that I was doing this – I must have been the most challenging employee he had ever come across so I'm pretty sure he was happy to receive it anyway. I went home feeling relieved that I was at least making tracks in my plan and was a step closer to not breaking any laws in a country where punishments would be unthinkable. Call me paranoid but I didn't trust that things were going to work out okay. I'd seen enough of this country to know that things were never smooth and more often than not, I was the victim.

And sure enough, Monday brought with it more challenges.

Frank called me to one side to discuss my resignation. Although I had said I would work my four weeks notice as contractually obliged, he tried to negotiate with me that I cut it down to five days instead as that was the pay cut off point and was convenient for them. As for my classes, as Aoife had none of her own, these would transfer immediately to her so really there was no longer a use for me in the school.

This should have been a great relief, to know I was leaving sooner. However, I had a dilemma in my head. My parents were arriving in five days time, staying for ten (which slipped us into June), and if I didn't get my notice paid, then I would have to pay an extra month's rent on the apartment just to tour guide my parents and I was dammed if the school was going to cost me more money.

I already had in mind that I had five days sick leave to 'use up' and was planning to use them whilst my parents were here anyway - thanks to the grabbing back of two days they had done to me anyway I didn't care that I was being petty too. And as for the visa/employment thing, I was already at-risk during May anyway, so I figured I might as well get the full whack salary because if anything, it would cover the fine I would have to pay if I was caught(!) This is crazy talk isn't it – but I wasn't thinking rationally. But basically, he was trying to force me to do the school a favour and save it money and I didn't feel inclined at that moment in time to agree because it didn't work for me.

I told him I would give it some thought and with that our meeting was over and Frank disappeared off in a huff. I assume, although it's hard to tell given his inability to show any real expression. Ten minutes later he finds me at my desk to hand to me back my holiday request form for the day I had booked to be with my parents with 'CANCELLED" written all over it. His explanation was that it had been reviewed and they had decided not to give it to me - but 'hey', he tells me sarcastically, 'if you take the five days notice period then you'll have all the time in the world to spend with your parents'. I resisted the urge to knock him out.

As it turns out, the situation was taken out of my hands. An hour or so later I get called to one side with Frank again. This time his face has cracked to smugness (which surprises me – I thought it was stuck) and he patronisingly informs me that Chinese labour laws state that if you have been working less than a month on a contract, you're apparently only entitled to a weeks' notice anyway. When I asked to see these labour laws and questioned why they were not referred to in my contract and doesn't he think they should have been seeing as they relate to the legalities of the contract, he waives me off and tells me they're all written in Chinese. Based on the fact I can't read Chinese what would be the point in showing it to me.

Again, I resisted the urge to knock him out, but it was considerably harder to control this time.

My response was to tell him that I would leave the school right that minute and that I want gardening leave. He agrees and asks me to wait around whilst he types me up a letter to formally accept my resignation, detail my final day of employment and that I could stay in the apartment until the end of the month. Cheeky man tries to whip a further two days off my notice period, so I get him to correct it, and with that done I finally leave the school for the last time. At that point in time I genuinely didn't even care if I eventually got paid for the work I'd have done or not. The feeling of it being over was so overwhelmingly good, loss of wages aside. I never had to go back there.

For the first time in months I felt like a weight had been lifted off my shoulders.

The relief didn't last long though – but then it never does in this tale does it?

THE UGLY

The
Beginning
of the End

L ess than 24 hours after I had been unceremoniously dismissed and granted my garden leave – the school was raided by the police and immigration.

On the Tuesday afternoon, a small army of police and immigration officers burst into the school armed with video cameras. They pushed their way into the teachers office, capturing on film all of my friends faces and demanding passports and visas. They interviewed Mole Noel who was just arriving at the school and questioned the accountant and Chinese staff at some length about foreign employees.

During their interviews they grilled my friends on the origins of their visas (which were issued from the City School where Mr Qing resides) and questioned at length the link between the schools to establish the validity of their visas. During their investigations and search of the premises they took documents, teaching schedules and records from the school away with them. All for the purposes of identifying illegal workers as part of their 100-day crackdown.

And who was the only one of the employees of the school not on the right visa? Me.

And who was the only one that wasn't in school that day? Me.

Thank my lucky stars.

Aoife kept me up to date with developments at the South East School that afternoon via phone and I'll be honest enough to say it made me tremble. My first thought after my initial relief that I wasn't there, was to contact Mitchell and make him aware. He was the only other illegal employee and although he was based in the City School, the authorities had been heavy on establishing the link between the schools and therefore it stood to reason that they would check City at any moment too.

Once Mitchell had been warned, Aoife rang to fill me in some more on the happenings. That's when I learned that the police had taken away paperwork and schedules from the school and I panicked. My name would be all over them surely?

My mind starting whirring…tomorrow I pick up my visa and then I actually have to walk into the heart of the lion's den to declare my existence to the police…what if they have my name to cross check against? What if they have already looked me up and have seen where I live? No-one expected a school raid in a million years, who's to say they won't come knocking at my door? And if the community has been encouraged to report all foreigners, legally residing or not, how do I know that if the police are active in this area, they aren't going to turn up right now?

My mind was totally flipping out on me… Something happened today that hadn't been heard of in Frank's ten years of teaching in China…in my head there were no boundaries now. And I felt sick.

The following day was the day that both Mitchell and I had to collect our passports and visas and then rock up to the police station in the 24 hours following. Needless to say, it was not something I was relishing doing.

I, very cowardly, made Mitchell do the trip on his own in the following morning to collect his documents and then, on his way home from the visa office, he was going to call and register his residency at his local police station. I was curious to hear if he had any problems or scrutiny to face. He was in a safer position than me anyway having not had his name raised to the police and I had no doubts that the boy could talk his way out of a plastic bag if anything came up. But I just wanted to check all the same.

His trip went smoothly so I started to relax a little about my own and began my own journey into the city to get my passport back. This was trouble free and had me home safe and sound within a couple of hours. The next trip was to the police station though, which was the bit I was most nervous about. Luckily Honey, Pete's Chinese girlfriend, had been an angel and written down for me, in Chinese, all the communications I would need to complete my registration on my own. And if I walked to the school, she would pop out, meet me and find me a taxi that she would direct. As I walked towards the school, I passed a police car. I felt sick.

As I got to the school, there was a police car outside. I felt sick. Then, when it proved difficult to get a taxi and seeing as it was a searingly hot day and I felt so sick with apprehension, I wondered maybe if I could just get it all over with and just hand myself in to one of these policemen, then maybe I'd get a lift to the police station and wouldn't end up melting on the street.

Thankfully it didn't come to that. Honey won in the end and sent me on my way. Honey truly was a good friend to me. If only she wasn't such a rare gem, I might have felt more settled in China, but alas.

And I'm sorry to report, for the purpose of it not being a more exciting story; I strolled in and out of that police station as if I didn't have a care in the world. Now officially legally re-registered and technically not employed, I should have felt relief. But despite this non-employment fact, I was still being processed on a payroll somewhere – and immigration and police had records of this, which indicated to the authorities that I HAD been illegally working. And just because they hadn't yet tied up their paperwork, didn't mean I wasn't still at great risk. The terrifying feeling, I had felt every day when I arrived in Beijing, was now firmly back inside me.

Thankfully none of the following sees me detained courtesy of the Chinese government. What it is though, is part of the final chapter of how leaving China behind couldn't have come soon enough.

My final two weeks in the country saw me free of the school and tour guiding my parents around Beijing, and in return, them sharing with me their shoulder to cry on whilst I finally had a breakdown over the stress of my past few months – I took full advantage of the comfort and the relief of them being with me that I cried on a daily basis. It was a hard two weeks for me personally, not wanting to spend any more time in the country that had treated me appallingly and that I now, more than ever, still feared, and desperately wished to escape the bad memories it held for me just as soon as their visit was over.

Every night after leaving them at their hotel and returning to my apartment, I felt depressed. These four walls held so many memories for me and aside from the great ones I had there, with my wonderful friend and saviour Aoife, gold hearted Amity and Rob - who I missed every day since he escaped China a few weeks previously – the four walls also represented the misery I had been through too.

Battles had been fought for the place, battles had been dissected in that place - and now all it held was ghosts which I didn't want reminding of. Every time I looked out of the window, I saw a world I hated, I could see the route to the school from my window where all my troubles began and ended, and every time I slept alone in my bed the sadness and mental exhaustion of the personal trials I had been through overwhelmed me.

So, needless to say, I wasn't the happiest tour guide for my parents (I certainly didn't deserve a tip - put it that way) but I did manage to prove to them the things I had written in my diaries were true, and it really was as challenging as I had described it to be. Call it an insider's view if you will. You won't find their experience in any travel brochures at your local friendly travel agent that's for sure.

Yes, they saw the spitting, the dead emotionless faces of the nation staring back at them, the disgusting sanitation in the seemingly modern metropolis, the unnecessary argy bargy on the subway, the complete lack of manners or customer service, the Gucci styled dogs, the country's less favourable delicacies, the ridiculous fashion sense and so forth.

But I think the memories of their trip that will be their most talked about are enough to explain my complete lack of love and sheer disgust for this country, and compound my desire to put it all behind me. These stories are yet to come…

During their visit to Beijing, I arranged a them fully guided and hand-held tour to Xi'an to see the Terracotta Warriors. I had booked them return flights so they didn't have to go through the trauma of the sleeper trains and related station nightmares.

A huge bonus of their trip away for me was that I could use their hotel room to hide away in whilst they were gone. Proper shower, lovely 5* food cooked for me, and a closeted existence from the 'real' Beijing for my last few days here, and I used this opportunity to start saying my goodbyes to my friends, knowing that within a few days of my parents return, I too would be leaving this country.

My first and most important goodbye was with Mitch. The person who had unwittingly entered this whole surreal saga by my side. And whilst I was hiding out at the hotel, he was a ten-minute stroll from me. We decided to meet at an Irish bar opposite the hotel around lunch-time, that Aoife and I had been to a couple of times after our lessons, a five-minute walk from the City School.

We met outside but he then immediately whisked me off to an area I had not been to before, about five-minutes down past his apartment block. It was a food centre and off the tourist track. He had been taking Mandarin lessons and was using meal times as a way to practice his newly acquired language in these very local places, where it was rare to find even an utterance of an English word. He carried with him a very tired looking A4 sheet of paper on which he had written a list of all the words he wanted to know, and his tutor had written in Mandarin their translation in pinyin. He didn't bother with sentences but so long as the key words were said he reckoned he could get by. His list of food translations filled much of the paper, and included the pinyin for dog and cat. I too knew these words however, so if he dared to try and order those for lunch, I would be crushing his windpipe.

We ended up with too much meat and too few vegetables. The amount of chillies in the hotpot broth was so strong we were both sweating, noses running and crying like babies by the end. Mitch admitted he may have underestimated the strength he had ordered and made a little note on his crib sheet not to order again. Too late for the linings of our digestive tracts - but it was so 'Mitch' it was hilarious. Bearing in mind I'd watched him sob, sitting on a kerb, after eating too much Wasabi, you'd have thought he would have learned.

Needless to say we needed something to neutralise the burn so Mitch suggested we go via a fruit and veg market on our way and buy ourselves ingredients to make smoothies back at his. So that's what we did. I begged him not to go for the stinking Durian fruit that was banned in so many upmarket establishments because of its stench and he thankfully resisted. Armed with a wide array of fruit, milk and yoghurt, we headed back to his apartment.

His apartment was in a low storey block and a lot less dodgy or oppressive looking than mine. Although there were still rickety bikes and discarded plant pots and the odd shoe discarded in the communal hallway, it had a more upmarket feel to it. The reason being that the two-bedroom apartment he had been given a room in by the school was the CELTA tutor's housing, so I'm guessing it had to make a better impression than most of our apartments did. It was a professional home. However, it did mean that the door was revolving and from one month to the next he would not know who he would be living with. His current roomie was coincidentally my own CELTA tutor who was taking some time out before the next course to do a little travelling, so Mitch was home alone for a while.

The apartment itself was relatively Western. Two bedrooms, a neat bathroom and a kitchen with an oven, which was very rare here. Unlike my apartment that only had a hob and a fridge, this was fully catered for with all mod cons and tasteful artwork on the walls. I felt he had landed on his feet after our initial debacle with this very central and maintained home. His only problem at the moment was an infestation of small, ant-sized maggot type insects that were flooding out of an unsealed hole in his shower. It was currently plugged up with toothpaste. Having tried shaving foam and toilet paper prior to this fix, toothpaste was the current winner as its staying power during a shower was apparently strong. He was pleased with his efforts.

As we (I) set about preparing our smoothies to quench the fire in our gullets, Mitch appeared with some nun chucks. In his time here, he had tried to embrace the Chinese ways of kung fu and other traditional arts. He had a fascination with Bruce Lee. But on attending the first few sessions of kung fu, a mixture of not understanding the commands and the lack of Bruce Lee finesse, he had given it up. Instead he bought nun chucks and was trying to teach himself via the power of YouTube, a lifetime art.

He had a playlist of Bruce Lee clips and tried to copy his idol. His first set of nun chucks were a serious weapon. Heavy, and long. A definite weapon that stretches your arm just holding them. He showed me them to me proudly and attempted to show me a few moves. Basically, just swinging them around in a weird and uncoordinated manner, narrowly missing light fittings. He apologised for not being particularly good and a little nervous, because during an earlier practice he had swung them round his head so fast they had wrapped round his body and smacked him so hard in the testicles he was concerned about having children in the future.

When that had happened, he had purchased a beginner's set that were lighter, made of rubber, and not so long against his short body that a body wrap would mean they could not threaten his groin.

On the other hand, his other typically Chinese hobby of table tennis was going fairly well and he was adept at persuading the visiting CELTA tutors to join him in the basement on the public tables. Thus, he was improving at something that would not cause him bodily harm and he was happy.

As for the teaching side of things, he was really enjoying it and getting stuck in. He took his work seriously and his success was the crucial key to him getting to Hong Kong. The school had promised him a legal visa when his came up for renewal in a few weeks and although he would have to find his own accommodation from thereon, he was not fazed. Life was treating him well and the challenges of China, although still incredibly frustrating for him, he relished as a challenge.

What helped was that he had also discovered a massage parlour that treated him like a King. He went a couple of times a week and because he was a Western male, he was always well serviced. He assured me that there was nothing untoward during his visits and that it was genuinely just a massage he was going for, but he did admit that the attention he got from the local ladies was boosting his ego one hundred-fold.

As he had not seen his girlfriend recently and was unsure where it was going, I think the attention boosted his confidence. He had found and paid for a lady who had translated into Cantonese a marriage proposal for him to approach his girlfriend with. But he had it done weeks ago, and having still not used it, I could see he was wavering. Being a white man in Asia was turning him in to a kid in a sweet shop and I could tell he was at risk of indulging... and he knew it too. He had stopped joining the rest of the school gang (teachers and admin staff) for dinners and nights out, because, by his own admission, he could not trust himself when he was drunk not to fall into the clutches of another lady, so he avoided the risk entirely.

As much as I am fond of Mitch, he's not what you would call classically good looking or someone you would necessarily strain your neck for if you saw him walking past you. He's one of these people that you have to get to know to then realise his attractiveness. But here in China, by the colour of his skin and his origin, he did not have to try for attention.

Girls would giggle and shyly smile as he walked down the street. Hairdressers, masseuses and shop workers would fawn over him. He didn't have to do anything more than be a Westerner. Because by being so, he had a higher status than that of a Chinese man and was assumed to be considerably richer. Western men were also the ticket out of the country for these girls to a life of relative luxury and opulence. Being a white man in Asia puts you on the stage of royalty. It was little wonder that his head was being turned. I did not judge him for a second. Better now he realised this than after marriage, let's be honest.

I, on the other hand, was considered the scum of the earth. I can assure you Mitch had never been spat on. When I first arrived I used to have the female admin staff at the school stroke my skin and tell me how beautiful it was. It was whiter than white after a long cold winter in England, and had a purer hue than their natural skin colour. I think that was the only time any part of me was envied out here. Since the sun had come out and my skin had turned browner and frecklier, I now only attracted disgusted looks. Freckles and a tan was my impurity coming out.

I was even more out of place here now, and getting more unattractive as the hot days went by. Adding insult to injury, I even had to get my mother to post me knickers because I just couldn't get them to fit out here, even as a UK size 10 which I had never considered large. But I was slowly becoming more and more the type of person that the Chinese men hate and fear. Huge, over-sized already, but now my pigmentation was definitely making me an even lower class - I was a nobody. Needless to say, whilst Mitch's self-esteem was soaring, mine was sinking.

China is also the first time I was ever offered a prostitute. Strolling at night through central Beijing back to the subway one day after school, I was approached by a gentleman who offered me a deal. I could pay him $10 and he would have sex with me. THAT is how far you have to go in this country as a white female to get laid, apparently. I understand the business logic of this now. White men have their heads turned by the flattery and feminine wiles of the local ladies and Chinese men have no attraction towards us white females what so ever. Lesbianism is illegal, so obviously engaging a prostitute is our only relief.

Mitch thought this was hilarious and said he'd do me for $5, you know, just to help me out.

Then, on a more serious note, we talked about what the future held for us both. Since doing CELTA, Mitch had adopted Aoife's full-time schedule of teaching, because he made the wise choice of not doing the course and instead commandeering the lessons and the parental relationships in her absence so well that the school had refused to hand them back to her when she finished the course. Therefore, Mitch had a full-time job to do and he was loving it. He was really passionate about the kids, imparting knowledge and I'm sure he enjoyed spending all that time not feeling like a short guy. Maybe that's why he liked Asia so much as a whole – he was big here. In more ways than one if the rumours were true about the natives, but I hadn't paid my $10 to find out.

He had also negotiated a genuine visa that he had just received back from the embassy so that he wouldn't have to look over his shoulder for the police or immigration every day. Unfortunately, being so far from home he could not get hold of his university certificate to support his application – largely because he didn't have one. However, he had mine and had photoshopped it effectively enough to pass muster. In a country where everything is faked, I'm pretty sure this is the lesser of the evils that have been forged.

So, I think Mitch is going to stay. He has no career back home, (probably through being busted for his dildo photoshopping skills at the local newspaper) he presumably still has a girlfriend in Hong Kong, and if not he is inundated with ladies here, he gets to play in the land of nun chucks, he's not going anywhere.

I, on the other hand, just know that I am leaving in a few days, and after the traveling comes to an end, my life is an open book.

We agree to keep each other posted on our adventures, not convinced we will actually write each other letters, but the power of social media will give us some insight into each other's lives. I know he will survive this. I know he will thrive on it. He's an absolute firecracker of a person.

When I leave him it is another emotional wrench. We survived effectively being people trafficked into this country, we lived in questionably dangerous environments, we fought back and we made it out the other side. There is no-one else in the world that went through that with me. He knows the fear, the frustration, the humiliation we put ourselves through. Another unbreakable bond of history.

We hug awkwardly and part ways, me in a cab, him walking back home. I watch him through the rear window of the taxi as we pull into the flow of traffic. He has his hands in his pockets and it looks like he's whistling, without a care in world. My view is temporarily blocked as he walks behind a sign at a bus stop... and he never reappears. It's almost like I imagined that funny little

London boy. I wonder if I did… the majority of our story was really quite unbelievable. I knew I was going to miss him, but knew I'd never be able to forget him.

I left Mitch because I was heading for a drink with Aussie Amity. We were the only two in the city without dates tonight, it would seem, and so we decided a few drinks, just us, would be a nice way to mark my trip shortly coming to an end.

We met in Sanlitun, the Western Quarter, and headed for a rooftop bar as the sun went down. It was one of the few places in the city that you could bask in the pollution in a rooftop beer garden. There were huge couches, a DJ and a mixture of Westerners and Chinese, but above all, a non-hostile environment, which often these places felt like.

It was a relatively clear night, although still no stars, but Beijing stretched out below us in all its glory. The traffic was heaving, the light pollution made the city glow like it was radioactive and there is no such thing as peace.

I don't know whether it's because I am leaving or I'm suffering from some sort of Stockholm Syndrome but I feel a sense of nostalgia. I feel like I missed out on so much here. What if I had given it a proper chance? Did I not try hard enough? Am I taking the easy way out? Has it all been a waste?

But I know deep down I have to go, this city, this country, is irreparably tainted for me. I can't trust this place. I have to leave before my faith in all of humanity dies along with my soul, and arguably before I'm arrested.

It's been a long time since I spent time with just me and Amity, without Aoife present and dancing around the living room like a crazy person. It's a welcome change and it's fun. I remember the first night I met her when she walked me home through the dark back alleys of the South East district. Since then she has been a hilarious playmate, a hairdresser, a tonic. Another genuine friend discovered out in this strange old world.

We talk for hours that night about the world and everything in it. She vows to keep us out long enough so we can head to Tiananmen Square and watch the raising of the flags at sunrise, just as Rob had done all those weeks ago. It feels like that is a farewell rite of passage. I doubt we will last that long but we will try.

It is then when I admit to her my sadness about Rob, which I had not had the courage to voice before now.

Despite being in regular contact since he had left, Skype, numerous emails and voice messages…in the last few days the trail had gone cold. I didn't question it because my attention had passed to my parents, and plus, I had expected it to happen at some point – he was starting a new life, investing in a new career, finding a home to settle into. It wasn't my place to demand regular contact when we both had opposing working or waking hours. But it had felt strange and a little abrupt. Our furious need to be in contact had virtually died over night – and not from my wishing.

The day my parents had left for Xi'an, I had woken up to a very long email from Rob. He'd apologised for his recent silence but he had something serious he needed to speak to me about.

The entire time he had been living in Beijing, and before in Singapore, he had always dated Eastern girls. And for some reason, he felt he needed to tell me that he can't lie to himself or me anymore, but his preference was for Asian women, and not me. My heart had completely broken. The one thing I had loved more than anything about my time out here was him. And he had just taken that away from me. We both knew we had no future together, we both acknowledged that we were going in different directions – so I was distraught at why he felt the need to confess this to me and damage the memories that we had made together. It was the final, most painful kick in the stomach that China could have given me. Whilst I admired his honesty, he had just destroyed 'us' and all our memories, in my eyes.

Amity and I go through periods of being drunk and dancing, to sober and serious and everything in between. And before we know it, the sky is getting lighter, neither of us noticing until the first rays of daylight peek through the haze. We stare open mouthed. The night has disappeared and we didn't even feel it passing. We know we can't make it to the square in time to watch the flag ceremony. So, we sit in silent awe as once again I watch another sunrise in Beijing, knowing that this is probably the very last time I will see it…it was a truly unforgettable evening.

My parents arrived back from Xi'an shell-shocked, but impressed, tired but willing to view more of the tourist sites seeing as they were here now and knew they would never be returning.

My Dad's leading story of their trip to Xi'an, was not the impressiveness of the Warriors, but a rather unfortunate poop incident. He regaled me in disbelief at what he had witnessed whilst waiting outside a public toilet at the airport. A mother, instead of taking her tiny child to the toilets a few strides away, saw fit to hoist the child into the air and let it defecate into a bin. (The child was wearing split pants, no nappy, which is standard out here). She then proceeded to wipe the child's bottom with her hand and stroll off, child in tow. No hand washing. No sanitisation. Nothing. Just a wipe on her clothing and she's good to go.

On the toilet theme, I was determined to prove the disgusting toilet situation to my Mum. So, when we passed one of the numerous public toilet blocks in a famous area of the city, I made her go in. Five holes in the ground, no cubicles, no doors, no paper, no hand washing facilities… and five women 'busy' whilst holding an apparently enthralling conversation. I regret to say she was almost sick at the accompanying stench, but I felt compelled to show her proof of my previous ramblings. She rapidly learned bladder control.

They came to my favourite local BBQ restaurant to savour the food I had raved about. The food impressed greatly as I knew it would, but the surroundings didn't. Spitting in the 'restaurant' rang out around us, the phlegm, rubbish, fag butts and meat bones littered the floor.

Using the bathroom there also took a further few years off Mum's life. They got lucky mind you, whilst I'd been there earlier in the week, someone had peed in the bin - next to the toilet (why?) - and we watched a seriously inebriated man be violently sick on the steps of the restaurant, wipe his sick soaked hands on his clothes and on the lady he later sat next to, before continuing with his food and drinking merrily with his work colleagues as if nothing had happened. (Part of the whole drink to impress the boss ethic which I never got around to detailing).

They also missed sightings of customers strolling in wearing their silk pyjamas – although we saw this eventually many times on the streets in broad daylight, I didn't feel they were too robbed.

Still, regardless of the above, the food at the BBQ remains the greatest in Beijing and they can now confirm this.

So what else did they witness? The sky rarely being blue thanks to the haze of pollution. They got off lightly by not experiencing a tasty pollution day, but they got the picture.

They witnessed taxi drivers ignoring the whiteys leaving us stranded at the roadside time and time again.

Which leads me on to the con. Not the original one that brought me out here, but a new one altogether. They say you haven't experienced Beijing until you've been conned, and they would be right. But they tried to con a girl who was so sick and angry of the city, that instead of us fearing for our safety, I think the conmen feared for their own. The ruse we got caught up in went: we couldn't get a taxi, as per normal.

The bus didn't turn up. We were offered, and took, a rickshaw ride back to the hotel. Me sat on my parents' knees whilst some poor guy cycled us home was a little harsh so we weren't surprised that when we hit a busy junction, we were divided up onto our own rickshaws. However, alarm bells started to ring in my head when the first driver we had agreed the price with, was no longer one of our drivers... and then they took the long way home. Mum first, Dad second, me third.

When I was deliberately separated from my parents I started to panic. The route wasn't the same, my parents were out of sight, and the rickshaw motor I was on kept 'failing', drawing more and more distance between me and my folks. I knew now we were going to be conned. Three rickshaws, three foreigners, back alleys... we were going to get robbed for a lot of money.

As my rickshaw finally rounded its last corner, with relief I saw my parents up ahead, dismounted and safe, but from the gestures from one of the Chinese drivers, I could see they were being asked to pay up.

I fumed. At this stage I didn't even have proof we were part of a con but I instinctively knew it. I shouted for them to not do anything until I came closer. And sure enough, for a £3 journey, they were asking over a £100 from us for the 'tour' (that had lasted three minutes). I was mad. At the end my tether, ready-to-murder-someone, mad.

Luckily being in Beijing and having had to navigate my way around a city I was deaf and dumb in and look after myself, I had learned the geography fast and I knew which direction the main road was in - and ordered my Mum to walk fast towards it whilst the aggressive pay dispute and squaring up was going on.

The conmen sensed, the second I ran towards them and my parents after dismounting the rickshaw early, that this was not going to be an easy mugging. Probably because of the way I was shouting for my Dad to put his wallet away and for my Mum to get the hell away, they turned their attention to me.

My immediate worry was for my Dad - his knees were so bad I knew he needed a head start to meet Mum if things were going to turn ugly, which they quite possibly could. I ordered him to start towards the road too (although he chose not to leave my side) whilst I dealt with the demands of the conmen who weren't happy their payday was trying to walk away. I have no idea what I thought I was going to do but there was no way I was going to let them do this to me or my parents.

The main road (and safety) was less than 100 metres away so I was pretty certain that I could move this situation nearer to the throngs of people and leave us less secluded and vulnerable. So, I grabbed my Dad and we started backing off, towards the main road and where I hoped my Mum would be waiting. That's all I wanted. Otherwise we could have lost a lot in that alley….

Thankfully, the conmen clearly have never heard the saying 'hell hath no fury like a woman scorned', so my next actions caught them off guard. I started shouting at them at the top of my voice and practically foamed at the mouth whilst they continued to demand money from us. As Dad and I continued to back off towards the main road, they began to focus their demands on me, the obvious spokesperson in their little party of victims.

They thrust fabricated price lists in my face and pulled on my arms to drag me back into their fold where they tried to surround me and intimidate me. My poor father stuck on the outside of a ring of four men surrounding his little girl.

It's fair to say they succeeded in their intimidation but I wasn't going to show them. (I had even managed to find time to remove my flip flops during this event so I was a little more mobile in case things got ugly). Yes, we could have paid up and handed over our wallets and purses, but I felt damned if I was going to let this country take any more from me than it already had, or do something despicable to my parents. Plus, the road (and presumed safety) was getting closer the more I dragged these men with me. (I'd also heard about this con before, and during my extensive research on the Chinese due to my earlier experiences, knew they were not at all prone to physical violence as they relied on verbal intimidation and bullying).

So, I fought back. I shook off their hands, shouted louder than them, wriggled out of their circle, and carried the argument on until we had rounded the corner and made sure we were within sight of the busy main road before I screwed up the notes for the originally agreed fare into tiny balls and threw them in their general direction.

It was as they scrambled for the money on the ground, that Dad and I picked up the pace in our backward walking until I could be sure the men were distracted enough counting the money, to turn and run. When we saw our chance, we turned and sped towards safety and my waiting and worried mother, who had been watching this all unfold in front of her eyes.

The conmen shouted and swore after us after realising they had only received the equivalent of £3, the agreed fare, but these gutless wonders were clearly used to meek and mild, confused tourists - not angry, mentally deranged, bitter and experienced Beijingers - that they gave up pursuing us any further. We had also made it to the 'safe zone' so to follow us would have exposed them to their next con victims which clearly made no business sense to their nasty little minds.

They made me want to spit on them in fury - just like I'd been spat on months earlier.

"They never reckoned on coming up against you, did they?" was the only phrase my dad uttered on our slow and shaky walk home.

Suffice to say, because I am writing this now, you know I'm not laid bleeding in a Chinese back alley. I'm simply left more glad that I'm no longer there and that my parents didn't have to experience that on their own. On reflection, our rickshaw rides were great fun and probably one of the highlights of our trip - up to the con bit of course. And yes, we were lucky to have come out unscathed. It's totally crazy how you react in adverse situations and in hindsight I can't believe that was my reaction. I had simply trusted in my knowledge of the city and the research I had done to save us from a sticky situation. But rest assured, the day the Chinese start being known to carry guns and knives, is the day I will gladly hand over my valuables. But until that day… screw you.

So what else did we experience that compounded my wish to get out of the country?

Other than being giving notice of eviction from my apartment, something else happened that epitomises my utter contempt for this country.

There was a viral video doing the rounds on the Internet and causing a moral uproar, of a two-year-old girl being hit and run over by a vehicle in one of the hutongs in china (the small narrow alleyways/roads that run between buildings), and left lying in the road, when a second vehicle runs over her and no less than 18 people walked past her bleeding body on the road - without batting an eyelid or helping the dying child. All caught on CCTV and aired on news channels across the world, apparently. But I wouldn't know - as I no longer lived in the free-world.

Could you think of anything more unspeakably disgusting than seeing a child be seriously injured - AND DOING NOTHING? Not rushing to their side, not calling an ambulance, just IGNORING a child in need? I think I am safe to say that no-one I know would ever be so barbaric and even the coldest of hearts would feel compelled to do something. But not the Chinese nation, apparently.

It's also in line with a Brazilian man witnessing a robbery in a district of Beijing and stepping in to protect the girl from her robbers - and then being beaten into hospital by a gang of a dozen men for his troubles. During which, streets of people in an area he was well known in, walked past as if nothing was happening. A Good Samaritan, hospitalised for doing the right thing, whilst the Chinese population turned a blind eye... I have nothing but hate inside me when I hear these stories. Whilst this story is not as heart-breaking as the poor bay girl who later died from her hit and run, it's another perfect example of how deeply into a moral decline this nation is sinking. (It also is an example of the Chinese being physically violent – which totally contradicts my statement about the conmen, but it genuinely is extremely rare).

There is much debate as to why this complete disregard for humanity happens, and why they don't apparently even care for their own fellow countrymen, and those theories have to do with corruption - the person who lends a hand is then sued by the 'victim' or their family for easy cash. Even if that person wasn't driving the car or wielding their own fists, they get the blame.

But to me? I wouldn't think twice about saving a child's life even if it meant I ended up monetarily poorer for it. And I'm pretty sure most of you readers wouldn't think twice either.

There aren't strong enough words to describe how I feel about any of this.

Some of you may be thinking back to the story of the UK man who was beaten to the ground by a Chinese gang after sexually assaulting the Chinese lady in Beijing – the one which supposedly prompted the visa crackdown? At first glance it may appear to further contradict the stories I've just told you. But whilst this publicised display of protectionism and unity and care for their neighbour is rare, it is generally pre-fabricated and planned and used as propaganda. It is also a good example of their hate of anything and anyone from outside their nation, and publicising incidents like these garners enough resounding hatred amongst the masses to encourage the efforts to remove infiltrators from their country. So, we know they have some sort of fight in them… but what a pity they don't display the same hatred for their own people who harm others in the same way.

What I'm trying to highlight, not very well admittedly due to my fury at the situation, is that unless there is a Westerner at fault, they do nothing to help their own people... you're on your own here.

This little diatribe brings me round to the final nail in my China experience's coffin.

One very rainy day towards the end of their trip, my parents and I, having just left the famous Temple of Heaven in Beijing (which was pretty in places, but mostly bland) we were looking for a taxi to get us back to the hotel before the skies emptied on us, on a particularly cloudy day.

Just as we were arriving at the central intersection of a six lane road to hail a cab going in our direction, I heard Mum scream in horror... simultaneously accompanied by a loud metal crushing sound. Dad and I looked in the direction of her stare in time to see a bicycle rolling across the road - and a young man, having been separated from it by a car, rolling in the opposite direction, about 50m from us.

Mum had been witness to a car knocking a cyclist off his bicycle and now the victim was laid in the foetal position on the road, not moving. We were helpless and three lanes of mental traffic away from the incident. As well as my heart pounding from fear for the man, it was sinking heavily towards my stomach. From what I had previously seen and learned of the Chinese thus far, I instinctively knew that no one would help this man or run to his aid. I was unknowingly commentating out loud my feelings and my predictions of what would happen next, and sure enough, the Chinese didn't disappoint. Or more rightly they did.

The only person to run to this poor injured guy's aid as he was still laying unmoving in the road, was a male Westerner who was a few feet away from the impact zone. Driver? Nothing. No movement. He stopped his car though, how nice, but he didn't get out to check on his victim. No-one else did either, they just drove round the new inconvenient obstacle. Not a single Chinese person ran to the aid of their injured fellow China man who was lying in the road…undoubtedly injured: potentially dying. None.

Worse still? There was a police car parked up on the opposite junction, directly across from where the accident happened. They must have heard it, they couldn't not have seen it, their patrol car was facing it for goodness sake. Did they help? Did they get out of their car? No. And no. They turned an ignorant and cold blind eye.

By the grace of God, it became apparent that this was not a fatal accident we witnessed. The victim was helped up by the Westerner, and after a few long minutes was escorted to the side of the road after having his bike retrieved by another Westerner, and by the time we had battled across the road, he had disappeared from sight.

So, all's well that ends well, huh? But how can it be? Goodness knows how injured that man really was whilst he forged on with his journey so as not to lose face. If that was my brother, or my father, or a friend, I would feel utterly sick at the thought that they suffered on their own after having their life quite literally flash before their eyes and had no-one to comfort them. Just seeing it happen to a stranger made me sick to the depths of my stomach. Was he actually even okay? Where did he go?

It was quite possibly the worst and most ugly experience of this country I'd had, and a stark example of the reality I had been living in. I no longer felt safe here and I didn't want my family here either. If anything happened to us, we'd be on our own. It wasn't worth the risk.

And that's when I finally realised my first dark few days in China were actually more risky than I cared to imagine. No one was going to help me, were they? I was right to fight for myself because no-one else was going to bother. Even the Western staff from the school, whom I begged to help me, had been in this cold-hearted country too long and had absorbed too much indifference to human plight to be of the use that I hoped they'd be. My close shave with this numb nation finally hit home.

It's all too sad when you have to finally admit that to judge other people by your own standards will only lead to disappointment. What a sorry place the world can be sometimes. And this particular world I needed to get out of once and for all. As soon as my parents were safely on their way home, I would be right behind them. I NEED them to leave and be safe again. No-one can protect me or my loved ones here. I knew that for sure now.

I'm just grateful that I got to this point in my journey when I can leave whilst there is still something other than an empty indifference to the world left in me. I have hope for other nations, but this one is terrifying and I want no part of it.

Mum and Dad need to go. I have to go. No question.

We are all flying tomorrow.

Goodbye Beijing. You disgust me.

EPILOGUE

I write this final diary from Phuket, Thailand. I left China a week ago, the same day my parents flew home, after tearful farewells to my fellow fighter Little Mitch and my rocks Aoife, Amity, Samuel, Pete, Honey, Holly and Lana.

I didn't cry for China when I left, I cried in relief that it was all finally over: The stress from waking up every day for months not knowing what the next day would bring, the constant battles, the sheer fear I felt passing through security on my way out of the country, the huge risks I was unwittingly forced to take and the little pieces of myself that the experience chipped away at.

Bearing in mind the time I've had to lick my wounds over the past week, writing these final China entries has been hard.

All I've told you about so far is my experience of China itself and the mess I got myself in to. The truth is there is a whole lot more behind the words... which will remain personal. Suffice to say, I don't feel like the person I was when I arrived in China, full of hope and excitement about my future. I feel a little bit broken, more than a little battle weary and with scars you can't see. Yeah,

I talk the good game sometimes but the truth is, I have really been struggling, and I'm not really that tough underneath.

In the week I've been here in Thailand, I have barely spoken to a soul and I have rarely left my room. I've been trying to rationalise everything that has happened but I realise now there is no point. I did however learn some valuable lessons through it all – unfortunately mostly about excruciating disappointment – from how I thought China would be, to how I naively believed better of people and of humanity. As a result, I feel let down and deflated and sad about a lot of it. A little bit of my faith in human nature has died.

But I also learned the good lessons, that when it comes to the crunch, I'm a fighter. A softie underneath, which is okay - but boy am I ballsy when it counts. I also tested my tolerance like never before, I found amazing friends - a bond built over tough times is a strong one, and I also firmly know that I will never again doggedly pursue something that is ultimately not worthy of my time, my effort and my heart. Life is too short and now I know to cut my losses sooner.

I now have two days left to pull myself together before I fly to Bangkok to join a four week organised tour through Cambodia and Vietnam with 15 strangers, after which I plan to settle in Hanoi to do volunteer work, bide my time, and then see where the world takes me.

I'm glad to say: China is history.

That is, until I've done my level best to make sure no-one else's child/sibling goes through what I went through. Watch this space whilst I take on that final fight.

In the meantime, before I leave for the rest of Asia – thank you all for supporting me on my China adventure. it's certainly been an emotional one – and not in the Swaziland-heart-warmingly-good way.

I hope my next tales to come read significantly less dramatic than this one.

Until my next adventure… take care.

ABOUT THE AUTHOR

Gemma Dunn has always been an avid traveller around her career as an Accountant. After qualifying in her mid-twenties she worked hard to raise sufficient funds to enable her to earn experiences abroad and take several career breaks and sabbaticals whenever possible.

The idea was borne after beginning her travels into the world with a short two months in Thailand during her university holidays, which was all she could afford by herself at the age of 19, through working several part time jobs alongside her studies. The travel bug bit her and she immediately knew she wanted to be more than just a traveller simply transitioning through various countries, and wanted to immerse herself in foreign countries and their cultures beyond the bars, beaches and hostels.

Her next major trip came a few years later and saw her spending two months as a volunteer teacher in Swaziland (now known as Eswatini) where she lived in a safari tent and supported a school in a remote village. After falling in love with the country, she returned a year later with her parents, to help build playground equipment at the same school, and plastering and painting the schoolroom walls.

After further periods of working, and squeezing in shorter European, American and Canadian travels when her work would allow, she earned her next major stint abroad: Teaching English as a Foreign Language (TEFL) in China, followed by volunteering at a school for Agent Orange sufferers in Vietnam, touring several countries in Asia and finally settling in Singapore as an Accountant for a year, to build her funds back up.

Returning home from Asia, instead of moving back to Reading, Berkshire where she grew up with her parents and three siblings, she decided to escape the hustle and bustle and follow her parents, sister and grandmother to the sleepy villages of Somerset where she still resides.

Following the unexpected death of her older sister and her beloved Grandparents within the space of two and half years, she took time out to continue her travels on a three month overland tour through Southern Africa, camping her way around nine countries.

A short period of working on her return now sees her taking a year off from everything corporate, and instead she is writing and following her dream of telling the world her stories and sharing her experiences - both good and bad.

And, obviously, incorporating a few more countries to her travel logs in her downtime...

Printed in Great Britain
by Amazon

25588147R00179